Evelyn Philip Shirley

Some account of English deer parks,

With notes on the management of deer

Evelyn Philip Shirley

Some account of English deer parks,
With notes on the management of deer

ISBN/EAN: 9783337808020

Printed in Europe, USA, Canada, Australia, Japan

Cover: Foto ©ninafisch / pixelio.de

More available books at **www.hansebooks.com**

SOME ACCOUNT

OF

ENGLISH DEER PARKS

WITH NOTES ON THE MANAGEMENT OF DEER

By ·EVELYN PHILIP SHIRLEY, Esq. M.A. F.S.A.

SOMETIME KNIGHT OF THE SHIRE FOR THE COUNTIES OF MONAGHAN AND WARWICK

LONDON
JOHN MURRAY, ALBEMARLE STREET
1867

The right of Translation is reserved

LONDON
PRINTED BY SPOTTISWOODE AND CO.
NEW-STREET SQUARE

The Great Elm Tree in the Park at Eatington, Warwickshire, 20 feet in circumference a yard from the ground.
Sketched by Selina Lady Heathcote, anno 1834.

PREFACE.

LTHOUGH there were several treatises written during the Middle Ages on 'the noble arte of venerie and hunting,' in which, perhaps, deer and deer parks may be said to be comprehended, while in the sixteenth and seventeenth centuries many books were printed on the same subject, yet neither then, or at a later period, has, I believe, any work appeared which treats on the management of the fallow-deer, or professes to give any account of the numerous parks for which England has been so long distinguished from the other countries of Europe.

This circumstance must plead my excuse for attempting, what I fear has been very imperfectly performed, a sketch of the origin and history of deer parks, and a list (for it is but little more) of most of these ancient and modern enclosures in the several English counties, with some few notes on the management of parks and deer at the present time.

For the purpose of obtaining information as to the present condition of English parks, I circulated among their owners a paper of queries with regard to the acreage and number of deer, as well as on the subject of management, and date or history of each particular park; and I take this opportunity of recording my obligations to those noblemen and gentlemen who were kind enough to notice my communication, or to allow their keepers to answer it. Among the number there are many to whom, for their great courtesy and kindness in affording information, a more particular expression of thanks is due; and here I desire particularly to mention the names of the Earl of Winchilsea and Nottingham, the Lords Farnham and Henniker, the Rev. Lord Saye and Sele, Sir William Heathcote, Bart. M.P., Sir Henry Dryden, Bart., the

Venerable Archdeacon Mildmay, Col. Wilson-Patten, M.P., W. W. E. Wynne, of Peniarth, Esq., N. Kendall, Esq., M.P., Octavius Morgan, Esq., M.P., Alex. Beresford Hope, Esq., M.P., George Legard, Esq., Charles Walpole, Esq., Charles Spencer Perceval, Esq., Kaye Dowland, of Mansfield, Esq., J. Gough Nichols, Esq., and the Rev. Henry Mills, of Pillerton, in the County of Warwick.

It appears as the result of the enquiries which I have made, that there are at present 334 parks still stocked with deer in the different counties of England ; among that number red deer are kept in about thirty-one parks.

With regard to the antiquity and size of these aristocratic enclosures in the present day, I have collected many particulars, by which it appears that there are parks whose origin is lost in the obscurity of early Norman times down to the date of the enclosure of yesterday, and that their extent varies from the stately area of more than two thousand acres to the little paddock of a few roods.

It is perhaps impossible to ascertain with accuracy the oldest existing deer park in England ; but if Lord Abergavenny's park at Eridge, in Sussex, may be identified with the *Reredfelle* of Domesday, there can be no doubt that it may lay claim to this unique distinction, there being no other Domesday park which appears in the category of existing enclosures stocked with deer.

The other point, as to extent, is more easily answered. From the returns which I have received it would seem, that with the exception of the Royal Park of Windsor, of about 2,600 acres, Lord Egerton of Tatton's Park, at Tatton, in Cheshire, containing 2,500 acres, is the largest in this country, though there are several others, such as Blenheim,[1] in Oxfordshire, Richmond Park, in Surrey, Eastwell, in Kent, Grimsthorpe, in Lincolnshire, Thoresby, in Nottinghamshire, and Knowesley, in Lancashire, which nearly approach it in size.

I have now only to add that I fear it is possible that the names of some existing deer parks have been inadvertently omitted; if so, I should be glad to be informed of the fact, and grateful for any corrections which may be forwarded to me. Many ancient and disused parks must also, of course, have escaped my attention; but such omissions must naturally attend an attempt of the present nature, and will, I hope, receive the indulgence of the reader.

LOWER EATINGTON PARK :
       April 30, 1867.

---

[1] Blenheim, indeed, contains about 2,800 acres, of which, however, but 1,150 are open to the deer.

CONTENTS.

CHAPTER I.

CHAPTER II.

CHAPTER III.

CHAPTER IV.

CHAPTER V.

CONTENTS.

CHAPTER X.

CHAPTER I.

SKETCH OF THE HISTORY OF DEER PARKS FROM THE CONQUEST TO THE BEGINNING OF THE SIXTEENTH CENTURY.

'The Bucke is a worthy Beast.'—GWILLIM.

CHAPTER I.

'And I will that every man be entitled to his hunting, in wood and in field, on his own possession ; And let everyone forego my hunting : take notice where I will have it untrespassed on, under penalty of the full wite.'—*Laws of King Cnut.*

S parks, or enclosed grounds for the preservation of deer, are incidentally mentioned in the general survey of Domesday undertaken soon after the Norman conquest of England, we may, I think, conclude that they were not unknown here before that period ; though we have (for the most part) no earlier means to distinguish them from the forests, woods, and hunting-grounds, which covered so large a portion of our island in pre-Norman times. And in confirmation of this view I would refer to Mr. Thorpe's ' Diplomatarium Anglicum Ævi Saxonici, a Collection of English Charters from the Reign of King Æthelberht of Kent A.D. DCV. to that of William the Conqueror.' Among the wills is that of Thurstân, of which the supposed date is 1045. He bequeaths to his ' *Chnites,* or pages, the wood at Ongar (in Essex) except the deer-hay or deer-park " *Derhaye*," and the stud which I

have there.'¹ Whitaker however, in his ' History of Craven,'² while treating
this subject with his usual good taste and judgment, leads us rather to
a contrary opinion, at least as regards the enclosure of any very considerable tracts. 'From a passage,' he writes, 'in one of the earliest
charters relating to Bolton Priory, it appears that the Forest of Skipton
was enclosed with a pale; the Chases of Blackburnshire were fenced in
the same manner. The Saxon forests, as far as I know, lay open, *and
the practice of enclosing these immense tracts must have been introduced
by the great Norman lords.* Musing on this circumstance, I was struck
by a passage of Columella from which it appears that the idea was familiar
to the ancient Princes of Gaul. "Hoc autem modo licet etiam latissimas
regiones tractusque montium claudere, sicuti Galliarum; locorum vastitas
patitur." The subject is treated by that author in a very lively and elegant
manner; the materials of the fence were cleft pales (vacerræ) of oak, cork
trees, &c., care was taken to enclose a supply of perennial water; as also
great plenty of mast-bearing and bacciferous trees, particularly the arbutus;
the animals nourished in these enclosures were the stag, the wild boar, the
fallow-deer, the roe, and the oryx; which last, from the account given of
his inverted mane by Pliny, can have been no other than the aurochs, or
wild bull still found in the Lithuanian forests. Beans, yet in use for the
winter fodder of deer, are particularly recommended; on the whole, I pro-
pound it as a subject of curious speculation, whether the practice of enclosing forests were not continued in France from the era of Classical Antiquity
to the Middle Ages, and whether the Norman lords, when they became
possessed of tracts equally wild and extensive in this country, did, by enclosing them, anything more than follow the example of their ancestors.
The forests of the French nobility at the time of the late Revolution
were uniformly open, but so have been our own during four or five
centuries.' From the above passage it would appear that fallow-deer were
included, together with red-deer, roe-deer, wild swine and wild cattle,

¹ 8vo. London, 1865, p. 574.   ² 2nd ed. p. 233.

among the denizens of the forests of Gaul, but it may be doubted whether they were indigenous to our northern latitudes, and I think the following reasons, gleaned from different writers, point with tolerable certainty to an opposite conclusion.

There are many varieties of the fallow-deer, but for our present purpose it will be sufficient to notice but two of them, the dark, and the spotted. The first are generally supposed to have been introduced into England by King James I. from Norway, 'where,' writes Bewick in his History of Quadrupeds,[1] ' having observed their hardiness in bearing the cold of that severe climate, he brought them into Scotland, and from thence transported them into his chases of Enfield and Epping ; since that time they have multiplied exceedingly in many parts of this kingdom, which is now become famous for venison of superior fatness and flavour to that of any other country in the world.' The spotted kind are supposed by Pennant, Bewick, and others, whose accounts are founded on that of Buffon, to have been brought from Bengal. But the Eastern origin of this species is now gen- erally denied ;[2] there appears to be no doubt that the *Cervus dama* or common fallow-deer is a native of Greece, and is still found there in a wild state, as well as in the forests of Italy ;[3] Cuvier writes of the fallow-deer, ' c'est devenue commune dans tous les pays d'Europe, mais elle paraît origi- naire de Barberie,' and in a note states, that since he penned the foregoing

---

[1] P. 143.

[2] There seems good reason to believe that one species of fallow-deer was known in Syria as early as the time of Solomon.

' And Solomon's provision for one day was thirty measures of fine flour, and three score measures of meal ;

' Ten fat oxen, and twenty oxen out of the pastures, and an hundred sheep, besides harts, and roebucks, and *fallow deer*, and fatted fowl.' —I *Kings* iv. 22, 23.

And long before the date of Solomon, in the enumeration of what may, and what may not be eaten, we have—

' These are the beasts which ye shall eat : the ox, the sheep, and the goat, the hart, and the roebuck, and the *fallow deer*, and the wild goat, and the pygarg, and the wild ox, and the cha- mois.'—*Deuteronomy*, xiv. 4, 5.

For the Dishon or pygarg, see Dr. Kitto's *Cyclopædia*, under Antelope, and the same autho- rity under Ail or Ajal, for the Cervus Barbarus or Barbary Stag, in size between our red and fallow-deer.

[3] Thompson's Natural History of Ireland, vol. vi. p. 32.

·he has received a specimen of a wild fallow-buck, killed in forestland to the south of Tunis.[1] Professor Owen, in a communication with which I have been favoured on this subject, remarks, 'that while he has derived abundant evidence of red-deer, roe-deer, and sundry extinct kinds, indigenous in Britain, he has never met with a fossil specimen, or one from marl or turbary, or cavern, of the fallow-deer, and considers this negative evidence as supporting the conclusion of the exotic origin of *Cervus dama.*'[2] ' Its enjoyment of summer,' adds Professor Owen, ' and sufferings in hard winters, show the fallow-deer not yet to have become thoroughly acclimatised; a rough shed, or some such shelter, and heat-engendering food (beans, maize, &c.) help to keep the herds in good condition, in our most favoured counties as to climate.'

But if not indigenous to Great Britain, there can be no doubt but that fallow-deer were introduced into England at a very early period. Æthelstân Ætherling, son of Æthelred II., mentions in his will his ' heahdeor,' or tall deer [Red Deer?], which seems to imply that he had also lesser, or fallow-deer, though roe-deer *may* be intended, and ' tall deer hounds' occur in the joint will of Byrhtric and Ælfswyth in the year 1045.[3]

If indeed we may regard that remarkable rhyming grant purported to be made by Edward the Confessor to Randolph Peperking for a genuine document of that age—and we appear to have the authority of Camden[4] for so regarding it—we have distinct evidence of the introduction of the fallow-deer into England before the Norman Conquest, if we may not conclude that the darker and hardier variety of the species is of native origin. The grant is as follows:—

> ' Ich Edward koning
> Have geven of my forest the keeping

[1] Régne Animal, i. (1829), p. 262.
[2] Hist. of British Fossil Mammals, 8vo. 1846, p. 483.
[3] Thorpe's Diplomatarium Anglicum, pp. 501 and 561.

[4] Camden's Britannia, under Essex. Gough's ed. vol. ii. p. 121. It is also admitted into Mr. Benjamin Thorpe's English Charters, 8vo. 1865, p. 420.

of the hundred of Chelmer and Dancing
to Randolf Peperking and his kindling,
with heorte and hinde, doe and bocke,
hare and foxe, catt and brocke,
wilde fowell with his flocke,
Patrich, fesant hen, and fesant cock,
with greene and wild stob and stock;
to kepen and to yemen by all her might,
both by day and eke by night,' &c.

The original, observes Camden, is in the Exchequer Records,[1] but the language softened by being frequently transcribed.

However, an undoubted evidence of the existence of the buck and doe in England in the middle of the thirteenth century is afforded by the curious agreement between the Earl of Winchester and Roger de Somery, which I have given at length at page 16 of this volume, and which is dated in the 31st year of Henry III. (1247); and in the 3rd year of Edward I. (1275) Sir William le Baud Knt. made a signal grant to the dean and canons of St. Paul's, London, of a doe yearly, on the feast of the Conversion of St. Paul, and of a fat buck upon the Commemoration of the same saint, to be offered at the high altar in St. Paul's by Sir William and his family, the reception of which buck and doe, it may be observed, was kept up even to the days of Queen Elizabeth, at the steps of the choir by the canons of St. Paul's, attired in their sacred vestments and wearing garlands of flowers upon their heads; and the horns of the buck carried on the top of a spear in procession, round about within the body of the church, with a great noise of horn-blowers, as the learned Camden upon his own view of both affirms.[2] From the beginning of the fourteenth century instances of the same kind abound, both in the legal writings of the period and in the poetry of that early age. Thus in the rhyme of Sire Thopas, in Chaucer's Canterbury Tales, we have

---

[1] Record. Hilar. Term. 17 Edw. II.   [2] Blount's Tenures, ed. Beckwith, p. 395.

> ' ᴴᵉ priketh through a faire forest,
>   therin is many a wilde best
>   ye both buck and hare.'

A little after (the quotation is pointed out by Whitaker in his ' History of Whalley' [1]), we find the following passage in the romance of Hippomedon :—

> ' Eppomedon he, with his hounded three
>   Drew down both buck and doo.'

and again :—

> ' All the game of the forest,
>   Hart and hynd, buck and doo.'

While Caxton was printing the 'Golden Legend,' he had a present from William Lord Arundel of a buck in summer, and a doe in winter; and about the same time they are mentioned by Dame Juliana Berners in many passages of ' The Book of St. Albans.'

The buck and the doe are also expressly mentioned in the ' Treatise on the Art of Hunting,' by William Twici, huntsman to King Edward II. Bell, in his ' History of British Quadrupeds,' has failed to give us any more exact information as to this disputed question, but his observations are so well and succinctly expressed that I cannot do better than repeat them. ' Whether this beautiful species (*Cervus dama*),' he writes, ' may be considered as indigenous to this country, or whether introduced at some remote period, appears to be a question which the lapse of time and the absence of sufficient historical testimony render difficult if not impossible of solution, and one upon which the most diligent search which I have been able to make has not thrown the smallest light. The circumstances which lead to the latter opinion are its restriction, in this country, solely to places which have been set apart for its reception, and the strong evidence which exists, both from the known foreign habitats of the species, and

---

[1] Whitaker's History of Whalley, p, 199,

from its comparative intolerance of our winters, that it must have been originally transplanted from a more genial climate. In this respect its habits differ essentially from those of the hardy stag and roebuck, which brave the cold of even Scottish winters, and live and flourish through them without the care and tendance of man. It is probable that it was brought to this country from the South of Europe, or from the Western parts of Asia, in which places it is found to attain to a larger size than in its semi-domesticated state in our parks. It is found, indeed, in a more severe climate than our own ; but it is only the dark brown variety, which is far more hardy than the usual one, and is well known to have been imported on account of this quality by James I. from Norway.'[1]

King James's claim to have reintroduced into this country, from Norway, the dark brown variety of fallow-deer, appears to rest on the dictum of Bewick, at least I have discovered no earlier authority for the assertion; it is confirmed, however, to some extent, by a letter in the State Paper Office, from Sir Roger Aston to Lord Salisbury, dated May 14, 1611, in which he writes that ' the king will not despatch the ship which brought the deer, before he knows what Salisbury gave for the last that came, and wishes Sir Thomas Lake to send word that the ship may be despatched;'[2] and in an original account which I have examined of ' divers extraordinary workes done since the first of May 1608,' I find the following, 'at Depthford for charge bestowed on the King's dog-house, and *conveying Deere to Theoball's w^h came fom the King of Denmarke, £30 5 1.'*[3] There is evidence also that the king presented 'pied' or spotted deer to the king of France ;[4] and his fondness for field sports, and particularly the interest which he took in his deer, invests the traditional belief on this

[1] Bell's History of British Quadrupeds, 8vo. 1837, p. 402.
[2] Calendar of Domestic State Papers. James I., p. 31.
[3] Original paper in the possession of the Baroness North.
[4] Warrant to pay to H. Seckford 100 marks for conveying certain pied deer to the French King. Docquet, March 30, 1608. Ib.

point with a great degree of probability, though that there were black, that is dark, deer long before his time in England, cannot admit of question, they are expressly noticed in Leland's Itinerary.[1]

Besides the parks noticed in Domesday, mention is frequently made of hayes in that invaluable survey; hayes,[2] derived from the Saxon, meaning literally a hedge, appear to differ from parks as being not intended for the permanent preservation of deer, but as a means to entrap them from the forests or woods in which they had roamed at large, in the same manner as elephants are caught at the present day in India, and deer in North America. From the hayes they could be transferred to parks securely fenced with wooden pales, whence they were hunted when it was the pleasure of the king or owner. In pre-Norman times, indeed, as we know from the laws of Canute and Edward the Confessor, the king arrogated to himself only his own forests, and permitted his subjects to hunt in their own lands; but the Norman conqueror assumed to himself the exclusive right of hunting, and very sparingly granted that privilege to some of his greatest nobles, both lay and clerical. For ages, indeed, the right of hunting in the Royal Forests was guarded with the utmost care; thus so late as the ninth year of Edward III., William de Montecute, who is described 'In armis strenuus, providus in conciliis, et in cunctis agendis, pronus, utilis, et fidelis,' received, for term of his life, the special reward of being allowed to hunt and sport in all the King's forests for one day during his journey to the Court.[3] The same privilege had been more generally accorded by the well-known concession of Henry III. to the Spiritual and Temporal Peers, as we find by the Charter of the Forest in the ninth year of his reign.

---

[1] Leland's Itinerary, vii. p. 40. Fol. 50.

[2] *Hay, Haia, Heia, Haga.* See an interesting note on this word in Whitaker's 'History of Whalley,' 4to. 1818, p. 205. That hays were used as means to entrap deer, or kids? is expressly proved by Domesday, *e.g.* 'Rogerius de Laci teñ Cortune, Ibi est haia capreolis capiend.'

Scirepescire, I. 256. 6. Haga, in the sense of hedge, is found in a charter of King Edward the Elder, anno 900, in Thorpe's 'English Charters,' p. 146.

[3] Patent Rolls, 9th Edward III., p. 123, 2nd pt.

The privilege of taking vermin in the royal forests appears to have been also the subject of royal grants; thus John de Beverle in the forty-second of Edward III., and the heirs male of his body, was licensed to take all kinds of vermin with dogs in the forests, chases, parks, and warrens of the king, and to hunt hares, and to use a certain horn of divers colours, viz. russet and black, which the king had given to him as a sign.[1]

Mr. Earle in his recent edition of the Saxon Chronicle, has well described the hunting of these early times:—'Now-a-days,' he says, 'men hunt for exercise and sport, but then they hunted for food, or for the luxury of fresh meat. Now the flight of the beast is the condition of a good hunt, but in those days it entailed disappointment. They had neither the means of giving chase or of killing at a distance, so they used stratagem to bring the game within the reach of their missiles. A labyrinth of alleys was penned out at a convenient part of the wood, and here the archers lay under covert. The hunt began by sending men round to break and beat the wood, and drive the game with dogs and horns into the ambuscade. This pen is the *haia* so frequently occurring among the *silvæ* of Domesday. Horns were used, not, as with us, to call the dogs, or, as in France, to signal the stray sportsman; but to scare the game. In fact, it was the *battue*, which is now, under altered circumstances, discountenanced by the authorities of the chase, but which in early times was the only way for man to cope with the beasts of the field.'

Of the thirty-one parks mentioned in Domesday, eight belonged to the king; these were in the counties of Surrey and Sussex, Hampshire, Devonshire, Buckinghamshire, Gloucestershire, Herefordshire, and Shropshire. The Bishop of Baieux had three parks, all in Kent; the Bishop of Winchester one at Waltham (afterwards called Bishop's Waltham), in Hampshire; the church of Pershore one in Worcestershire; and the church of St. Albans another near that place, in the county of Hertford. The Earl of Ow had

---

[1] Patent Rolls, 42 Edward III.

a park at Wiltingham, in Sussex; the Earl Roger four parks, in the counties of Sussex, Worcester, and Southampton; Roger de Lacy one at Wibelai (Webley), in Herefordshire; Hugh de Grentemaisnil one at Ware, in Hertfordshire; Peter de Valongies one at Belintone (Benington), in the same county; Walter Giffard one at Credintone (Long Crendon), in Buckinghamshire; the Countess Judith one at Chertelinge (Kirtling), in Cambridgeshire; the Earl of Britanny one at Burch (or Borough), in the same county; Goisfred de Magneville one at Enfield, in Middlesex; Hugh de Belcamp one at Stachedene (Stagsden) in Bedfordshire; Suen of Essex had a park in the Hundred of Rochefort, in that county; Robert Malet one at Eiam (Eye), in Suffolk; the Earl of Moretaine one at Cotescia (the modern Cossay), in Norfolk, and Esnulf de Hesding one at Rislepe (Riselip), in Middlesex.

The haiæ or hays noticed in the Great Survey occur chiefly in Worcestershire, Herefordshire, Shropshire, and Cheshire; more than seventy are recorded, occurring generally in groups of two, three, four, five, and even of seven; they were held by persons of all classes both in Church and State. Eyries of hawks are sometimes noticed with the haiæ, an evidence of the early connection of the sports of hunting and hawking. In one place [1] we find Stabilituras (stands) mentioned in connection with hays in a wood, the earliest notice probably of the ancient hunting-stand so general in the Middle Ages, and still in common use on the Continent. The size of these hays, with one exception, is not recorded in Domesday; that exception is the hay of 'Donnelie,' the modern Beldesest in Warwickshire, belonging to the Earl of Mellent, which was half a mile long and the same broad, and which was appraised at 20, and afterwards at 30 shillings. The use of them is very plainly declared : ' iii haiæ capreol capiendis:' 'una haia in qua qđ potest capere captat ;' 'ibi est haia capreolis capienđ;' &c. explain, as I have before observed, their object and their distinction from the park or chase.

[1] Domesday Book, i. 269.

Before we take leave of the '*Parci*, or *Parchi*,' of Domesday, the venerable predecessors of the almost innumerable parks which at one time were found dotted about in every corner of the island, it may be well to notice a very common error as to the park at Woodstock being the oldest in England, and which Sir Henry Ellis, in his valuable 'Introduction to Domesday,' appears to have been the first to notice and detect. 'Stow, in his Annals' (ed. 1631, p. 143), remarks Sir Henry, 'and Sir William Dugdale in his History of Warwickshire (ed. i. p. 182), appear to have been misled by John Ross (Rous) into the opinion that the Park of Woodstock in Oxfordshire, said to have been made by King Henry the First, was the earliest in England.' Dugdale's authority is so great, that one cannot wonder that this error should be so universal, and he is quite borne out by the author on whom he relied, and whose statement I have given in a note,[1] though we know it is without foundation.

The devotion to the chase by which our Norman kings and their nobles were distinguished, and the severe, nay cruel Forest Laws, which was the consequence of that passion, need not be illustrated here. It will be sufficient to observe that both forests, chases, and parks (we hear nothing of hays at least in their original sense) multiplied after the Norman Conquest,[2] though we have no means accurately to enumerate or

---

[1] 'Eciam in Anglia parcum de Wodstok (Henricus Primus fecit) cum palacio infra prædictum parcum, qui parcus erat primus parcus Angliæ, et pro eo fiendo plures villæ destructæ sunt, et continet in circuitu septem milliaria Anglicana. An erant ibi aliquæ ecclesiæ vel capellæ destructæ nescio. Et constructus erat circa annum xiiii. regni hujus regis vel parum post. Hujus rei exemplo ceteri domini imparcáverunt certas terras suas. Unde Henricus comes Warrewici parcum de Wegenok juxta Warrewyk incepit, et in principio solum terram quæ usque hodie "the old Perke," dicitur, continebat ; sed modo valde dilatatur.'—*Joannis Rossi, Hist. Regum Angliæ,* ed. Hearne, 8vo. Oxon, 1745, p. 138.

[2] It has been supposed, by some antiquaries, that one reason for the great number of parks which existed in England in early times may be attributed to domestic economy, and that their original purpose was for the fatting of the deer driven in from the forest, the venison of which was salted down for the winter supply of the lord's household. That such was sometimes the practice is proved by the following extract from the Close Rolls of the 26th Edward I. (1298): 'Rex custodibus Episcopatûs de Ely (at that time vacant) mandamus, quod

trace them, further than the reign of John, beyond which period the Patent Rolls in which many of them are recorded do not extend; licenses from the Crown for imparking,[1] a source both of profit to the sovereign, and a convenient, indeed necessary,[2] privilege to the subjects who could afford to purchase them, are very generally found enrolled from this period, and extend to the middle of the seventeenth century. The right of having a deer-leap (saltatorium)[3] is sometimes granted, and with regard to enclosures in forests, in order to allow free ingress to the royal deer, a reservation made as to the depth of the foss or ditch, and the height of the pale or hedge, with which the ground was to be fenced:[4] 'To the ancient economy of our Royal and Baronial Castles,' observes Whitaker,[5] ' usually belonged two parks, one a park enclosed with a wall, probably for fallow-deer, after the introduction of that species; the other for red-deer, fenced with a hedge and paling, or, in the words of Bracton,[6] " Vallatum fuit et inclausatum fossato, haia, et pallatio." '

in parcis Episc. prædicti 100 damos in instanti pinguidinis seisona capi, saliri, siccari, et eos salitos et siccatos in doleis poni, et salvo custodiri faciatis,' &c.—*Dalloway and Cartwright's Rape of Arundel*, p. 247.

[1] *Imparking.* The Latin *imparcus* and *parcus*, of the Patent Rolls, may perhaps sometimes mislead. In the north of England, in Devonshire, and in Ireland, a park may mean a paddock or small field near the town or house, without any connection with deer. It is possible, therefore, that in some instances a simple license to enclose should be understood.

[2] Roger de Rannes was amerced forty marks for the park which he had made without the king's leave. This was in the 5th Stephen. —*Maddox, History of the Exchequer*, i. 557.

[3] *Saltatorium.* Saltory, or deer-leap, i.e. a pit-fall ; an old and well-known contrivance for taking deer, generally on the edge of a forest or chase, often granted by charter, and often, too, used by deer-stealers without any right. One of the Articles of Inquiry in the Court of Swain-

mote was : ' Item, whether any man have any great close within three miles of the forest, that have any saltories or great gaps, called deer-lopes, to receive deer into them, when they be in chasing, and when they are in them they cannot get out again.' An example of a chartered deer-leap, still exercising its privileges, is at Wolseley in Staffordshire, on the edge of Cannock or Cank Chase ; and Whitaker, in his ' History of Whalley,' describes a hollow in the ground within the demesne of Habergham, which tradition points out as a pitfall, dug for impounding stray deer when the two families of Townley and Habergham lived upon terms of bad neighbourhood. — *Whitaker's History of Whalley*, 4to. London, 1818, p. 276.

[4] If a man have license to enclose any ground within the forest, he may not enclose the same *cum altâ haiâ et fossato, vel cum alto pallatio.*— Assiz. Forest. de Lancaster, 12 Edward III. Manwood, c. 10.

[5] History of Whalley, p. 205, note.

[6] Bracton Institutes, 2 c. 40, No. 3.

A large proportion of our ancient parks were for the especial use of the bishops and dignified clergy, who, while they were forbidden by the canon 'de clerico venatore,' to hunt 'cum canibus aut accipitribus, voluptatis causâ,' were permitted to do so 'recreatonis aut valetudinis graciâ,' —a rather subtle distinction. The archbishop of Canterbury had more than twenty parks or chases, attached to the see,[1] and most of the bishops, abbots, and priors are found to have been in the enjoyment of one or more of these privileged places for the aristocratic sports of the field.

The ancient Treatise on Hunting by William Twici, the huntsman of Edward II.,[2] and the curious and more elaborate work on the same subject called, 'Le Livre du Roy Modus, et de la Royne Racio,' without mentioning other authorities, give us some quaint details of the various ways of hunting carried on by our ancestors. These treatises are in question and answer, and are written in Old French. Perhaps a better idea will be formed of the practice on these occasions by the woodcuts which I have given in this work, copied exactly from some illustrations in an early MS. of 'Le Roy Modus' in my possession, than from any passages from the text itself, which, it must be confessed, are somewhat long and tedious. They describe the manner of

[1] Spelman's 'English Works,' 1723, p. 110.   [2] Privately printed by the present Sir H. Dryden, Bart. Sm. 4to. Daventry, 1843.

hunting deer with bloodhounds and with greyhounds, the huntsmen being represented both on foot[1] and on horseback; also the various modes of approaching deer with the bow; sometimes in ambush, 'where one ought

to be dressed the same colour as the wood.' It is to be observed that the common long-bow, and not the cross-bow, which was afterwards used in shooting deer in parks, is represented in these ancient illuminations.

The following translation of an agreement between Roger de Quincy, Earl of Winchester, and Roger de Somery, Baron of Dudley, defining their mutual rights of hunting in Charnwood Forest and Bradgate Park, Leicestershire, affords an illustration of another kind as to the 'noble science,' and is an evidence at the same time of the importance which was attached to it :—

'This is the Agreement made at Leicester, on the day of St. Vincent the Martyr (22nd of January), in the 31st year of the reign of King Henry, the son of King John (anno 1247). Before Sir Roger de Turkilby,

---

[1] King Henry V. is said, in Harrison's Description of Britain (p. 108), to have disdained to follow any fallow-deer with hounds or greyhounds, but ' to have tired them by his own travails on foot, and so killed them with his hands.' See the 1st ed. of Holinshed's Chronicles (1577).

Master Simon de Walton, Sir Gilbert de Preston, and Sir John de Cobham, Justices then there itinerant, between Roger de Quincy,[1] Earl of Winton, and Roger de Somery: To wit; That the aforesaid Roger de Somery hath granted for him and his heirs, that the aforesaid Earl and his heirs may have and hold his Park of Bradgate so enclosed as it was enclosed in the octaves of St. Hilary, in the 31st year of the aforesaid King Henry, with the Deer-leaps (Saltatoriis), then in it made; and for this Agreement and Grant, the same Earl hath granted for him and his heirs, that the same Roger de Somery and his heirs may enter at any hour on the Forest of him the Earl, to chase or hunt in it (ad bersandum), with nine bows and six hounds, according to the form of a cyrograph before made, between the aforesaid Roger Earl of Winton, and Hugh de Albiniaco Earl of Arundel, in the Court of the Lord the King at Leicester. And if any wild beast, wounded by any of the aforesaid bows, shall enter the aforesaid Park by any deer-leap or otherwise, it shall be lawful for the aforesaid Roger de Somery and his heirs to send one or two of his men, who shall follow the aforesaid wild beast, with the dogs pursuing, within the aforesaid Park, without bows or arrows, and may take it on that day whereon it was wounded, without hurt of other wild beasts in the aforesaid Park abiding; so that if they be footmen, they shall enter by some deer-leap or hedge; and, if they be horsemen, they shall enter by the gate, if it shall be open; and otherwise shall not enter before they wind their horn for the keeper, if he will come. And further the same Earl hath granted for him and his heirs, that they for the future shall every year cause to be taken a brace of bucks, in the buck season, and a brace of does in the doe season, and them

---

[1] 'The priors of Ulvescroft had a special grant from Roger de Quincy to hunt at their pleasure in Charnwood *usque ad saltum*, unto the *saulte* of the parks of Bradgate, Groby, and Lough-borough. The Earl's Dyke, in this forest, still remaining, was a work of considerable magnitude, and though the precise period of its forma-tion can only be conjectured, its object was apparently to serve the double purpose of a well-defined boundary, and mutual *deerfence*, between the Earls of Leicester and Chester. Its bank was doubtless surrounded by a paling.'—*Potter's Charnwood Forest*, p. 177.

cause to be delivered at the gate of the aforesaid Park, to any one of the men of the aforesaid Roger de Somery and his heirs, bringing their letters patent for the aforesaid deer. The aforesaid Earl hath also granted for him and his heirs, that they for the future shall make no park, nor augment the park beyond the bounds of the hunting ground of the aforesaid Roger de Somery and his heirs, besides the ancient Enclosures of the aforesaid Forest : and the aforesaid Roger de Somery hath granted for him and his heirs, that they for the future shall never enter the aforesaid Forest to chase, save with nine bows and six hounds; and that their Foresters shall not carry in the wood of the aforesaid Roger de Somery and his heirs, barbed arrows but piled arrows, (sed pilettas).[1] And that his men of Barwe (Barrow) and foresters, within the octaves of St. Michael, at the Park ford, shall do fealty every year to the bailiffs of the aforesaid Earl and his heirs, and other things which to the aforesaid forest belong, according to the purport of the cyrograph between the aforesaid Earls of Winchester and Arundel before made. And this Agreement is made between the aforesaid Earl and the aforesaid Roger de Somery saving to the same Earl and his heirs, and to the aforesaid Roger de Somery and his heirs, all the articles in the aforesaid cyrograph made between the aforesaid Earls of Winchester and Arundel contained. And further the said Earl hath granted for him and his heirs, that the one or two of the men of the aforesaid Roger de Somery and his heirs, who shall follow the aforesaid wild beast wounded, with the dogs pursuing it into the aforesaid Park, with the aforesaid wild beast, whether they shall have taken it or not, may with the aforesaid dogs, freely and without hindrance, go out thro' the gate of the aforesaid Park; and the aforesaid Earl and his heirs shall cause some one of their servants to give notice to the aforesaid Roger de Somery and his heirs at Barwe, on what day he shall send for the aforesaid deer to the aforesaid place, at the

---

[1] *Pilettas.* From *pila*, a ball. In our ancient forest laws, an arrow which had a round knob a little above the head, to hinder it from going far into the mark.

aforesaid times; and this notice they shall cause to be given to them six days before the aforesaid day. In witness whereof each to the others writing hath put to his seal.

'And it is to be observed, that the time of buck season (tempus pinguedinis),[1] here is computed between the Feast of S. Peter ad Vincula (August 1) and the Exaltation of Holy Cross, (Sept. 14), and the time of doe season (tempus firmationis)[2] between the Feast of S. Martin (Nov. 11) and the Purification of the Blessed Virgin (Feb. 2).'[3][4]

The above is, as I suppose, one of the earliest and most curious instances which can be adduced of a Hunting Agreement, and evinces the minute care and attention with which such agreements were carried out. No doubt there are others extant, but this will be sufficient for our present purpose, the illustration of the deer-hunting of our ancestors. Hunting, indeed, during the Middle Ages appears to have been carried on with much deliberation, not to say solemnity. Deeds were engrossed and sealed, and the most searching and exact enquiries made as to the state of the game in every forest and chase, as appears by the wardmotes, some of which are still preserved. Warrants for the due delivery of venison were written and signed with legal accuracy, and letters, at a period when letter-writing was a rare accomplishment and confined to the clergy, were despatched

---

[1] *Tempus pinguedinis,* translated grease time, or the fat season. Richard II. granted to the abbess of Wherwell, in Hampshire, two bucks 'de grees,' and two does 'de firmeson,' 'annuatim, a foresta de Chuyte' (Chute), in the seventh year of his reign.—Patent Rolls.

[2] *Firmatio,* the doe season ; *a* supplying with food.—Leg. Inæ. c. 34.

[3] Potter's 'Charnwood Forest,' 4to. 1842, p. 117, and Blount's 'Tenures,' Ed. Beckwith, p. 426.

[4] Although our ancestors defined very clearly

the lawful seasons of the chase, they did not always observe them. Thus, we find in the household roll of Eleanor Countess of Leicester, A.D. 1265, under date of the 10th of May, the following entry : 'pro expensis canum, per Michaelem de Kemes (inge), in capiendo i cervum vi[d].' This proves that venison was used in the spring as well as at the proper periods.—*Manners and Household Expenses of England in the thirteenth and fourteenth centuries.* Roxburghe Club, 1841.

from royal and noble persons to their dependents, the knightly, and gentle keepers of parks.

Gradually, and in proportion to the increasing power of the subject, and in inverse ratio to the decrease of the forests and wastes of the realm, which were generally held from the Crown by the greater nobility at the pleasure of the reigning sovereign, the impaled parks of England increased to a considerable extent, though restrained by the license for enclosing, which the laws rendered ever essential, and which the Commons, as appears by the Rolls of Parliament, in the sixth of Henry IV. (A.D. 1404), endeavoured unsuccessfully to abrogate. At this period, by far the larger number of the parks throughout the realm were held directly under the Crown, a large proportion were still the inheritance of the Church, the remainder divided between the different orders of the greater and lesser nobility, the latter including the knightly and gentle families of England.

The following letters, written by command of Queen Margaret of Anjou, may not be out of place here :—

' By the Queene.' ' To the Keeper of Oᵣ Park of Apechild[1] or his Depute there.' ' Wel beloved, we wol and expressly charge you that, for certain considerations moving us, our game within our parc of Apechild, wherof ye have the saufe garde and keping, ye do, with all diligence, to be cherishsed, favered, and kept, without suffryng eny personne, of what degre, estat, or condicion that he be, to hunte there, or have course, shot, or other disporte, in amentising[2] our game above said, to th' extent that, at what tyme it shall please us to resorte thedor, yoᵣ trew acquital may be founden for the good keping and replenishing therof, to th' accompissement of oᵣ intencion in this partie. And that in no wise ye obeie ne serve eny other warrant, but if hit be under our signet, and signed with oᵣ owne hande. And if eny personne presume t' attempte to the contrarie of the premisses, ye do

---

[1] Apchild, or Abfield, in the parish of Gt. Waltham, Essex.

[2] *Amantise, amortise,* alienate ?

certiffie us of their names : and that ye faill not herof, as ye will eschew
our displeasure, at yor perill, and upon forfeiture of the kepyng of o^r said
park.

'Yeven at Plasshe,[1] the xxviii day of Auguste, the yere etc. xxvii
[1449.]'

'By the Quene.' 'To my lords sqüier and ours, J. D. Keper of Shene
Parke,[2] or his Depute there.'

'Trusty and welbeloved. For as moche as we suppose that in short
tyme, we shall come righte negh unto my lords menoir of Shene, we desire
and praye you hartly that ye will kepe against our resortinge thedor, for
oure disporte and recreation, two or iii of the grettest bukkes in my lord's
parc there, saving alweyes my lord's owne commandment there in presence.
As we trust etc.'[3]

To a date a little subsequent to that of the preceding letters, the latter
part, namely, of the fifteenth century and the beginning of the sixteenth,
we may, I think, ascribe the erection of 'Lodges,' built for the purposes of
hunting and retirement, in uncultivated and romantic chases and parks at
some distance from the castles and manor houses of the noble and knightly
owners—quiet seats, where the lord might indulge his silvan tastes free
from the cares of his household and retainers.

Leland in his Itinerary, the earliest, and I had almost said most
agreeable, of English Topographers, constantly mentions the 'pratie loggis'
which adorned the parks of his day. Of these the well-known inscription
at Wortley, in Yorkshire, preserves 'a pleasant record, which speaks much
to the imagination,'[4] and of which Hunter, in his 'Hallamshire,' has given us
the following account :—

'Wharncliffe is five miles from the Town of Sheffield to the north, it is

---

[1] Plasshe, Pleshey, the ancient seat of the
Bohuns Earls of Essex, and afterwards of Thomas
of Woodstock Duke of Gloucester, in Essex.

[2] Shene Park, i. e. Richmond, in Surrey.

[3] Letters of Queen Margaret of Anjou, printed
by the Camden Society in 1863, pp. 100—137.

[4] Quarterly Review, vol. xxxvii. (1820).

partly a Forest, and partly a Deer-Park, and is still a member of the great estates of the Wortley family. The *sea* of *wood* and its command of a prospect of almost unrivalled extent and magnificence, render it one of the most grand and imposing scenes imaginable. If in the midst of such truly magnificent scenery the mind can turn to objects so insignificant, three seats may be discovered cut in the solid rock, *vivoque sedilia saxo,* and probably intended to accommodate those who sought to enjoy this enchanting scenery ; near to them, and also cut in the living rock, or on what is technically called a ground-fast stone, is the inscription below. For more than two centuries it was exposed to every blast that blew; but having been originally cut in a fine bold character, it is still legible, and it has long been protected from any further injury from the weather by a small shed built over it by the late Mr. Edward Wortley Montague.'[1]

Pray for the Saule of
Thomas Wryttelay, Knyght,
for the kyngs bode to Edward
the forthe, Richard third, Hare the bii. and Hare biii.
hows saules God pardon. Whyche
Thomas cawsyd a loge to be made
hon this crag the mydys of
Wanclife for his plesor to her the
hartes bel, in the yere of owr
Lord a thousand cccccy.

Of this same Sir Thomas Wortley, the Family Pedigree narrates, ' Also he had much delite in huntinge, that he did build in the middest in his forest of Wharnclife, a house or lodge, at which house he did lye at, for the most part of the grease tyme ; and the worshipfull of the country did ther resorte unto him, beinge ther with him pastime and good cheere : many tymes he would go into the forest of the peeke and set up ther his tent with

---

[1] Hunter's Hallamshire, fo. 1819, p. 2, *note.*

great provision of viteles, having in his company many worshipfull persones, with his owne famylye, and would remaine ther vii. weeks or more, hunting and makinge other worthy pastimes unto his companye.'[1]

[1] Hunter's South Yorkshire, vol. ii. p. 311.

CHAPTER II.

SKETCH OF THE HISTORY OF DEER PARKS FROM THE
BEGINNING OF THE SIXTEENTH CENTURY
TO THE PRESENT TIME.

CHAPTER II.

*Sketch of the History of Deer Parks from the beginning of the
Sixteenth Century to the Present Time.*

ARRISON, in the curious description of England prefixed to the
first edition of Holinshed's Chronicles, gives us a valuable, but
I think an exaggerated account of the number of Deer Parks in
his time, the early part of the sixteenth century :—' In every
shyre of Englande,' he writes, ' there is great plentye of Parkes, whereof some
here and there appertaine unto the Prince, the rest unto such of the nobilitye
and gentlemen as have their lands and patrimony lying neere unto the
same; I would gladly have set downe the just number of these inclosures
to bee founde in every countye, but sith I cannot so doe, it shal suffice to
say, that in Kent and Essex only are to the number of a hundred, wherein
great plenty of fallowe Deere is cherished and kept.'   And again :—' Our
Parkes are generally inclosed wyth strong pale made of oke, of which kinde
of woode there is great store cherished from tyme to tyme in eache of them,
onely for the maintenaunce of the sayde defence and safe keeping of the
Deere from raunging about the countrey. The circuite of these inclosures in
lyke maner containe oft times a walke of foure or five myles, and sometimes
more or lesse, whereby it is to be seene what store of ground is employed
upon that vayne comoditie which bringeth no maner of gaine or profit to
the owner, sith they comonlye give awaye their fleshe, never taking penny
for the same, because venission in England is neither bought nor soulde by
the right owner, but maintained only for hys pleasure, to the no smal
decay of husbandry, and diminution of mankinde : For when in times
past, many large and welthy occupiers were dwelling within the compasse
of some one Parke, and therby great plenty of corne and cattell seene, and

to be had amongst them, beside a more copious procreation of humaine issue, wherby the realme was alwaies better furnished with able men to serve the Prince in his affaires; now there is almost nothing kept but a sort of wilde and savage beasts, cherished for pleasure and delite, and yet the owners styll desirous to enlarge those groundes, do not let daily to take in more, affirming that we have already to great store of people in England, and that youth by mariying to soone, doe nothing profite the countrey, but fill it full of beggars.'[1] He proceeds to say that 'The twentieth parte of the realme is employed upon Deere and Conies already.' This is probably an exaggeration, nevertheless there is abundant evidence to prove that there were a vast number of parks in England during the sixteenth century, though towards the end of that period they had begun to decline; upwards of seven hundred are marked in Saxton's maps, engraved between the years 1575 and 1580, besides twenty-one, which are marked in Wales; but yet it is plain by the accounts of Lambard, in his ' Perambulation of Kent,' printed in 1576, and Carew, in his ' Survey of Cornwall,' printed in 1602, that a great number had been within the memory of men disparked, the owners, in the quaint language of the Cornish Squire, ' making there Deere leape over the pale, to give the bullockes place.' Stow in his Annals (1592), and Moryson in his Itinerary (1617), confirms what has been stated above, the former quoting Andrew Bourd,[2] 'that there be more Parks in England than in all Europe beside,' and classing ' Deare red and fallow,' with goats and conies, ' for every where there is jolly maintenance of those kinds of beasts, because it is full of great woods, whereof there riseth pastime of hunting, greatly exercised, specially by the Nobility and Gentlemen.' Moryson observes :—' The English are so naturally inclined to pleasure, as there is no Countrie, wherein the Gentlemen and Lords have so many and large Parkes onely reserved for the pleasure of hunting, or where all sorts of men alot so much ground about their houses for pleasure of Gardens and

---

[1] Holinshed's Chronicles, 1st ed. 1577, p. 89.   [2] Stow's Annals. Ed. Howes, an. 1631, p. 2.

Orchards.' And again :—' The King's Forrests have innumerable heards of Red Deare, and all parts have such plenty of Fallow Deare, as every gentleman of five hundreth or a thousand pounds rent by the yeere hath a Parke for them inclosed with pales of wood for two or three miles compasse. Yet this prodigall age hath so forced Gentlemen to improve their revenewes, as many of these grounds are by them disparked, and converted to feede Cattell : Lastly (without offence be it spoken) I will boldly say, that England (yea perhaps one county thereof) hath more fallow Deare, than all Europe that I have seene.'[1]   In another place Moryson writing of Ireland, adds, ' The Earle of Ormond in Mounster, and the Earle of Kildare in Leinster, had each of them a small Parke inclosed for Fallowe Deare, and I have not seene any other Parke in Ireland.'[2]   A striking difference between the condition of the sister kingdoms,

I could not better illustrate the domestic economy of a large deer park at this period than by giving the following extracts from an Original Roll[3] on paper, containing the accounts of Richard Chambyr, Park Keeper of Framlingham, in Suffolk, from the year 1515 to 1518, and for which I am obliged to Charles Spencer Perceval, Esq., F.S.A. Framlingham at this time belonged to the Duke of Norfolk.

In the vij yere of our soferen lord kyng herry the viii and in the xxiij yer of rychard chambyr þker of framlingham.

Item my lord of Norwyche . i buk	Item the A'bbot of Sypton[4] . 1 buk
Item my lórd Wylleby . . ij bukkis	Item S[r]. Wylliam Rows . . 1 buk
Item be the commaundment of	Item the Abbas of brvsyzard[5] . 1 buk
my lord Wylleby S[r]. lyenell	Item the mastyr of metyngham . 1 buk
demok . . . . . 1 buk	Item Iohan Henyngham . . 1 buk
Item my lády Vere . . . 1 buk	Item S[r]. Arthur hopton . . 1 buk

---

[1] Moryson's Itinerary, part iii. pp. 147, 148.
[2] Ibid. p. 161.
[3] *Penes* Ph. Frere, Esq.

[4] Sibton, Cisterc. Abbey, Hund. of Blithing, Co. Suff.
[5] Brusyard Minoresses, Co. Suff.

Item S^r. Edmond Jeney . . 1 buk

Item S^r. John Wyllebye . . 1 buk

Item Anthony Hansart . . 1 buk

Item S^r. Robert cotton . . 1 buk

Item S^r. tomas lovell . . . 1 buk

Item the prior of hey and the scoell mastyr . . . . 1 buk

Item for Iohan teye . . . 1 buk

Item the balys [1] of ypswyche . 1 buk

Item robert cheke . . . 1 buk

Item the gyld of framlyngham . 1 buk

Item the abbot of bery . . ji bukkis

Item the prior of buttley . . 1 buk

Item the prior of. Seynt petyrs . 1 buk

Item the prior of Wood brege . 1 buk

Item the prior of elye . . 1 buk

Item edmond Wyngfeld and hn 1 buk

Item Wylliam Jeney . . . 1 buk

Item Crystoper harman . . 1 buk

Item edmond gelgatt . . . 1 buk

Item robert forthe the helder . 1 buk

Item doctor call . . . 1 buk

Item the parson of framlyngham for his tythe . . . . 1 buk

Item my lord curson was her and kylled a buk and a sowrell . 1 buk and I gaue the sowrell to lord cursons seruauntis and S^r. rychyard Wentforthys seruauntis

Item S^r. rychard Wentforthe . 1 buk

Item S^r. Anthony Wyngfeld . 1 buk

Item S^r. rychard cawndysche . 1 buk

Item S^r. iohan Awdeley . . 1 buk

Item S^r. iohan glemham . . 1 buk

Item S^r. Iamys framyngham . 1 buk

Item the townschepe of ypswyche 1 buk

Item mastyr lane . . . . 1 buk

Item the towne of Wodbrege . 1 buk

Item the priories of Campsey . 1 buk

Item mastyr Commysary . . 1 buk

Item be a warrant of my lordis Iohan draper gentylman . 1 buk

Item be a warrant of my lordis

Iohan mascall of the chancery 1 buk

Item be a warrant of my lordis rychard Warton . . . 1 buk

Item the person of orforthe and Johan garlond . . . 1 buk

Item be a warrant of my lordis . 1 buk

Item S^r. edward Ichyngham . 1 buk

Item regnold lytylprow . . 1 buk

Item Iohan Rychere of bongay . 1 buk

Item S^r. crystofer Wyllebye . 1 buk

Item herry kooke . . . 1 buk

Item my lady bowser . . 1 buk

Item be warrant of my lordis mastyr chauncy . . . 1 buk

Item mastyr lucas . . . 1 buk

Item thomas benet and robert mellis . . . . . 1 buk

Item M^r. thomas fyncham . 1 buk

Item Wylliam mekylfeld . . 1 buk

Item M^r. prior of thelforthe . 1 buk

Item Robert browne . . . 1 buk

Item thomas sporne . . . 1 buk

Item the towne. of harleston . 1 buk

Item S^r. thomas tyrrell . . 1 buk

Item thomas cok for hys dow-tyris marryage . . . 1 buk

Item for mastrys marget hasset 1 buk

Item edmond rookwood . . 1 buk

Item nycholas call . . . 1 buk

Item be a warrant of my lordis Wylliam crane gentylman . 1 buk

Item humfrey everton . . 1 buk

Item thomas Russche . . 1 buk

Item S^r. thomas Wysche . . 1 buk

Lossys thys somer ded of the wyppys.

Item of buks . . . . iij

Item of sowers v

Item of preketys . . . i

Item of dooys . . . . viij

Item a dog came in and kyllyd a do

Item dallyng of laxfeld merser

---

[1] Bailiffs.

ij doggis of hys came in and
kyllyd a doo and a fawne.
Item on holy rood evyn I found
in the parke Sʳ. Iohan bowse
parysch pryst of tanygton with
hys bow bent and an arrow in
yt betyng at the herd.

These be the doys [does] that I have kyllyd
thes seson.

Item my lord Wylleby .	. ij doys

+

Item for the Awdyt . .	. ij doys
Item to my lordis grace to lam-	
bethe	. viij doys
Item aftyr that the second tyme	vj doys
Item at the iij tyme .	. vj doys
Item my lord Wyllebye .	. j do
Item [&c. &c. preseiits of does .	
set down as the bucks. In all	
64 does.]	

[Losses in all 31 head.]

My lord Wylleby cam from london and he schewyd me that
my lordys grace was content
thatt he sholde kyll doys her,
and for as many doys as he
kyllyd heere he schulde put
quyke doys¹ in hersham² park
for them as wyche he had   . x doys

Also he seyd my lordys grace
was content thatt my lord
byrsschope schuld haue .   . ij doys
he seyd that my lordys grace
schulde haue to putt in hersham parke . . . . vj doys
Also he schewyd me that my
lordys grace was content that
Iohan henyngham schuld haue
iij doys and he schulde put in
hersham parke for them. . viij doys

Thees be the lossys thatt I have had thys
wynter

Item of bukkys . .	. vij
Item of sowrellys .	. iiij
Item of preketys .	. x
Item of dooys . . .	. xvij
Item of fawnys . .	. iij scor xj

Thes be dede be candylmes

Thes be the lossys sythe candylmes

Item of bukkys . .	. iij
Item a buk dyed drownyd in	
the moote . . .	. [i]
Item [sowrells ij—sowers j—pre-	
kettys iiij—doys v.]	
Item of ye last yer fawnys mor-	
kyns	. xlixᵗᵉ

Thes be ded syn Wytson day
[End of viiᵗʰ year.]

1516 (*in a modern hand*). *In the viij yer [Hen. 8, and 24th year of*
Richard Chambyr.]

Lossys this fawning tym.

Item of fawnys . . . . xlxᵗᵉ

Thes be the bukkys yⁱ I haue kyllyd thys yer.
Item the frensche quene . . 1 buk

Item ij fawnys.
Item she sent to me for a fawne.
Item the duke sent to me for a . 1 buk
Item the quene cam agayn and
kyllyd . . . . . iiij bukys

¹ Live does.
² *hersham.* So probably for Horsham, Co.
Sussex, where the Dukes of Norfolk had two

parks, very near the town.—See Dallaway and
Cartwright.

Item [&c. to various persons in
all, including the foregoing, 99
bucks, 2 sors, 3 sorrells, a pricket, 2 docs, and a fawne.]

Thes be y° lossys thys somer of the garget.

(Abstract) 9 bucks, 3 sores, 4 sorrels, 1 pricket.
Item doys dyed of fawning and
the garget xi

*Thes be the dere that I have begon to kyll
this seson.*

[To various persons . . . 9 does]
      +
Item for the audyte . . . ij dois
Item to my lordys grace to Lon-
don before the awdyte and
aftyr . . . . xxxvj doys
[To various other persons . . 25 does]

*Thes be the dere that be ded in the same
place.*

[Bucks 7, sowers 3, sowrells 5, prekettys viij,
does 23, fawns 59.]

Item. Johan pulsham thelder cam rydyng
be the wey and fownd a do without and hys
doge kyllyd *hym* [*sic*] and he hyng hys dog.

Also Watyr Warnere, the sone of Ane
Warnere of Denyngton, forstallyd my lordys
dere wan I was settyng them home and put
hys byche to hyr and browt hyre in to the
parke and kyllyd here.

Also on seynt markys day Iohan foxe
and yonge thomas hyllys, laddys, and Wijl-
liam tendyclone, they went forthe to the
releffyng [?] of the hare and had a sowre,
and browt hyr in to the parke and kyllyd
a do with fawne and a nother fawne.

    End of 1516.

[(1517 Modern hand) 6th of Henry 8.˙ 26 of
Richard Chambre.]

*Thes be the deere that I haue kyllyd thys
somere.*

Inter alia.
Item my lord Edmond howard . vi bukkys
Item for the comyng of my lord
 cardenall . . . . i buk
Item he cam trow the parke and
 kyllyd '. '. . . 1 buk and a do
Item on the next day I was
 sygned to kyll for hym . . xij bukkys
 In all 93 bucks, 1 doe, 1 sorrell.

[Dead of the Garget.]

[11 bucks, 6 sowers, 7 sowrells, 43 prickets,
67 does, 50 fawns.]

On the thouris day after mycholmes daye
at night I toke the persone of ketylwerjs
brege in the parke.

[Killed for various persons 22 does.]

*These be the lossys that I had of quyke deere
to Wyndferdyng for my lorde of Surrey.*

[viz.]
[121 deer taken at seven different times of
the following descriptions :
Bucks, sowers, sowrells, does, prickets
' malefawnys,' ' rascall fawnys.']

[*Deer had to Hersham for my Lord of
Norfolk at four times.*
Summa. 6 score and one ' quyk dere.']

[*Dead this winter in Framlingham Park.*
44 bucks, 19 sowers, 28 sowrells, 54 prickets,
89 does, 165 fawns.]

    End of 1517.

[1518, 10th of Henry 8, 26th of Richard Chambre.].
[Deer killed] 68 bucks.
[Died of the Garget and 'the Rotte thys somore,' 15 bucks, 6 sowers, 9 souarellys, 4 prickettis, 11 ' of dooges.']
[Losses of fawns in fawning time and this summer, 31 fawns.]

[*Does killed for various persons*, 93, *including*]
Item for my Lorde of Norffolks grace to lambeth afore the audite and senys [since]   . xxx doys
Item the abbot of Bery sente to me for a doo, upon sent Johan is daye in Cristismes, and I kyllyd hyr and delyveryd hyr to Iohan Crispe and to Johan Chyrie ? and in the whey home-ward they toke a corse in Hol-fereth and broute a souerell in to the parke and kyllyd hyme ther.   At wich I toke up the one doge in the parke and keppyd hym, they made labor to Sir Wylliam Rowces for the dog and I delyueryde the dog to hym   .   .   .   . *1* doo

[*Losses in the winter in Framlingham Park.*
23 bucks, 16 soures, 19 souerelys, 16 pricketys, 38 doyes.   'Item of faunys lx xxxv.' [*sic*]
A doe and 9 fawns killed by dogs.]
End of 1518.

[1519. 11 H. 8. 27 R. C.]
Losses this fawning time.
1 fawn killed by 'a mastife beche and a spanyell.'
53 fawns died.]

Bucks killed for various persons.
Viz. 96 bucks, including
Item Sr Iohan Rows for syng-ynge of his fyrst messe . . 1 bucke
Item George Baker for his mariage . . . . . 1 bucke

[*Losses this summer, viz.*
3 bucks, 'a bowre,' 2 sowrellis, 9 dooes.]
Item the mundaye afore mychaelmes daye cam in a dogge of Iohnsons of denyng-tone, the schoe maker, and kyllyd ij dooes, and there the dogge was take up, and I sende to hym to wete wether he wold have the dogge agayne and he sende me word naye, and then I hynge hym upon a tre.

The Northumberland Household Book also, which was begun to be compiled in the year 1512, gives a very particular account of the parks and deer appertaining to the great house of Percy, by which it appears, that exclusive of the parks in Sussex and other Counties in the South there was a total of 5,571 deer in 21 parks and forests in the counties of Northumberland, Cumberland and York; of this number there were required for the supply of 'the House in Winter,' 29 does, and of ' bukks in Somer' 20; the number appointed from every park being most accurately stated, according to the size of each.[1]   No doubt other great families, though few could compare at that period with the splendour and wealth of the Houses of Howard and Percy, had, in their several degrees, parks of deer of proportionate size and number, but the larger parks generally in the southern and midland counties, were old royal domains, or belonging to the Crown by right of the Duchy of Lancaster, and for the most part leased out to those of the nobility and gentry who had interest at Court.   The keepership of a royal park, with its ' herbage and pannage,' the right of so many fee deer, &c., was a prize eagerly sought for at a period when the younger brothers of knightly families were glad to be provided for by being appointed keeper of the family park, and being put in possession of the lodge attached to it.   Thus the celebrated Sir Thomas Smith, the unfortunate grantee of 'the Ardes' in the county of Down in Ireland, offers in 1575 to resign his grant to the Crown, or to exchange it for a manor in Essex 'with a park,' 'because it was never my chance yet to have a Park, or the keeping of a Park.'[2]   A lesser privilege of this nature, but one which was no doubt also greatly appreciated, was the right to kill a buck or doe yearly in another person's park, of which the grant to John Bohun, Esq., in the park of Heveningham, in Suffolk, is a curious illustration :—

' To all faithful people to whome thys present writing shall come. John Hevyngham, Knyght, Dame Alice, his wife, Anthony Hevyngham, sone and heire apparant to the same Sir John, sends greting in our Lord God Everlastyng Kyng. Knowe ye, that I the said Sir John, in performaunce of a certaine covenaunt and agreement on my parte to be pformed, specifyed, and conteyned in an indenture made betwyn me on the oon parte, and oon Nicholus Bohun Esquier, on the other parte, bearing date this syxte day of this present monyth of Octobere, have given and graunted, and by theis

---

[1] See the Northumberland Household Book, ed. 1827, p. 112.

[2] Shirley's Territory of Farney, 4to. 1845, p. 52.

pr̃sents doo gif, and graunte to the said Nicholus, a yerly fee of oon buk in
somer, and oon doo in wynter to be taken of my gifte within my parke at
Heveyngham, in seasonable and convenyent tymes in the yer: to have and
enjoye the said fee of oon buk, and oon doo yerly, to be taken in such tyme
and place as is aforesaid to the said Nicholus and his assyngs during his
life naturall: and that it shall be lefull to the same Nicholus, at his own
plesure to kille yerly the said buk and doo in convenyent tymes of the
yer, with hys houndys, grey houndys, or long bowe. Soo always the same
Nicholus be there present in his own person, and so that the said Nicholus
do gif convenyent knowledge to the keper of the seid parke for the tyme
being of his comyng their to hunte and kyll as is aforeseid, or ellys the
same buk and doo to be killed by the same keper, and delivered to the
seid Nicholus or his assigns at the seid park. And we the seid Dame Alice
and Anthony and eyther of us do fully assinte and agre to thys presente
graunte, and doo satisfye and confirme the astate of the seid Nicholus of
and in the premises, to have and to enjoye the seid fee to hym and his
assignes during his life naturall, in such wise and forme as is before
expressed. In witness wherof we, the seid Sir John, Dame Alice, and
Anthony, have unto sett our seales, upon the eyght day of Octobre, in the
fyve and twenty yer of the reygn of our Sovereyne lord, King Henry
the eight.

'I. HEVENYNGHAM. A. HEVENYNGHAM. By me ANTHONY HEVE-
NYNGHAM.'[1]

Though during the reign of Elizabeth, as we have seen, parks began to
decline in number, yet there were new ones sometimes enclosed. The
following instance, which describes at length both the expense connected
with the undertaking, and the manner in which its completion was celebrated, needs no apology for insertion here :—

' The booke of Remembrance when Astwelle parke [2] was first created

[1] Suckling's Suffolk, vol. ii. p. 387.
[2] In Northamptonshire, on the confines of Whittlebury Forest, then the seat of Thomas Lovett, Esq.

D 2

and inclosed, and wheare and at what tyme the pale was bought for the same, &c.

'Imprimis, bought at Borseley woode, in the first yeare of the reigne of kinge Edward the sixt, by John Oltams of my Lorde Windesowes Woodewarde there, the number of six thousand pale wch cost xxxiii^s iiii^d a thousand.

'Itm. in the seconde yeare of the reigne of the saied Kynge, bought in Perrey parke xx^ti okes to make pales of the deputies of Sr Nicholas Throgmorton, Knight, wch coste vii^li.

'Itm. in the thirde yeare of the saied Kinges reigne bought in the saied parke other xx^ti okes, wch cost vi^li. xiii^s. iiii^d.

'Itm. in the fourth yeare of the saied Kynges reigne, of my Lord Marquesses Woodwardes in the forest xx^ti okes, wch cost vi^li xiii^s. iiii^d.

'Itm. bought of Mr Gifford at three parkes, xx^ti okes, wch cost vi^li.

'Itm. the saied parke was impaled by one James Fawkener of Sireshm, who died in the yeare of O^r Lord God 1560.

'M^d. In a statute made in anno V^to R^ne Eliz. in Cap. 21, ther is enacted the charter of the same parke, wch acte toke effecte at Pentecost followinge the said acte made in the saide yeare.

'Itm. In Julye then followinge, Thomas Lovett, owner of the saied parke, made sute to the Right Honorable the Lord M'ques of Northn, to come to vewe and peruse the same for a testimony of thinges to come, the wch should approve that the saied parke was fynished before that daie, whiche saied Lord Marques did come the saied monthe and yeare, accompaned wth many of the most worshipfull of the saied shire, and other of other shires, whose names do hereafter followe, that is to saie: The Lord Marques of Northn, Sir John Spencer, Sir John Fermor, Sir Robert Lane, Sir Robert Stafford, Knights. M^r. Mighell Poulteney, M^r. Throgmton, Sient of the Hawkes, M^r. Richard Knightley, M^r. Thoms Piggott, M^r. Jerome Ferm^r Esquiers. With many and dyvers others, at wch tyme the saied Honorable Lorde Marques of Northn ther wth his bucke houndes did kyll three buckes, and his companye killed one bucke; wch saied foure buckes were killed in Astwell parke aforesaid in July aforesaid, and next after the saied estatute toke effecte, beinge in anno 1564.'[1]

The Act here referred to was intended for the preservation of deer and deer parks, and subjected any person breaking into 'an empaled park used for the keeping breeding and cherishing of deer,' to imprisonment for theee months, and made him also liable 'to pay to the partie grieved his treble damages.' But an Act of more importance to the owners of parks had been passed in 1536 (27th Henry VIII.) enacted with a view to encourage the breed of horses, and which interfered, in what would now be considered a very arbitrary manner, with the rights of the subject. This Act appears to have fallen into disuse, but was revived in the reign of Elizabeth. It will be explained by the following 'Instructions to Commissioners appointed by the Queen's Majesty for the ministering of Horses in all places w^{th}in the Realm, &c.' (dated Nov. 10. 1577):—' Item you shall take orders that every man that hath a Park of his own, or in Lease or in keeping for term of life of the compass of one mile, shall keep in the same two mares, and every man that shall have a Park of the compass of four miles, shall keep four mares, according to the scantling appointed in the statute, and you shall do what you can to procure every man that hath a Park of the compass of two miles and upwards to four miles, shall keep three mares of that scantling, which we take to be the meaning of the Statute.'[2][3]

From the original in the possession of the Earl Ferrers.

[2] Original instructions *penes* Lord Willoughby de Broke.

[3] In illustration of the habits of our ancestors as regards their park-keepers at this period, the following appointment of one may be taken as an instance. In 1584, George Shirley, Esq., granted unto Joseph Crispe, gent, for a term of forty years 'the parkershippe of the park in Staunton, wth all the profitts of the same—viz.

one fat bucke and one fat doe, with two closes, and dispasturing for twelve kine, and one bull, one gelding or nayge, and one stalking mare within the said parke, with the House called the Lodge, standing within the said parke, and also sufficient firewood to be taken within the said part of the browse or windfall wood, to be spent only within the said Lodge.' (From the original grant at Staunton Harold *penes* the Earl Ferrers.)

Buck-hunting in parks appears to have been the most fashionable
disport of the Elizabethan period. The forests, and their primeval inhabitants the red-deer, had been much reduced; the nobility, that is,
archbishop, bishop, earl or baron, coming to the court at the summons
of the sovereign, and passing by the forests, could no longer easily
exercise their privilege, as they were empowered by the old charter of
King Henry III., of ' killing one or two of our deer by view of our Forester,
'f he be present; or else he shall cause one to blow an Horn for him, so
that he seem not to steal our Deer.' [1] Those days were gone, but in their
place every gentleman could ' enjoy his own hunting in his own grounds,'
as it had been in pre-Norman times, and many, it must be confessed, did
little or nothing else. Thus of Henry Lord Berkeley it is recorded that
in the month of July in the first year of Elizabeth (1559), ' He came with
his Wife and Family to Callowden his house by Coventry, when the first
work done, was the sending for his buckhounds to Yate in Gloucestershire; his hounds being come, away goethe he and his wife a progress of
buck-hunting to the Parks of Berkswell, Groby, Bradgate, Leicester Forest,
Tiley and others on this side his house; and after a small repose, then the
parks of Kenelworth, Astley, Wedgnock and others, on the other side of
his house, and this was the course of this Lord, more or less, for the thirty
next summers at least.' [2]

Queen Elizabeth inherited from her father a taste for these silvan sports,
and her ' progresses ' afford us many pleasant glimpses of her enjoyment of
them. The following incident, which took place in 1574, relates also to Henry
Lord Berkeley, and proves her resemblance to her father in other and more
dangerous characteristics :—' Queen Elizabeth in her progress, in the 15th
year of her reigne, came to Berkeley Castle, what time this Lord Henry
had a stately game of red-deer in the park adjoining, called " *The Worthy* "
whereof Henry Ligon was keeper, during which time of her being there,

---

[1] Charter of the Forest, 9 H. III. cap. xi.   [2] Smyth's Lives of the Berkeleys, 1821, p.
188.

such slaughter was made as twenty-seven stagges were slayne in the toyles
in one day, and many others, on that and the next stollen and havocked;
whereof when this Lord (Henry) being then at Callowden, was advertized,
having much set his delight in this game, he sodainly and passionately
disparked that grownd; but in a few months after he had a secret friendly
advertisement from the Court "that the Queen was informed how the same
was disparked by him, on repining at her coming to his house (for indeed it
was not in her jests), and at the good sport she had in the park, advising
this Lord to carry a wary watch over his words and actions, least thus that
Earl (meaning Leicester) that had, contrary to her set justice, drawn her to
his Castle, and purposely had caused that slaughter of his deare, might
have a further plot against his head and that castle, whereto he had taken
no small likeage, and affirmed to have good title therto, and was not far
from his Manor of Wotton, lately recovered against him." [1]

When Frederick Duke of Wirtemberg came to England in August 1592,
he visited Queen Elizabeth at Reading. His private secretary wrote and
published an account of his Highness's travels which have been lately
translated into English by Mr. Rye of the British Museum, from whose
entertaining volume I make the following extract relating to the sports of
the Field at that time in fashion, and with which His Highness was
entertained:—

' It had pleased her Majesty to depute an old distinguished English lord
to attend his Highness, and she had commissioned and directed him not
only to show his Highness the splendid Royal Castle at Windsor, but also
to amuse him by the way with shooting and hunting red-deer, for you
must know that in the vicinity of the same place Windsor, there are
upwards of sixty parks (?) which are full of game of various kinds, and
they are so contiguous, that in order to have a glorious and royal sport the
animals can be driven out of one inclosure into another, and so on; all

[1] Smyth's Lives of the Berkeleys, p. 203.

which inclosures are encompassed by fences. And thus it happened: the huntsmen who had been ordered for the occasion, and who live in splendid separate lodges in these parks, made some capital sport for his Highness. In the first inclosure his Highness shot off the leg of a fallow-deer, and the dogs soon after caught the animal. In the second they chased a stag for a long time backwards and forwards with particularly good hounds, over an extensive and delightful plain; at length his Highness shot him in front with an English cross-bow, and this deer the dogs finally worried and caught. In the third, the greyhounds chased a deer, but much too soon, for they caught it directly, even before it could get out into the open plain. Then these stags were brought to Windsor and presented to his Highness; one of them was taken to his lodging, and sent as a present to Mons. de Beauvois, the French Ambassador.'[1]

In 1591, the Queen was at Cowdray in Sussex, the seat of Viscount Montague. An account of this visit has been preserved which describes how, 'on Monday August 17, at eight of the clocke in the morning, her Highness took horse, with all her traine, and rode into the parke; where was a delicate bowre prepared, under the which were her Highness' musicians placed, and a cross-bowe by a nymph, with a sweet song, delivered to her hands, to shoote at the deere, about some thirtie in number, put into a paddock, of which number she killed three or four, and the Countesse of Kildare one.—Then rode her Grace to Cowdray to dinner, and aboute sixe of the clocke in the evening, from a turret, sawe sixteen buckes, all having fayre lawe, pulled downe with greyhoundes in a lawnd: all the huntinge ordered by Meister Henrie Browne, the Lorde Montague's thirde sonne, Raunger of Windsor forest.'[2] The position of a 'delicate bower' of this description, is still pointed out at Cowdray, and tradition asserts that her Majesty dined under it, affording an apt illustration 'of the place where and howe an assembly should be made, in the presence of a Prince, or

[1] England as seen by Foreigners, 1865, p. 15.   [2] Progresses of Queen Elizabeth, vol. iii. p. 91.

some honourable person,' described by Gascoigne in his 'Booke of Hunting,' first printed in 1575, in the following pleasant verses :—

> Who list [by me] to learne, Assembly for to make,
> For keysar, king, or comely queene, for lord or ladies sake ;
> Or where, or in what sort, it should prepared be,
> Marke well my words, and thanke me then, for thankes I crave in fee.
> The place should first be pight, on pleasant gladsome greene,
> Yet under shade of stately trees, where little sunne is seene :
> And neare some fountaine spring, whose chrystall runing streames,
> May helpe to coole the parching heate, ycaught by *Phœbus* beames.
> The place appointed thus, it neither shall be clad
> With Arras nor with Tapystry, such paltry were too bad,
> Ne yet those hote perfumes, whereof high courtes do smell,
> May once presume in such a place, or Paradise to dwell.
> Away with fayned fresh, as broken boughes or leaves;
> Away, away, with forced flowers, ygathred from their graves :
> This place must of itselfe afforde such sweete delight,
> And eke such shewe, as better may content the greedy sight :
> Where sundrie sortes of leaves, which growe upon the ground,
> May seeme (indeede) such tapystry, as we (by art) have found.
> Where fresh and fragrant flowers, shall need no courtiers cost,
> To daube himselfe with Syvet, Muske, and many an oyntment lost.
> Where sweetest singing byrdes, may make such melodye,
> As *Pan*, not yet *Apollo's* arte, can sounde such harmony.
> Where breath of westerne windes, may calmly yeeld content,
> Where casements neede not opened be, where ayre is never pent,
> Where shade may serve for shryne, and yet the sunne at hande,
> Where beautie neede not quake for colde, ne yet with sunne be tande.
> In fine and to conclude, where pleasure dwels at large,
> Which Princes seeke in Palaces, with payne and costly charge.[1]

Gascoigne's work on 'The Noble Arte of Venerie or Hunting' appears to have been for the most part translated from early French works on this subject, founded upon some of the very ancient treatises to which I have before referred.[2] This, perhaps, may account for the retention of the very ancient, but even in the Elizabethan age, one would suppose, very

---

[1] Gascoigne's Noble Arte of Venerie. Ed. 1st, p. 98.   [2] Page 15.

The Report of a Huntsman upon the sight of an Hart, in pride of grease.
From Gascoigne's Book of Hunting 1575.

unpleasing practice of the Huntsman presenting the 'fewmèts' or ordure !
of the Hart to the Queen Majesty herself! as represented in the accom-
panying woodcut from Gascoigne's Book.   Here the Queen is seen in a
'standing,' surrounded by her Court, the Huntsman on his knee before her :
his business is thus described in verse :—

> Before the Queene, I come report to make
> Then hushe and peace, for noble Trystrams sake.
> From out my horne, my fewmets fyrst I drawe,
> And theas present, on leaves, by hunters lawe :
> And thus I say : my liege, behold and see
> An Hart of tenne, I hope he harbor'd bee.
> For if you marke, his fewmets every poynt,
> You shall them finde, long, round, and well annoynt,
> Knottie and great, withouten prickes or eares,
> The moystness shewes, what venysone he beares.[1]

Afterwards other huntsmen made their several reports, and presented
their fewmeshings, and after this curious inspection, it was for the ' Prince
to choose which of the Harts he will hunt, and which he thinks most
likely to make him best sport.'

The queen sometimes, and as an especial mark of favour, honoured
some of her favourites with the deer killed by her own royal hand.   Thus
on one occasion we are told in a letter from Robert Duddley to Archbishop Parker, that he had sent him by the queen's command, ' a great
and fat stag, killed with the Queen's own hand, but which, because the
weather was hot, and the dere somewhat chafed, and dangerous to be
carried so farr without some help, he had caused to be parboyled in this
sort, for the best preservation of him.'[2]

The taste of King James I. for hunting, and in particular the interest
which he took in his deer, has been already alluded to.[3]   History gives us
numerous proofs.   The following in point of date should have precedence,
and is a characteristic example of the royal taste :—

[1] Gascoigne, p. 96.   [2] Ant. Rep. ii. p. 166.   [3] P. 9.

' His Majestie having a little while reposed himselfe ' at Widdrington
Castle [in Northumberland] ' after his great journey, found new occasion
to travel further; for as he was delighting himselfe with the pleasure of
the parke, he suddenly beheld a number of deere neare the place: The
game being so faire before him he could not forbear; but according to
his wonted manner forth he went and slew two of them : which done he
returned with a good appetite to the house, where he was most Royally
feasted and banketted that night.' This was altogether a most unsports-
manlike proceeding, having taken place on Friday, April 8, 1603, on the
king's journey from Scotland to take possession of the Crown of England ; [1]
and a few days afterwards at Worksop he is related to have offended
against the laws of the chase in like manner.[2]

But perhaps the 'Proclamation against Hunters, stealers and killers
of Deare within any the King's Majesties Forests, Chases or Parks,' which
was 'given at Our Honour of Hampton Court the 9. day of September
Anno Dom. 1609,' will still more completely illustrate King James's incli-
nation and the royal habits with respect to the chase :—

' We had hoped,' it quaintly commences, ' seeing it is notorious to all
our subjects, how greatly we delight in the exercise of Hunting, as well
for our recreation, as for the necessary preservation of our health, that no
man in whom was either reverence to our person, or fear of our Lawes,
would have offered us offence in those our sports, considering especially,
that the nature of all people is not onely in things of this qualitie but in
matters of greater moment so farre to conform themselves to the affection
and disposition of their Sovereigne, as to affect that which they know to
be liking to them and to respect it, and to avoyd the contrary : and we
must acknowledge that we have found that Gentlemen and persons of the

---

[1] Nichols's Progresses of King James I., vol. i.
p. 68.   Sir Robert Long was the owner of
Widdrington at this time.   The narrative is by
T. Millington.

[2] Nichols's Progresses of King James I., vol. i.
p. 85.

better sort (who know best what becometh their duetie) have restrained
their owne humors, and framed themselves therein to give us contentment :
yet falleth it out notwithstanding, that neither the example of them, nor
respect of the Lawes, nor duety to us, hath had power to reforme the cor-
rupt natures and insolent dispositions of some of the baser sort, and some
other of a disordered life ; By divers of which condition (since our offence
manifested against those that trespasse in that kinde) and since our last
comming forth into this Progresse, in places where wee lately tooke our
pleasure in our owne grounds, and neare our owne houses of abode, there
have bene more frequent offences offerred in that kinde, then at any time
heretofore, or in the late Queenes dayes were attempted : Neverthelesse,
howsoever in her later dayes (being a Lady whose sexe and yeares were not
so apt to that kinde of recreation, having no posteritie, and therefore lesse
carefull of conservation of that kinde of Royaltie, which her progenitors
kings of this Realme had maintained) people might perhaps for those
respects presume of more libertie then became them, or the Lawes of the
Realme doe permit ; yet in our time, being a Prince that have manifested
our affection and delight in that exercise, and having posteritie like to
continue in the same disposition, when either their recreation or their
exercise shall require it : It seemeth strange that men will now attempt to
offend with more licentiousnesse, then at any time heretofore, and offer to
us in our grounds, that which they will not endure each at others hands
in their owne.   We are not ignorant, that there are some passions in mens
mindes so strong, as hard it is but they will breake foorth at times beyond
the bounds of reason, where commoditie, pleasure or revenge provoketh :
But this offence being a trespassing against reason which hath no end in it,
whereof can redound to the offender neither profit or pleasure, honour
or other recompence : we cannot interprete that the transgressions that
are done therein doe proceed, but either out of a barbarous and uncivill
disposition, not fit to bee suffered in an ordered Estate, or out of an insolent
humor and unrespective to our person, no wayes to be endured.'

His Majesty proceeds to threaten 'the severitie we intend to use hereafter,' and concludes by declaring that he will 'extend against them all penalties whatsoever, which by the Lawes of the Forrests, or by any other Lawes or Statutes of the Realme are to be inflicted upon them.'

In the autumn of 1613, John Ernest, Duke of Saxe-Weimar, visited James I. at Theobalds: an account of his journey was printed in 1620, and the following extract from a translation in 'England as seen by Foreigners,' will further illustrate the royal method of hunting at this period :—

'The King and Prince then went down and out through the pleasure ground [at Theobalds], where horses and carriages were waiting. The King and young Prince seated themselves in one carriage, his Highness took his place in the other; and thus they proceeded to the hunt; the other earls and lords rode on horseback. When they came to the hunting-ground, the King, the Prince, and his Highness also mounted on horseback; his Majesty had provided a fine palfrey for his Highness. The hunt generally comes off in this way: the huntsmen remain on the spot where the game is to be found, with twenty or thirty dogs; if the King fancies any in particular among the herd, he causes his pleasure to be signified to the huntsmen, who forthwith proceed to mark the place where the animal stood; they then lead the dogs thither, which are taught to follow this one animal only, and accordingly away they run straight upon his track; and even should there be forty or fifty deer together, they do nothing to them, but chase only the one, and never give up till they have overtaken and brought it down. Meanwhile the King hurries incessantly after the dogs until they have caught the game. There is no particular enjoyment in this sport. Two animals only were caught on this occasion : one was presented by the King to his Highness, which was eaten at his lodging. His Majesty, however, now and then uses long bows and arrows, and when he is disposed, he shoots a deer.' [1]

---

[1] England as seen by Foreigners, p. 154.

We may give one more example of James I.'s love of 'woodcraft' towards the end of his reign.

Mr. Chamberlain writes to Sir T. Carleton, April 24, 1619:—'The King removed from Royston to Ware, being carried part of the way by the Guard in a Neapolitan portative Chair, given him by Lady Hatton, and the rest in a litter. He came the next day in the same way to Theobalds; weak as he was, he would have his deer mustered before him.'[1]

Charles I., the munificent patron of the fine arts, took less interest than his father in the maintenance of the royal parks; nevertheless there can be no doubt but that the royal forests, chases, and parks, as well as the parks belonging to the nobility and gentry generally, were well preserved and in good condition till the era of the Great Rebellion in 1641. The distractions of that unhappy period resulted in the almost total destruction of not only the royal preserves, but of those of all who were of the loyal party; in other words, of the parks and deer of the greater number of the lords and gentlemen of England; various papers written at the Restoration, and preserved in the State Paper Office, abundantly prove what has been stated above. Some extracts are here given:—

In August 1660, Mr. John Ellis makes suit for the keeping of the king's New Park near York, 'where great devastation of wood and deer has lately been committed.'[2]

In November 1660, Sir Henry Wood begs for a grant of fifty deer, to be taken within a year from Heveningham Park, Suffolk, (the estate of the traitor William Heveningham), to his own little park at Lowdham, which he has re-inclosed, 'the pales being broken down, and the deer sold during the Usurpation.'[3]

In the Royal Park of Easthamstead in Berkshire, 'the deer had been universally destroyed, and it is almost impossible to procure any.'[4] In Waltham Forest the deer and game were totally destroyed during the

[1] S. P. O. Domestic.   [3] S. P. O. Domestic.   Cal. 1660, p. 400.
[2] S. P. O. Domestic, Cal. 1660, p. 243.   [4] S. P. O. Domestic.   Cal. 1661, p. 67.

late wars.[1] In the New Forest also the decay of deer is mentioned during the late distractions ;[2] and in 1662, June 30, an order was given 'to repair the destruction of deer in Thorney Wood, Sherwood Forest, and other forests; no fee deer of any kind to be taken, by colour of any warrant, unless the king be present in person.'[3]

In consequence of the destruction of deer during the Usurpation, the state papers show that deer were brought from Germany and elsewhere, to replenish Windsor and Sherwood Forests.[4] On the 13th of November 1661, a warrant was signed for the payment of 1000*l.* to Sir William St. Ravy for expenses of transporting red and fallow-deer. On this occasion, by a righteous retribution, the parks of the Roundheads were obliged to repay some of the losses which had been occasioned by the disloyalty of their owners. July 7, 1662, a warrant was issued to Robert Child and William Bowles, Masters of the Toils, to order the taking of fallow-deer in the parks of the Earl of Northumberland, and twenty-six others, and of red-deer in those of Lord Paget and Mr. Winwood, and the conveying them to the Royal Parks. 1700*l.* was ordered to be paid for this service.[5]

A curious illustration of this subject is afforded by a letter from Lord Chancellor Clarendon to Secretary (Morice ?) preserved in the State Paper Office, and dated ' Worcester House, August 4, 1666.' It relates to a baronetcy granted to the son of Dr. Peyton of the Isle of Ely, a loyal man, who had given His Majesty deer to re-stock his parks, and on whom a baronetcy was conferred in consequence.

But perhaps the following statement of the losses incurred by William Cavendish, Duke of Newcastle, describes with more minuteness the condition of many a once well-wooded park at this disastrous period :—' Of eight parks that he was possessed of before the wars, all but Welbeck Park, were quite destroyed, and that was saved by his brother, Sir Charles Cavendish,

---

[1] S. P. O. Domestic. Cal. 1661, p. 46.
[2] S. P. O. Domestic. Cal. 1662, p. 353.
[3] S. P. O. Domestic. Cal. 1662, p. 423.

[4] S. P. O. Domestic. Cal. 1662, p. 145.
[5] S. P. O. Domestic. Cal. 1662, pp. 431, 491.

who bought out his lordship's life in it. Clipston Park, wherein he had formerly taken much delight (it being seven miles in compass, rich of wood, watered by a pleasant river, running through it, full of fish and otters [?] ; as also well stocked with deer and all sorts of game), was quite defaced, there being not one timber tree left in it, which were the tallest in the country, and valued at 20,000*l.* When he beheld the ruins of this seat, though he was remarkable for his patience under misfortunes, he was observed to be much troubled ; but only said, *he was in hopes to have found it not so much defaced*, and gave present orders for repaling it.'[1]

A little before this period, we have the following notice of Kirtling, commonly called Catlige or Catlage, in Cambridgeshire, on the borders of Suffolk, at that time the seat of Dudley Lord North, and of the manner of hunting the buck there :—' At Kirtling was a very large and well-stocked Deer Park ; and at least twice a week in the season, there was killing of a deer ; the method there was for the keeper, with a large cross-bow and arrow, to wound the deer, and two or three disciplined park-hounds pursued till he dropped.'[2]

This continued a common method of taking deer in parks till the middle of the eighteenth century, though hunting them with buck-hounds as well as coursing with grey-hounds was also practised generally, as appears by the prints in ' The Gentleman's Recreation,' printed in 1721.

Another method, which appears to have been founded on the German fashion, is thus described in the Travels of Cosmo III., Grand Duke of Tuscany, who visited England in 1669 :—' On first entering the park (Hampton Court), he was met by Prince Robert (Rupert), who was likewise come thither for the diversion of seeing the hunt. After the usual compliments, His Highness went forward, Prince Rupert remaining in the place appointed for him under the shade of a tree, on a stage a little raised from the ground, which is the same where the King stands to see this amuse-

---

[1] Collins's Historical Collections of the Noble   [2] Lives of the Norths, 2nd ed. vol. i. p. 47.
Families of Cavendish, &c.   Fo. 1752, p. 42.

ment. When the huntsmen had stretched out the nets, after the German manner, inclosing withⁿ them a considerable space of land, they let the dogs loose upon four deer, which were confined there, who as soon as they saw them, took to flight; but as they had not the power of going which way they pleased, they ran round the nets, endeavouring by various cunning ·leaps to save themselves from being stopped by the dogs, and continued to run in this manner for some time to the great diversion of the spectators, till at last the huntsmen, that they might not harass the animals superfluously, drawing a certain cord, opened the nets in one part, which was prepared for that purpose, and left the deer at liberty to escape.'

In Chafins' Anecdotes of Cranbourn Chase, I find frequent notices of buck-hunting in the early part of the eighteenth century. It appears that in those days even the judges on their circuits engaged in this fashionable sport, which was generally carried on in the summer evenings after an early dinner at two o'clock, 'the deer at that time being more easily found and more able to run and shew sport, and as the evening advanced, and the dew fell, the scent gradually improved, and the cool air enabled the horses and the hounds to recover their wind, and go through their work without injury.'[1]

About the beginning of the eighteenth century a fashion was introduced of making small paddocks or parks for deer, generally near the house, where the land was mostly rich and good, (whereas in former times the parks were almost always at a distance from the residence of the proprietors, and often of great extent, occupying the worst and wildest lands of the manor;) of this new fashion, which was very prevalent till the latter part of the last century, the prints in ' Noveau Theatre de la grande Britagne' afford many examples. One which has existed to the present day is well known, adjoining the College of S. Mary Magdalen at Oxford. However from the period of the Restoration parks decreased not only in

---

[1] Chafins' Cranbourn Chase, p. 29.

size but in number, or at least never attained to the importance which they had occupied in former ages.   The royal domains, including ancient but generally disused parks in various parts of England, previously wasted during the evil days of the Usurpation, had been much reduced in consequence of the prodigal grants made by Charles II., and in fact a considerable proportion had passed from the Crown before the accession of the House of Hanover.   At length in 1701 (1 Anne, c. 7) the Civil List Act was passed, by which the Crown was restrained from further grants in fee. From the date of the Restoration also licenses for imparking gradually became obsolete, though it is laid down in the law-books to this day that none can make a chase or park without the king's license, 'for that is *quodam modo* to appropriate those creatures which are *feræ naturæ et nullius in bonis,* to himself, and to restrain them of their natural liberty, which he cannot do without the king's license.'[1]   Nevertheless a large proportion of the parks of the present day have probably been impaled since the beginning of the last century, and although for many years gradually decreasing, occasionally new ones are enclosed and old ones restored ; some particulars on this point will appear in the notes which follow on the ancient and present existing parks in England.

[1] Coke's Reports, ed. 1826, vol. vi. p. 164.

CHAPTER III.

NOTES ON DEER PARKS IN THE COUNTIES

OF

MIDDLESEX,	KENT,
SURREY,	ESSEX, AND
SUSSEX,	HERTFORD.

'Lord ! who would live turmoiled in the Court,
And may enjoy such quiet walks as these ?'
SHAKESPERE, *Henry VI.*

Facsimile of the Brass of JAMES GRAY, Keeper of Hunsdon Park. From the original in Hunsdon Church, Hertfordshire.

'James Gray, servant to the Right Honorable the Lord Chamberlaine and Keeper of the Great Parke at Hunsdon, was buried in Hunsdon Churche the xiii of december 1591.'

P. P. HUNSDON.

CHAPTER III.

MIDDLESEX.

HE Survey of Domesday records the names of two parks within the small metropolitan county. Goisfred de Magnaville had one in the manor of *Enfield*, and Ernulf de Hesding a park of wild beasts (ferarum) at *Rislepe* (*Rislip*), in the hundred of Elthorne. Alluding to the former, two parks are marked near the Chase of Enfield, in Saxton's map of Middlesex of 1575, and but two others at *Mariburne* and *Hyde Park*. One of the Enfield parks, called 'The Old Park,' 'The Frith,' and sometimes 'Parcus intrinsicus,' or 'the Home Park,' to distinguish it from the Chase, or 'Parcus extrinsicus,' contained, according to a survey made in 1650, 553 acres, and was disparked before the reign of William III., by whom it was granted to the Earl of Portland. The other, called 'The New, or Little Park,' adjoined to Enfield House, and must have been taken out of the Chase, and enclosed subsequent to the Earl of Rutland's conveyance to Henry VIII.: it contained in the year 1641, 375 acres, when it was sold by Charles I. to the Earl of Pembroke ; it had been so long disparked, and converted into meadow and tillage, that the very site of it was unknown in the time of Lysons.[1] Norden, in his description of Middlesex, written in 1596, observes : 'This shire is plentifully furnished with her Majesty's parkes, for princely delight, exceeding all the kingdome of Fraunce, wherein are not so many (if the discourse be true which is made of a debate betweene an heraulde of England and a herauld of Fraunce),[2] where it is affirmed that there are in all that region but two parkes. In Middlesex are ten of her Majesty's—*St. James's Park, Hyde Park, Marybone Park, Hanworth Park, Henton Park, Hampton Court Parks* (two), *Enfield Parks* (two), *Twickenham Park*, disparked.[3] The park walk of St. James's, enclosed by Henry VIII., is mentioned together with 'Mariburne Parke,' by Leland in his Itinerary ;[4] and by Hentzner in his Travels in 1598, who says, 'In this park (St. James's) is great plenty of deer.'[5] Evelyn in his Memoirs, writing in 1665, observes also of St. James's Park : 'There were also deer of severall countries, white, spotted like leopards, antelopes, an elk, red-deer, roe-bucks, staggs ;'[6] and deer

---

[1] Lyson's Environs of London, 2nd ed. vol. ii. p. 186.
[2] By J. Coke, printed in 1550.
[3] Norden's Middlesex, ed. 1723, p. 14.
[4] Leland's Itin. vol. iv. p. 131, fol. 192*b*.
[5] Hentzner's Travels, Strawberry Hill ed. p. 34.
[6] Evelyn's Memoirs, vol. i. p. 356.

are represented in Kip's view of St. James's Palace in 1714, in the park beyond the mall.[1] The deer in Hyde Park remained there in the memory of many of the present generation ; they were removed about 1831, 'in consequence, as it is said, of the number of pet dogs which were shot by the keeper, and which occasioned a great many complaints.'[2] Norden, in 1572, describes Hyde Park as 'substancially impaled, with a fayre lodge and princelye standes therein ; it is a stately parke, and full of fayre game.'[3]

Maryburne Park, which occupied the site of the present 'Regent's Park,' contained 543 acres and 17 perches. It was disparked during the Usurpation, and never afterwards restored.[4]

William, Earl of Pembroke, was keeper of the Royal Park at *Hanworth* in the first year of Queen Mary I. (1553-4), and here Queen Elizabeth dined and hunted in September 1600.[5]

Kenton or *Kempton Park* was granted to Sir Robert Killigrew (October 27, 1631) in fee form, at the yearly rent of 18*l.* 1*s.*, with the condition, 'that he shall maintain the said park stocked with 300 deer for his Majesty's disport.'[6] There were deer here about thirty years ago. There had been once two parks here, as appears by the custody of them being granted to Christopher and Edmund Water, in the year 1461.[7]

Of *Hampton Court* Norden says, 'There were two parkes, one of them for deere, the other of hares, both invironed with walls of bricke, the south side of the deere park excepted, which is paled, and invironed with the Thamise.'[8] There were afterwards three parks at Hampton Court, '*Bushy Old Park, The Middle or North Park,* and the *New Park* :' two of these have been joined, and go by the name of '*Bushy Park.*' Timothy Bennett, of Hampton Wick, tried and achieved the right of free passage through this park about the year 1752.[9] There are said to be 1,100 acres, well-stocked with deer. Evelyn mentions it in 1662, that 'it was formerly a flat, naked piece of ground, now planted with sweete rows of lime trees.'[10] Of Enfield Chase he also observes, 'A solitarie desert, yet stocked with not less than 3,000 deere.'[10]

Speed's map of Middlesex, engraved in 1610, adds only two to this list of parks ; '*Osterley Park,*' and another at 'Dorman's Well,' a little north of it. The house at Osterley was erected by Sir Thomas Gresham, and finished about the year 1577 ; 'and standeth,' says Nor-

---

[1] Of the Park of St. James's the well-known anecdote is told, that Caroline, Queen of George II., had wished to shut it up, and asked Sir Robert Walpole what it would cost to do it ? he replied, 'only a crown, madam,'[a]
[2] Mr. E. Jesse, in 'Once-a-Week,' part 68, p. 156.
[3] MS. Harl. 570.
[4] At that time there were 124 deer of several sorts, sold for 130*l.* 1,774*l.* 8*s.* 0*d.* was re-

[a] Lord Orford's Memoirs of the last ten years of George II. Vol. ii. p. 61.

ceived for the timber. See Lyson's Environs, vol. ii. p. 542.
[5] Nichols's Progresses of Queen Elizabeth, vol. iii. p. 513.
[6] S. P. O. Domestic, Cal. 1631-3, p. 172.
[7] Lyson's Middlesex, p. 273.
[8] Norden's Middlesex, p. 26.
[9] Lyson's Middlesex, p. 72. The fee of Keeper of Bushy Park is 4*d.* per diem ; Paler of the Park, 11*s.* 3*d.* per annum ; Moyer of the Brakes, 4*d.* per diem. There was a lodge in Bushy Park as early as 1628.
[10] Evelyn's Memoirs, vol. i. pp. 336, 456.

den, 'in a parke by him also impaled, well wooded, and garnished with manie fishe ponds.'[1] The Bishop of London had also a park at *Hornsey*, with a hill called Lodghill, ' for that thereon sometime stoode a lodge when the parke was replenished with deere.'[2] In former days there had been a park at ' *Pynnor*,' in the parish of Harrow, of which I find the following account in an original Roll of Woods, &c., belonging to Sir Edward North,[3] March 20. 2d Edward VI. (1548) : —

'In Pynnor Park be growyeng ccxl. okes of lx. yeres, and xxiiii. yeres growth, whereof xxiiii. valued at xx*d.* the tree, xxiiii. at xii*d.* the tree, and xxiiii. resydue at viii*d.* the tree not here chardged for, bycause the same were solde to John Byrde, farmer of the said parke, by the Archbishope of Canterburye.' To which see the park originally belonged. Nicholas, abbot of Westminster, was made

keeper of Pinner Park in 1383 ;[4] it was alienated by Dudley Lord North in 1630, and has long been converted into tillage.[5]

In 1714 there was a small park or paddock of deer at *Dawley*, in this county, then the seat of Lord Ossulstone.[6] But two parks containing deer now remain in Middlesex— *Bushy* and *Hampton Court.*

Twickenham Park, though disparked according to Norden in his Description of Middlesex, written in 1596, is marked in Speed's map of 1610. In 1547, Robert Bouchier was made keeper of it, then called ' *Isleworth Park*,' alias ' The New Park of Richmond.' The name, ' Twickenham Park,' still exists, though it has been so long without deer. It was sold in lots, according to Lysons in 1805.[7]

Existing Deer Parks in the County of Middlesex.

BUSHY AND HAMPTON COURT, belonging to Her Majesty the Queen.

SURREY.

BUT one park is recorded in Domesday as existing in the county of Surrey, that namely at *Stocha*, or *Stoke*, and which belonged to the king. Stoke, near Guil-

ford, is here intended; no trace of the royal park remains. The place is identical with Stockton or Stoughton, where Henry de Gildeford had license to im-

---

[1] Norden's Middlesex, pp. 36, 37.
[2] Several events in English history were connected with this park of Hornsey. Here the Duke of Gloucester, the Earls of Warwick, Arundel, and others met in a hostile manner, in 1386, to oppose King Richard II. Here the Lord Mayor of London met Edward V. after his father's death, and here

Henry VII. was also met on his return from Scotland, and conducted into the City in like manner.
[3] *Penes* the Baroness North.
[4] Lamb. Reg. Canterbury, fol. 51*a.*
[5] Lyson's Environs, vol. ii. p. 384.
[6] Kip's Views of Seats.
[7] Lyson's Environs, vol. ii. p. 775.

park 160 acres of land in the third year of Edward II.[1] The royal park of *Guilford* is in the neighbourhood; it was enclosed by Henry II;[2] and in 1299 was with the manor assigned to Queen Margaret, the second wife of Edward I., in part of her dower, and on her death reverted to the Crown. In the third year of Henry VII. the custody of this manor and park was given to Sir Reginald Bray; in the reign of Queen Elizabeth it was in the keeping of the Viscount Montague; in 1620, James I. granted it to George Murray, afterwards Earl of Annandale; and in the sixth of the following reign, the fee simple, including the whole stock of deer then in the park, was also conveyed to him, with power to dispark the woods, a power however which does not appear to have been exercised till about the year 1709, when the property was purchased by the Hon. Thomas Onslow.[3] Norden, in 1607, thus describes it: 'This Table comprehendeth Guldeforde Parke, lyinge in Surreye, Sr Thomas Gorge is the keeper therof, — Caster under keeper. This Parke hath 600 Fallow Deere, about 80 of antler, and not above 30 Buckes. The circuite of this Parke is 6¼ miles. It paleth 7½ mile. Meanlie timbered, not sufficient to mayntaine the pale: It contayneth in quantitie 1620 acres; the most reasonable good grounde.'[4]

The other royal parks in this county were, *Byfleet, Woking, Witley, Chobham, Bagshot, Henley, Potnells, Otelands, Banstead, Nonsuch,* and *Mortlake* or *Rich-*

mond. Most of these parks are laid down in Norden's map of Windsor Forest.[4] *Byfleet Park* is mentioned as early as the fifty-first year of Henry III. It was afterwards attached to the Duchy of Cornwall, and by Henry VIII. added to the 'Honor of Hampton Court.' It was in the keeping of Mr. Askew in the reign of Elizabeth.[5] Norden, in his MS. Survey of Windsor, taken in 1607 (Harl. MS. 3749), observes of 'Byflete, wherof Sir Edward Howard is chiefe keper, And hath about 160 fallow deere, about 36 of antler, and 14 buckes; This park is in circuite 3¼ mile, and so muche it paleth, few or no timber trees to mayntaine the fence: It contayneth in quantitie about 380 acres meane ground: The hooping birde, vulgarlie helde ominous, muche frequenteth this parke.'

Woking. — Here in the 9th of Edward I. was a small park of 40 acres, of the yearly value of 0*l.* 13*s.* 4*d.* In the 20th of Edward II. it was described as fit to maintain 40 deer.[5] The Earl of Lincoln was the keeper of Woking Park in the reign of Elizabeth.

Witley, or *Whitley.*—This park is mentioned in the 21st of Henry VI.,[6] and was in the keeping of Mr. Jones in the reign of Queen Elizabeth.[7] It was a large park on the borders of Hampshire.

Chobham Park, in Chertsey Walk, was sold by Queen Mary to Nicholas Heath, Archbishop of York, for 3000*l.* It contained 500 acres of land enclosed by a

[1] Manning and Bray's Surrey, vol. i. p. 166, 169.
[2] Manning and Bray's Surrey, vol. i. p. 22.
[3] Brayley's Surrey, vol. i. p. 304.
Harl. MS. 3749.
[4] Manning and Bray's Surrey, vol. i. p. 117, and Brayley's Surrey, vol. i. p. 52, and vol. ii. p. 153.
[5] Manning and Bray's Surrey, vol. ii. p. 42.
[7] Brayley's Surrey, vol. i. p. 52.

pale. The timber was valued at 800*l*. It has long been disparked, and divided into farms.[1]

Bagshot Park is mentioned in records of very early date; its custody had been granted to Henry Uvedale, Esq., and the reversion was given by Henry VIII. to William Fitzwilliam, Earl of Southampton; it afterwards reverted to the Crown; and in the reign of Elizabeth Sir Richard Creswell was keeper. James I. and Charles I. occasionally resided here for hunting. It was disparked by order of the Parliament, and reinclosed by order of Charles II.[2] In 1685, Evelyn, in his Memoirs, records that this park was ' full of red deer.'[3]

Henley Park, in the parish of Ash. In the 11th of Edward III. John de Molyns had a license to impark his woods at Westgrove and Godarde's Grove appertaining to his manor of Henley, and 300 acres of land adjoining.[4] Henley Park was sold by the Crown in the year 1633, with license to dispark or assart the land.[5] It is a little north-west of Guilford.

Potnells, or *Portnell Park*, anciently belonged to the Crown. In 1528, this park is described ' as not then enclosed, but had been lately so, and was then as waste within the Forest of Windsor.' It was granted by Henry VIII. to Sir William Fitzwilliam.[6]

Otelands Park is in the parish of Weybridge. The manor was conveyed to Henry VIII. in 1538, and it afterwards became a royal park. Here Queen Eliza-

beth is traditionally said to have shot with a cross-bow,[7] and here was the scene of the famous exploit of John Selwyn, the keeper of this royal park, who died in 1587, and is represented on his tomb in the adjoining church of Walton riding on a stag. The story was first told by Grose in the Antiquarian Repertory (vol i. pp. 1, 2). Selwyn is said to have been famous for his skill in horsemanship; and attending before the Queen in the Park of Otelands, he, in the heat of the chase, suddenly leaped from his horse upon the back of the stag, both running at the time at their utmost speed; and not only kept his seat gracefully, but drawing his sword, and coming near the Queen, plunged it into his throat, so that the animal fell dead at her feet.[8]

Otelands Park was considerably increased by James I.; and about the year 1608, I find 900*l*. was paid for purchase of lands for the enlargement of it,[9] besides 198*l*. 17*s*. 10*d*. for repairs.[9] The lands were disparked during the Interregnum, but the park appears to have been restored by Henry Clinton, 7th Earl of Lincoln, about the year 1725.[10]

Banstead.—Here was a park belonging to Hubert de Burgh, in the reign of Henry III., which became vested in the Crown from the second year of Edward I. It was granted to Sir Nicholas Carew of Beddington, by Henry VIII.

Nonsuch, in the parish of Cuddington. Two parks were enclosed in the reign of Henry VIII. The Great Park, 911 acres,

[1] Brayley's Surrey, vol. ii. p. 160.
[2] Ib. vol. i. p. 465.
[3] Evelyn's Memoirs, vol. i. p. 570.
[4] Cal. of Patent Rolls, p. 130.
[5] Brayley's Surrey, vol. i. p. 428.
[6] Brayley's Surrey, vol. ii. p. 297.

[7] Progresses, vol. iii. p. 598, note.
[8] Brayley's Surrey, vol. ii. p. 328.
[9] Original Accounts *penes* the Baroness North.
[10] Brayley's Surrey, vol. ii. p. 382.

and the Little Park, 671 acres. The king erected the Palace of Nonsuch in the latter. In Queen Mary's time it was granted to the Earl of Arundel, and from him passed to the Lumleys, who sold it to the Crown. It was the residence of Lord Lumley in the reign of Queen Elizabeth, in whose time (1586) Camden wrote the following agreeable account of it: 'The house is so surrounded by parks, so full of deer, delicious gardens, artificial arbours, pastures, and shady walks, that it seems to be the spot where pleasure chose to dwell with health.' Hentzner, in his travels, visited it in 1598, and describes it in the same words. Nonsuch Palace was destroyed during the Rebellion; it was surveyed by order of the Parliament in 1650, when it appeared that there were in the Little Park 108 fallow-deer, valued at 240*l*.[1] Evelyn mentions it in his Memoirs and Diary in the year 1666, and notes the avenue planted with fair elms; but he adds, 'The rest of these goodly trees, both of this and of Worcester Park adjoining, were felled by those destructive and avaritious rebels in the late war.' Nonsuch was granted in 1671, by Charles II. to Viscount Grandison and others. It was disparked before 1709 by the Duchess of Cleveland, for whom it had been held in trust.[2]

Richmond, or Shene, and Mortlake Parks.—There were two parks at Shene and Mortlake in the reign of Henry VIII. That at Shene (the name of which was changed to Richmond by Henry VII.) had existed for a long time; and I have already quoted a letter from Queen Margaret of Anjou to the keeper there,[3] written about the middle of the fifteenth century. These parks were united by Charles I. in 1637, and considerable additions made to them, but not without the very serious opposition of many of the proprietors whose lands were affected by the proposed enclosure. Lord Clarendon, in his History of the Rebellion, has given us a particular account of this transaction, which is also quoted at length with some additions in 'The History of the Making of Richmond New Park in Surrey;'[4] a pamphlet written in 1751, in consequence of some attempts which were made at the time to prevent the free ingress of the people into this park. The present Great Park at Richmond is between 8 and 9 miles in circumference, and is said to include 2,253 acres; fallow-deer, 1,600; red-deer, 40 or 50.[5]

Of Episcopal Parks within the county of Surrey, we have *Croydon* and *Burstow*, belonging to the Archbishop of Canterbury; *Farnham* and *Esher*, appurtenant to the bishoprick of Winchester.

Croydon, for ages the country palace of the Archbishop of Canterbury, was sold by Act of Parliament in 1780, when Addington was purchased in lieu of it. Walworth, the famous Lord Mayor of London, was appointed keeper of Croydon Park by Archbishop Courtenay in 1382.[6]

Burstow Park, on the borders of Sussex, was an ancient park belonging to the same see; in the reign of Elizabeth it had been alienated to Sir Thomas Sherley.[7]

---

[1] Archæologia, vol. v. p. 438.
[2] Brayley's Surrey, vol. iv. p. 406.
[3] See page 21.
[4] 8vo. London, 1751.

[5] Brayley's Surrey, vol. iii. p. 65.
[6] Ib. vol. iv. 7.
[7] Ib. vol. iv. p. 293.

There were formerly two parks at *Farn-ham*; the Old Park contained about 1,000 acres; it was disparked and divided into farms in the reign of Charles II. The Little Park, adjoining to the eastern side of the castle, occupies 300 acres, and contains a herd of about 320 fallow-deer. In ancient times there were various officers in connection with Farnham Castle, appointed by the bishop,[1] as Keeper of the Castle, Keepers of the Parks, Keepers of the North and South Chase, and of Frensham Ponds, with the swans in them; and these offices were frequently held, singly and collectively, by persons of distinction in the county.[2]

Esher Park contained about 180 acres of land, and was annexed by Henry VIII. to the Honor of Hampton Court in 1540; here William Waynflete, Bishop of Winchester, erected a palace within the park from 1447 to 1486.[3]

There were many other ancient parks in Surrey: brief notes of those which I have met with are here subjoined.

West Horsley.—The park is not marked in the maps of Saxton or Speed, but the park is very ancient; in the seventh of Edward I. (1279) Sir Ralph Berners claimed from the grant of Henry III. to Hugh de Windsor the right to have two parks here, which claim was admitted before the king's judges at Guilford.[4] I find the park again recognised in a grant to Richard, son of Sir James Berners, knight, in the first of Henry IV.[5]

Alfold Park, near Ridgewick in Sussex, once the park of William Longespée, whose father was a natural son of Henry II.; it contained about 300 acres, but has been long disparked.[6]

Iwood or *Ewood Park.*—Here was a mansion and park of about 600 acres in the parish of Newdigate, which had belonged to the Earls of Warren and Surrey, and afterwards descended to the Fitzallens, Earls of Arundel, and afterwards again divided and went to coheirs.[7]

Merton.—In the 20th of Edward I. the prior of Merton had a license to assart and impark forty acres of woodland adjoining to his park of Merton, Northwood, and le Frith.[8]

Gatton Park was imparked by John Tymperley in the 27th of Henry VI. (1449) by the king's license, 'for his good and faithful services, and in consideration of 40 shillings.' The license comprehended ' 360 acres of land, 80 acres of wood, 20 acres of marsh, 80 acres of pasture, and 40 acres of meadow at Gatton; and 40 acres of wood, 100 acres of land, 80 acres

---

[1] In the 14th of Edward III. the Bishop of Winchester granted to William 'Parker,' in fee, the custody of the Hundreds of Farnham and Crundall, and all the fallen and dead wood in his park of Farnham, with liberty to keep there two heifers, six oxen, three cows, and three steers, during the whole year, and pannage of fourteen pigs, with other ample fees, for an annual rent of eighty hens.—*Cal. of Patent Rolls,* p. 88.

In 1609 (Dec. 2), John Norden (the surveyor?), wrote to Lord Salisbury, in whose keeping it seems to have been, about the reparation of the pales, lodges, &c., in Farnham Park, and the negligence of the keepers in punishing robbers of the same.—*Cal. of Domestic Papers, James I.*

[2] Brayley's Surrey, vol. v. p. 267.
[3] Ib. vol. ii. p. 426.
[4] Ib. vol. ii. p. 72.
[5] Cal. Patent Rolls, p. 237.
[6] Brayley's Surrey, vol. v. p. 115.
[7] Ib. vol. iv. p. 289.
[8] Cal. Patent Rolls, p. 55.

of pasture, and 30 acres of meadow, at Merstham.'[1]

Woodcote Park, at Horton in Epsom. —License for a park was granted by Henry VI. to John Marston and Rose his wife. In later times it became a seat of the Calverts, Lords Baltimore ;[2] but there appears to have been a former park here, as Henry I. or Henry II. licensed the abbots of Chertsey to have their park here shut up whenever they would, and that they might have all the beasts which they could take therein.[3]

Vachery Park in Shere, and *Baynard's Park* adjoining. The great park of Vachery, from *vaccaria,* a dairy house, appears to have appertained to the Manor House of Shere ; in early times it belonged to the great family of the Butlers of Ireland, and afterwards to the famous Sir Reginald Bray.[4] Evelyn mentions Baynards in the year 1657, as ' a house of my brother Richard's, a very faire noble house built in a park, and having one of the goodliest avenues of oakes up to it that ever I saw.'[5]

Beddington Park, the old seat of the Carews, near Croydon.—Evelyn mentions it as ' a fine park,' though in decay ; it was between three and four miles in circumference, well wooded, and, until very recent times, abounded with deer.[6]

At *Carshalton,* near adjoining, containing 145 acres, there is a herd of fallow-deer. It was enclosed about the year 1746.

Clandon Park and *Sutton Park,* adjoining.—Imparked by license of Henry VIII. (May 25, 1531) to Sir Richard Weston, of

Sutton Place, where there was also another and smaller park. Clandon contained 600 acres of land and pasture, 50 acres of wood, 400 acres of furze and heath in Marrow and Clandon. Sir Richard erected a hunting-lodge in his new park, but the land was afterwards disparked, and sold in 1642 to Sir Richard Onslow, by whom the park was again enclosed ; his grandson made it his principal seat. George, first Earl of Onslow, enlarged Clandon Park about the year 1776. The Old Park comprised about 183 acres, and the New Park about 45 acres; until a few years since, it continued to be well stocked with deer, and was celebrated for its venison.[7]

Loseley Park was imparked by license under the Privy Seal from Henry VIII., dated December 24, 1533 ; there were 200 acres licensed 'to be surrounded with hedges, ditches, and pales.' Red deer were once kept here, but the park has been for many years disparked.[8]

Pirford, in Woking.—The enclosure of the Lord's Park is mentioned in the 13th of Edward IV.[9] ' This park,' says Aubrey, writing in the middle of the reign of Charles II., ' is a very delightful place, three miles about, it is well wooded and stored with deer.' It was afterwards in the Parkhurst and Onslow families; the two parks at Pirford having been in the keeping of the Earl of Lincoln in the reign of Queen Elizabeth ; between sixty and seventy years ago the house was pulled down and the park converted into farms, by George Lord Onslow.[10]

[1] Brayley's Surrey, vol. iv. p. 309.
[2] Ib. vol. iv. p. 350.
[3] Manning and Bray, vol. ii. p. 611.
[4] Brayley's Surrey, vol. v. p. 186.
[5] Evelyn's Memoirs, vol. i. p. 295.
[6] Brayley's Survey, vol. iv. p. 69.
[7] Ib. vol. ii. p. 59.
[8] Ih. vol. i. p. 411.
[9] Manning and Bray, vol. i. p. 134.
[10] Brayley's Surrey, vol. ii. p. 147.

Ryegate.—Here was a park in the keeping of the Lady Howard in the Elizabethan period ;[1] in Evelyn's time it belonged to Lady Peterborough ; he observes that the park was then much defaced.[2] By a survey taken in 1622, it is said to have contained 150 acres, and then was well stocked with timber trees and replenished with deer.[3]

Betchworth Castle.—Sir Thomas Browne was owner of the park here in the reign of Queen Elizabeth.[1]

Stoke d'Abernon, 'M[r] Liefields Park, to be enquired whether it be of the compass of a mile.' (This was with reference to the Act of the 27th of Henry VIII. for the encouragement of the breed of horses.)

Albury Park is not marked in the ancient maps; in Evelyn's time it was the seat of Mr. Henry Howard, and was often visited by that distinguished scholar, who in his Journal, July 2, 1662, remarks, ' we hunted and killed a buck in the park, Mr. Howard inviting most of the gentlemen of the country neare him.'[4]

Starburrow, on the borders of Kent and Sussex, called also Prinkham, it is in the parish of Lingfield ; here was a park in the 47th of Edward III., held by the Berkeley family.[5] The Lord Burrowes was the owner in the reign of Elizabeth.

Blechingley, not far from Ryegate, here was a park belonging to the Lord Howard at the same period. ' *Park silver* ' is mentioned in the accounts here in 24th of Edward I.[6]

Ashstead Park.— Evelyn mentions in

1684 ' S[r] Robert Howard's new built house, which stands in a park in the downe.'[7] This is one of the very few parks still existing in Surrey ; the area is 136 acres. In 1864 there was here a herd of 300 deer ; it is now the property of the Honourable Mrs. Howard.

South Lambeth.—There was a park here in the reign of James I., made by Sir Noel Caron, ambassador from the States of Holland, which is said to have extended to Vauxhall and Kennington Lane.[8] I do not find it marked in Speed's map.

Wonersh Park.—Formed by the first Lord Grantley, who died in 1789, not of great extent, but luxuriantly wooded; there was here a herd of about 80 head of deer.[9]

Peper-Harow Park, about 285 acres; until lately well-stocked with deer, it was disparked in 1851-2, but is now (1866) being restored ; it is the seat of Viscount Midleton.

Ottershaw Park, described in 1819 as comprising 430 acres, stocked with deer.

Morden Park, Sir William Clayton's park, now disparked.

List of existing Deer Parks in the County of Surrey.

1. RICHMOND   . The Queen.
2. FARNHAM .   . The Bishop of Winchester.
3. ASHTEAD .   . The Hon. Mrs. Howard.
4. CARSHALTON   . Mr. Taylor.
5. WONERSH .   . Lord Grantley.
6. PEPER-HAROW . Viscount Midleton.

---

[1] Brayley's Surrey, vol. i. p. 52.
[2] Evelyn's Memoirs, vol. i. p. 286.
[3] Manning and Bray's Surrey, vol. i. p. 287.
[4] Evelyn's Memoirs, vol. i. p. 336.
[5] Manning and Bray's Surrey, vol. ii. p. 340.
[6] Manning and Bray, vol. ii. p. 290.
[7] Evelyn's Memoirs, vol. i. p. 536.
[8] Progresses of Queen Elizabeth, vol. iii. p. 440, note.
[9] Brayley's Surrey, vol. v. p. 151.

SUSSEX.

PARKS at *Reredfelle, Wiltingham, Walburgetone,* and *Waltham,* are recorded in the Domesday Survey as existing in the county of Sussex. The first, afterwards called Rotherfield, belonged to the king, and is supposed to be identical with Eridge, the present wild and beautiful park of the Earl of Abergavenny ; Wiltingham belonged to the Earl of Ow, and Walburgetone and Waltham to Earl Roger.

Eridge Park appears to have been part of the Forest of Waterdown, and is mentioned in an Inquisition in the time of Edward III. on the death of Hugh le Despencer, which found among other things 'that the manor of Rotherfield (Redefeldde) was then held by two members of the Le Despencer family, and that there was a certain park there, and a tenement called Eridge, parcel of the Park.'[1] The present park of Eridge contains 928 acres, and there is a herd of 300 deer, including a few red deer.

Walburgetone or *Walberton,* was evidently part of the park of the Earl Roger attached to the possession of Arundel Castle. This ancient park contained 842 acres; it is now a farm. The new or present park was made in 1786; it is in extent 1,145 acres, and is capable of containing a herd of 1,000 deer. Soon after the Conquest there were two parks at Arundel, distinguished as the large and

small parks ; besides these, sixteen other parks surrounded the castle in every direction within the limits of Western Sussex ; they were as follows :— Ruele, Betworthe, Selershe, Est dene, West dene, Wythe, Dounle, Alfrithe, Cockyng, Woolavington, Shullinglegh, Westholte, Vilereswode, Stanstede, Bygenor, and Meredone.[2]

Waltham, five miles and a half southeast of Petworth, was, after the Conquest, parcel of the possessions of the see of Chichester ; the ancient park within the demesne of the castle of Amberley has been usually demised under the same lease with Rackham and Cold-Waltham.[3]

Wiltingham, supposed to be identical with Wilting in the parish of Hollington, near Hastings. There is no other record of a park here.

The Archbishops of Canterbury possessed two ancient parks in Sussex — *Slindon* near Arundel, and *Mayfield* near Ashdown Forest. The former was given to the see by King Henry I. In the year 1272 it was agreed that the Earl of Arundel was bound to deliver to the Archbishop at this manor, 13 bucks or stags, and 13 does or hinds in proper season, in compensation of the Archbishop's right of free warren. This right was commuted for a money payment in 1366, by Archbishop Islip, who has been blamed for making away with the privi-

---

[1] See the proceedings before the Court of Common Pleas, February 8, 1847, Morgan and Another *versus* the Earl of Abergavenny.

[2] Cartwright's Rape of Arundel, p. 93, note.

[3] Cartwright's Rape of Arundel, p. 289.

leges of the see.[1] Leland thus mentions this place in his ' Itinerary:'—' There is a faire wod longging to the Bishop of Canterbyri, and a park, and an auncient place in it cawled *Shydon*, on the right hand in the way almoste betwixt Arundle and Chichester.'[2] Slindon was exchanged with the Crown in 1543, and was granted with the park to Sir Thomas Palmer in 1553.[1]

Mayfield.—The park is recognised in the Patent Rolls of the 28th of Edward III., and a park was attached to this manor at the period of its alienation in 1537.[3]

The following notes relate to other parks in this county, in the several rapes of Chichester, Arundel, Bramber, Lewes, Pevensey, and Hastings.

In Chichester Rape is *Halneker.* Here in the third year of Edward III. was a park of 130 acres, valued at 6s. 8d. beyond the keep of the deer.[4] By a survey taken by order of Thomas Duke of Norfolk, in the time of Elizabeth, it is stated that it was 4 miles in compass, ' wᶜʰ may yerely sustaine viiiᶜ deare with some provision of haie in winter, yf maste ffayle ; and there be at this survaye viiiᶜ deare as yt is enfourmed us.'[5]

This place is called ' Halfnaked,' in Saxton's map of 1375. Adjoining to Halneker is *Goodwood*, an ancient park purchased of the family of Compton of East Lavant by Charles first Duke of Richmond, before 1720. The whole circuit of the park is enclosed by a lofty flint wall.[6]

Shelhurst Park, to the north of Halneker, was one of those attached to the castle of Arundel, as was also *East-Deane Park*, a little to the north-west ; both have been long disparked.

To the west of Goodwood on the borders of Hampshire are *Stansted* and *Merden*, both also originally belonging to Arundel Castle. Stansted was laid out about 1686 in the formal style then lately introduced from the forest of Chantili ; there are three avenues of great width and extent, particularly the central or western, which is equalled only as a magnificent street of trees by that of Oakley Grove in Gloucestershire ; one of the parks anciently belonging to Stansted is converted into farms ; the present park comprehends 630 acres, exclusive of 960 acres of forest land.[7]

North of Stansted a park called ' Harting ' is marked in the ancient maps ; this I conclude to be *Up Park*, in the parish of East Harting, one of the most beautiful situations in the south of England. It is a park of 890 acres, half of which is covered with fern, and ornamented with the finest beech timber ; there is a herd of 800 or 1,000 fallow-deer.

Speed marks parks at *Dounley* to the east of Harting, and near Aylworth to the south of Stansted. The former was attached to the castle of Arundel.

Cowdray Park, near Midhurst, the old seat of the Brownes Viscounts Montague, was anciently part of the domains appen-

1 Dallaway's Rape of Chichester, p. 140. Sussex Archæological Collections, vol. ii. p. 232. Cal. Patent Rolls, p. 175.
2 Itin. vol. vi. p. 31, fol. 32.
3 Sussex Archæological Collections, vol. ii. p. 232.
4 Dallaway's Rape of Chichester, p. ·131.

5 Original Survey, *penes* Lord Willoughby de Broke. Printed for the Sussex Archæological Collections, vol. ix. p. 224.
6 Dallaway's Rape of Chichester, p. 135.
7 Ib. pp. 158, 162, and Nichols's Progresses of Queen Elizabeth, vol. iii. p. 97, note.

F

dant to the castle of Midhurst, which belonged to the Bohuns; and although it is said in the license for imparking granted in 1533, to Sir William Fitzwilliam, that it should in future be called *Cowdray*, there is sufficient evidence of the manor having been called by that name in the reign of Edward III. Three separate parks are stated to belong to Thomas Earl of Arundel as parcel of the Barony of Midhurst in the reign of Henry VIII., viz. Cowdray, sometimes called 'le Shingle,' and Shingle Park, and the two north parks.[1] Cowdray contains 600 acres within its present bounds, and there is a herd of 500 fallow-deer.

This park is remarkable for the chesnut ' races,' and for other fine trees; the present house was originally the keeper's lodge, used as the residence of the family after the fire at the old mansion in 1793.

In the north-west corner of the rape of Chichester is *Rivers Park*, which is marked both in Saxton's and Speed's maps. Leland observes, ' one Rivers was owner of Rivers parke in the quarter by Petworth, but the maner place was sumwhat withoute the parke, as yet apperith in the paroche of——;' and in another place he says it ' longgid to the Dikes.'[2]

Shillinglee Park, in the rape of Arundel, was one of the parks which were especially retained by the Earls of Arundel, and it was frequently granted in dower to their widows. In 1342, William Earl of Arundel exchanged it with Henry VIII., when Richard Bowyer was appointed

parker for the Crown. After many changes it came to the ancestors of the Earl of Winterton, the present possessor.[3]

Michelham Park, adjoining to Shillinglee; is no longer impaled.

Petworth has now two parks. 'The Stag Park, about thirty years since,' says Dallaway, ' was cleared of trees and drained, and then divided by hedge-rows into farms.' Here Leland mentions that there was ' a log of the Great Park of Petworth where one Syr William Redmille a knight dwelled.'[4] At present a high stone wall encloses 9½ miles in extent, within which are about 2,042 acres.[5]

Below Petworth Speed marks the parks of *Woolavington, Downton*, and *Burton*; the last contained 210 acres, and was supposed to have been enclosed by Sir William Goring, Bart. at the suppression[6] of monasteries.

More south is *Bignor*, where there was a park enclosed from the great forest of Arundel in the reign of Henry III.; it was one of the parks appendant to the castle of Arundel.

Parham Park, the venerable seat of the Bishops, and now of their descendant Curzon, Baroness Zouche, is not marked in the ancient maps of Saxton and Speed; it is, however, a most beautiful and romantic park of wild and broken scenery, dotted with old pollard oaks, and once said to have enclosed 800 acres, now much reduced in size; there is at present a herd of 200 fallow-deer.

Near Arundel were the parks of *Badworth* and *Angmering*. The former be-

---

[1] Dallaway's Rape of Chichester, p. 243.
[2] Leland Itin. vol. vi. p. 17, fol. 18.
[3] Dallaway and Cartwright's Rape of Arundel, p. 368.
[4] Lel. Itin. vol. vi. p. 31, fol. 32.

[5] Dallaway and Cartwright's Rape of Arundel, p. 330.
[6] Dallaway and Cartwright's Rape of Arundel, p. 65.

longed to Arundel Castle; the latter, of considerable extent and beautifully wooded, in the parishes of Angmering, Rustingham, and Patching, was an appendage to Michelgrove House, the ancient seat of the Shelleys.[1]

Near Horsham in the north-western part of the rape of Bramber, is St. Leonards forest, marked in the ancient maps as surrounded by a pale; adjoining and within this forest, were the following parks, once the inheritance of the great house of Braose, which by a survey made in 1608, were found at that time to be disparked,— *Chesworth Park,* 223 acres. In 1549 there were here 100 deer, at the time of the attainder of the Lord Admiral Seymour.[2]—*Sedgwick Park,* 624 acres; here were also 100 deer in 1549.—*Beaubush Park,* 757 acres, of which Maurice eighth Lord Berkeley died seized in 1523, 100 deer in 1549.— *Shelley Park,* 647 acres.[3] 'In the little park in the Forest' there were 80 deer in 1549. John de-Mowbray received a grant of the free chase of St. Leonards in the sixteenth of Edward III.[4]

Speed marks a park at *Slynfold,* in the north-eastern part of the rape of Bramber, and others are marked at *Westgrinsted, Fawhurst, Henfeld,* and *Blackston. Westgrinsted,* in the Elizabethan period the seat of a younger branch of the Sherleys of Wiston, afterwards passed to the Carylls, and then to the Burrells, the present possessors. The park is remarkable for its fine maple trees ; its extent is 300

acres, and there are the same number of fallow-deer.

The park of *Wiston,* inherited by the Sherleys from a branch of the great house of Braose, is marked in Speed's map of 1610 ; it contains at present 170 acres, with a herd of 300 head of deer, and now belongs to the family of Goring.

At *Warminghurst,* a little north of Wiston, a park was enclosed in the early part of the eighteenth century, which has been long disparked.[5]

The rape of Lewes contained many parks. In the northern part in Worth Forest was *Tylgate,* and three other parks adjoining, one of them called Wourthe or Worth ;[6] more south were two parks at *Slaugham,* and two more near Cuckfield ; others at *Hurst* and *Danny;* these are all marked in Speed's map, the two last only by Saxton. At *Ditchling* was also an ancient park, where Edward Prince of Wales, afterwards Edward II., kept 'his colts ;' the site of it is known as ' Park Farm,' and it is marked in Saxton's map. In the 13th century it belonged to the de Warrens, and by their gift to the Priory of Lewes. In 1415, it was in dower to Beatrix, widow of Thomas Fitzalan, fifth Earl of Arundel, when it contained by estimation 300 acres. In 1476 it belonged to Edward Lord Bergavenny, and in 1597 was in the same family ; no traces of a park or its boundaries now remain.[7]

The rape of Pevensey, besides the forests of Ashdown and Waterdown, contained,

---

[1] Dallaway and Cartwright's Rape of Arundel, p. 330.
[2] Sussex Archæological Collections, vol. xiii. pp. 124-125.
[3] Cartwright's Rape of Bramber, p. 335.
[4] Cal. Patent Rolls, p. 144.
[5] Cartwright's Rape of Bramber, p. 256.

[6] These parks were called also 'the south, north, east, and west parks of the forest,' as appears by a note of fees of keepers in the British Museum. Cotton MS. Titus B. vol. iv. fol. 236.
[7] Sussex Archæological Collections, vol. xiii. p. 240, vol. xvi. p. 134.

according to Speed, fourteen parks; of these *Eridge* and *Mayfield* have been already noticed. Adjoining to Ashdown Forest, sometimes called *Lancaster Great Park*, were *Bolbrook* and *Stonland* Parks; also *Buckhurst*, the ancient seat of the now extinct family of Sackville, and now the inheritance of their descendant, the Earl de la Warr. Buckhurst Park appears to have been enclosed by Andrew de Sackville in the 29th year of Edward I.[1]

Lancaster Great Park was so called from having been enlarged by John of Gaunt Duke of Lancaster; though it is mentioned as a park in the reign of Edward II., who occasionally resided here. On a rising ground, the ' King's standing' is still pointed out; where, according to the well-known custom of the chase, the game was driven before him. According to the Parliamentary survey made in April 1658, this park contained 13,991a. or. 37p. After the Restoration, the fences, which had fallen to decay, were attempted to be restored; but 'by the crossness of the neighbourhood,' the attempt seems to have been unsuccessful. The park has been long disparked, and for a time resumed its forest character; sixty years ago there was said to have been twelve or fourteen hundred head of deer still left— the last, a doe, was killed about the year 1808.[2]

To the south of Ashdown Forest, and partly enclosed within its bounds, was *Newnd Park*.

Further south still, parks are marked at *Uckfield* and *Ifield*; and near them a cluster of five parks, of which the prin-

cipal was *Plashet*, an ancient park, noticed also in Saxton's map; a small portion of the park of *Plashet* was restored by Lord Gage in 1825, containing 94 acres, with a herd of 100 head of fallow-deer.

Another park is marked by Speed, near *Haylsham*, on the borders of the rape of Hastings.

But two ancient parks are given by Saxton and Speed in the rape of Hastings, those of *Hurstmonseux* and *Ashburnham.* The park of *Hurstmonseux* is of great antiquity, and was increased bv Royal license in the first year of Henry V.[3]

Ashburnham, a still existing park of the noble and very ancient family of that name, is in the parishes of Penhurst and Catsfield, and contains an area of about 500 acres, with a herd of 200 fallow-deer, with a small herd of red-deer.

List of existing Deer Parks in the County of Sussex.

1. ERIDGE	.	. Earl of Abergavenny.
2. ARUNDEL	.	. Duke of Norfolk.
3. ASHBURNHAM	.	Earl of Ashburnham.
4. PETWORTH		. Lord Leconfield.
5. UP-PARK	.	. Lady Fetherstone.
6. PARHAM	.	. Lady de la Zouche.
7. WISTON	.	. Rev. J. Goring.
8. COWDRAY	.	. Earl of Egmont.
9. WEST-GRINSTED		Sir Percy Burrell, Bart.
10. CUCKFIELD	.	Colonel Sergison.
11. DEN	.	. Mr. Eversfield.
12. PLASHET	.	. Lord Gage.

---

[1] Cal. Patent Rolls, p. 62.
[2] See the Sussex Archæological Collections, vol. xiv. p. 35, for a valuable account of Ash-

down Forest by the Rev. Ed. Turner.
[3] Cal. Patent Rolls, p. 262.

KENT.

THREE parks are noticed in the Domes-day Survey in the county of Kent, at Wicheham (*Wickham*), Esledes (*Leedes*), and Certh (*Great Chart*), all belonging to the Bishop of Baieux in Normandy, who was half-brother to William the Conqueror and Earl of Kent. At Leedes, the park may still be said to exist, though at present without deer, surrounding the historical castle of that name, belonging to Mr. Wickham-Marten, and originally founded by Sir Robert de Crevecœur, in the early part of the twelfth century.

Lambard, in his 'Perambulation of Kent,' written in 1571, observes of this county : ' Parkes of fallow-deere, and games of gray conyes, it maynteyneth many, the one for pleasure, and the other for profit, as it may wel appeare by this, that within memorie almost the one halfe of the first sorte be disparkedt and the number of warreyns continueth, if it do not increase dayly. As for red-deere and blacke conyes, it nourisheth them not, as having no great walkes of wast grounde for the one, and not tarying the tyme to rayse the gaine by the other; for blacke conyes are kept partly for their skins, which have their season in winter; and Kent, by the nearnesse to London, hath so quicke market of young rabbits, that it killeth this game chiefly in summer.'[1] Lambard proceeds afterwards to give a list of Kentish parks, distinguishing those which were at that time disparked; and which were, *Panthyrst, Brasted, Henden,*

Hever, Broxam, Wrotham, Ightam, Cage, Postern, Sutton, Langley, Alington, Mere-wood, Lye, Folkston, Stonehyrst, and *Oxenhoth,* where there had been two parks, now disparked. The parks existing in Lambard's time were, three parks in the south and north frythe, or forest, in the south-western corner of the county, two parks at *Otforde,* one at *Knoll,* one at *Gromebridge,* and at *Penshirst, Cooling, Byrling, Cobham, Grenewiche,* three at *Eltham,* one at *Ashowre,* at *South-parke, Lullingstone, Calehyl, Leedes, S. Augustines, Bedgebury, Westenhanger, Halden, Hamswell, Hungershall, Shorland, Stowting, Saltwood, Posting, Ashford, Sissinghirst,* and *Glassenbury.*

The Royal parks were those of *Greenwich* and *Eltham.* The former was founded by license granted by King Henry VI. in the eleventh year of his reign (1433), to Humphry Duke of Gloucester and Alianor his wife, to crenelate the mansion of his manor of East Greenwich, and to impark 200 acres of land and pasture ; this license was confirmed by Act of Parliament passed in the fifteenth of the same reign (1436). Hentzner, in his travels in 1598, thus mentions Greenwich :—' Near this palace is the Queen's Park, stocked with deer ; such parks are common throughout England, belonging to those that are distinguished either for their rank or riches. In the middle of this is an old square tower called MIREFLEVR, supposed to be that mentioned in the

[1] Lambard's Perambulation of Kent, p. 9.

romance of Amadis de Gaul; and joining to it a plain where knights and other gentlemen use to meet at set times and holidays to exercise on horseback.' This tower was built by Humphry Duke of Gloucester, and repaired by Henry VIII. in 1526. 'It became at one time the habitation of some of the younger branches of the Royal Family; sometimes the residence of a favourite mistress; sometimes a prison, and sometimes a place of defence.'[1] The Observatory now occupies the site. Kilburne, in his Survey, informs us that ' King James' [the First] ' walled the park with brick.'[2]

The kings of England had a palace at *Eltham* at a very early period. The Great Park at Eltham contained 596 acres, according to the survey taken in 1649. Patrick Maule, Esq., Groom of the Bedchamber, was then Ranger and Master of the Game. The Little, or Middle, Park contained 333 acres ; Horne, alias Lee, Park, in Eltham and Lee, 336 acres. The deer in all these parks had been destroyed by the soldiery and common people. In the three parks, 3,700 trees had been marked for the navy. A book, called ' The Mysteries of the Good Old Cause,' published in 1660, says, ' Sir Thomas Walsingham had the Honour of Eltham given him, which was the Earl of Dorset's, and the Middle Park, which was Mr. White's ; he has cut down 5000l. worth of timber, and hath scarcely left a tree to make a gibbet.' Sir Theodore Mayerne, physician to the king, had been for many years chief ranger and master of the game

of Horne Park, and resided in the lodge (now a farmhouse). During the reign of Charles I., before 1649, he had removed to Chelsea, and left an undertenant in the lodge, as is stated in the Survey.[3]

Of episcopal parks in Kent there were *Otford* and *Aldington*. At Otford there were two parks adjoining the palace, ' whiche of long time belonged to the Archbishops of Canterbury,' and of this place Lambard narrates, that as ' Thomas a Becket walked on a time in the Olde Parke (busie at his prayers), that he was muche hindered in devotion by the sweete note and melodie of a nightingale that sang in a bushe beside him, and that therefore (in the might of his holynesse) he injoyned, that from thenceforth no byrde of that kynde shoulde be so bolde as to sing thereaboutes.'[4] Otford was exchanged with Henry VIII. by Archbishop Cranmer.[5]

Aldington Park is mentioned by Leland in his ' Itinerary,' ' where Archbishop Moreton builded.'[6] It was also alienated from the Church by Archbishop Cranmer in the thirty-first of Henry VIII.

St. Augustine's, adjoining to Canterbury, appears to have been appendant to the celebrated abbey there, which after the Dissolution came to the Crown : the park was existing in 1576.

Of the deer parks noticed by Lambard as existing in 1576, three only remain at the present time—*Knole*, *Cobham*, and *Lullingstone*. Knole, at one time a palace of the Archbishops of Canterbury, afterwards exchanged by Cranmer with the

[1] Lyson's Environs, vol. i. p. 519.
[2] Kilburne's Survey of Kent, p. 115.
[3] Lyson's Environs, vol. i. p. 479.
[4] Lambard's Perambulation of Kent, p. 375.
[5] The keeper of the Great Park at Otford

had a yearly fee of 6l. 3s. 4d., and the keeper of the Little Park had a yearly fee of 6l. 1s. 8d. —Cotton MS. Titus B. vol. iv. fol. 236.
[6] Leland's Itin. vol. vii. p. 138, 139.

Crown, and long the principal seat of the Sackvilles Dukes of Dorset, is celebrated for its extensive park, ornamented with the finest beech trees, and 'covered with as fine a turf as any in the world.' The park of Knole at present contains 1,000 acres, more than half of which is covered with timber; there is a herd of 400 fallow-deer. (Adjoining Knole is *Wilderness*, the seat of the Marquis Camden. Here Lord Chief Justice Pratt, who died in 1724, enclosed a park; disparked after the decease of the first marquis in 1840.)

Cobham, the ancient seat of the Cobham family, and now of the Earl of Darnley, near Gravesend: the park contains about 530 acres, and a herd of 800 fallow-deer.

Lullingstone, a fine old park with ancient oaks, and fine hawthorns, containing 650 acres of beautifully broken ground, and a herd of 400 black and fallow fallow-deer.

Penshurst, the old Sidney seat, at present I believe without deer, claims however, from its historical character in ancient times, some notice among the parks of this country:—

Thou hast thy walks for health as well as sport,
Thy mount to which the Driads do resort,
Where Pan and Bacchus their high feasts have
    made,
Beneath the broad beech and the chestnut
    shade;
That tall tree which of a nut was set
At his great birth where all the Muses met.[1]

The tree here alluded to was called 'Bears-Oak,' and was planted at the birth of Sir Philip Sidney in 1554.

Besides Lambard's list of ancient Kentish parks, Saxton, in his map of that

County dated in 1575, marks parks at *Tunbridge, Ulcum, Hemsted, Hasting-ligh,* and *Forde*; the last a little north of Canterbury, one of the minor palaces of the Archbishops of Canterbury. In Speed's map, early in the reign of James I., other parks were noticed at *Bromley, Scott's Hall, Hanger, Bocton-Malherbe, Through-ley,* and *Eastwell.* Leland, in his 'Itinerary,' notes also a park at *Sutton Valance* by Boxley, in this county, belonging to the Cliffords,[2] though he has very incorrectly described the situation of the place, Sutton Valance being four or five miles south of Boxley.

The Patent Rolls preserve also a few notices of parks in Kent. In the forty-sixth year of Henry III. William de Say received license to impark his Wood of *Hangre*, within the bounds of the forest of Pembury. This is the park before alluded to, and marked in Speed's map of the county.

In the eighteenth of Edward II., David de Strabolgi, Earl of Athol, had license to impark his wood of *Northwood* in the Hundred of Whitstable in this county. In the fifteenth of Edward III., Walter de Say had license to impark one hundred acres of land and wood in 'Bierlenge,' and a certain road through the midst of them. This regards the ancient seat afterwards of the Nevill family at *Birling* in this county. In the thirty-third year of the same reign the king confirmed to the Archbishop of Canterbury the grant made to him by William Morant, who engaged that neither he nor his heirs would make any park in his domain lands in Chevening to the prejudice of the archbishop's free chase there. Morants Court, the ancient

---

[1] Ben Jonson's Forest.   [2] Leland's Itin. vol. vi. p. 27, fol. 28.

seat of the family of Morant, adjoins Chevening, and is in that parish, in the liberty of the archbishop.

In the *forty-first* of Edward III. Stephen Ashway obtained leave to increase his park at Brokesham in this county.

Among the Kentish parks which were imparked in the sixteenth, seventeenth, and eighteenth centuries, we have *Eastwell*, one of the largest and perhaps most remarkable of deer parks in the south of England. It appears to have been imparked by Sir Thomas Finch in the reign of Elizabeth. Though not marked as a park in Saxton's Survey, we find it in that of Speed in the beginning of the reign of James I.; and Catherine, daughter of Sir Thomas Moyle of Eastwell, and widow of Sir Thomas Finch, is said to have died seized of the capital messuage called Eastwell Place, with the garden and '*Park*,' in 1586-7.[1] The present park contains nearly 2,300 acres, within its outer fence, which stretches for nearly four miles along the high-road from Ashford to Faversham; about 1,500 or 1,600 acres are open to the deer. This park exhibits great variety of ground and abrupt differences of character and soil, being in some parts stiff clay, in others loams upon chalk, and in others chalk downs, with scarcely any soil to cover the substratum. This great variety of soil and pasturage has an excellent effect upon the deer, and insures the extraordinary quality and flavour of the venison for which this park is remarkable.

Eastwell Park is also remarkable for the great height of the fern, which flourishes here in the greatest luxuriance, in a wood of gigantic beeches, now unfortunately much decayed, cut into eight avenues, and known as 'the Star Walk.' Specimens of fern have been gathered measuring more than fourteen feet in height. In favourable years, the fern will reach to a man's shoulders on horseback, completely concealing fallow-deer, which can only be traced by their bounds. Eastwell Park contains both red and fallow-deer of every variety, and is celebrated for a breed of powerful greyhounds peculiar to this park, and used for catching the deer after the rutting season is over, and then turning them into a paddock in order to supply the London market. The method of doing this is described elsewhere.[2]

Surrenden-Dering, supposed to be an ancient park, contains 350 acres of land, with a herd of 150 fallow-deer.

Mereworth Castle, also an ancient park, though not so marked in the ancient maps of the county; a small park of from 90 to 100 acres, with from 80 to 100 head of fallow-deer. This park was restocked from Ireland about the year 1852.

Chilham Park, said to have been first enclosed in the year 1616; it contains an area of 228 acres, with a small herd of from 65 to 70 fallow-deer.

Mersham-Hatch Park, enclosed by a grant from James I. in 1618; a park of 380 acres, with a herd of from 200 to 220 fallow-deer.

Waldershare Park was enclosed in the reign of Queen Anne, probably by the Furnese family, the then proprietors. It is a park of 500 acres without 'the Wilderness,' with a large herd of fallow-deer.

---

[1] Collins's Peerage Ed. Bridges, vol. iii. p. 379.

[2] Information of the Earl of Winchilsea and Nottingham.

Godmersham Park.—The total extent is 696 acres; 560 acres open to the deer; imparked in the years 1742-3. There is a herd of 500 fallow-deer, which are said to have come from the Grange in Hampshire, but before that place was permanently disparked.

The Mote Park.—It is uncertain when this park was first enclosed. It contains 480 acres, of which number 140 are free of tithe, in consequence (as it is said) of that being the original deer park. The deer have been reduced from 600 to 400, and now to but 86, all fallow-deer.

Hall Place Park, in the parish of Leigh. This park contains about 150 acres, with a herd of about 80 fallow-deer.

Boughton Park.—A very small park, containing but very few deer.

Existing Deer Parks in Kent.

1.	GREENWICH	. The Queen.
2.	KNOLE .	. The Countess de la Warre.
3.	COBHAM .	. The Earl of Darnley.
4.	LULLINGSTONE	Sir Perceval Hart Dyke, Bart.
5.	EASTWELL	. The Earl of Winchilsea.
6.	SURRENDEN-DERING,	Sir Edward Dering, Bart.
7.	MEREWORTH	. Viscount Falmouth.
8.	CHILHAM	. Mr. Hardy.
9.	MERSHAM-HATCH,	Sir Norton Knatchbull, Bart.
10.	WALDERSHARE	The Earl of Guilford.
11.	GODMERSHAM	. Mr. Knight.
12.	THE MOTE	. Earl of Romney.
13.	HALL-PLACE	. Mr. Baily.
14.	BOUGHTON	. Mr. Rider.

ESSEX.

THAT Essex 'is full of Parks,' was remarked by Norden in his Survey of that county in the year 1594, and a glance at the map will prove that this observation was well founded, no less than forty-five being marked by him, and forty-four in Saxton's map dated in 1576. The county was indeed completely studded with parks in the Elizabethan period; the number has been gradually reduced, there being at present, I believe, but eleven deer parks in Essex, the sole representatives of that great hunting field or forest which we are told[1] in ancient times comprehended almost the whole of the county, an area greatly reduced by a charter or grant of King John,

dated the 25th of March, in the fifth year of his reign, and again by a perambulation made in the twenty-ninth of Edward I. in pursuance of the Charta de Forestâ.

But one park in Essex is noticed in Domesday, that belonging to Suein, in the Hundred of Rochefort. A park is marked at '*Rocheford*' both by Saxton and Norden in the reign of Elizabeth. The principal Royal parks in this county were those in the parish of Great Waltham, called '*Pleshey* and *Apchild*,' and at *Havering*, called *Havering atte Bower*, an ancient and favourite seat of Royalty. But the Patent Rolls abounding with licenses to

[1] See the 15th Report of the Commissioners on the Woods and Forests, anno 1793.

enclose parks in Essex, and the hundreds of the county being small and inconveniently numerous, perhaps the best method of noticing them first will be in chronological rather than topographical order, beginning, as they do, as early as the reign of King John, in the fifth of whose reign the Bishop of London obtained license to impark his wood of *Ratendon*,[1] within the bounds of the forest of Essex; and in the twenty-second of Henry III., the same park is recognised as belonging to the Bishop of Ely.[2] In the sixth of John the park of *Langley*, belonging to William Gray,[3] occurs. In the twenty-eighth of Henry III. Philip Basset obtained license to assart and impark ten acres of wood in *Westwoode* beyond the bounds of the Great Park of *Aungre*.[4] In the thirty-second of the same reign the Abbot of Stratford had license to impark his wood of *Lugton*, within the bounds of the forest of Essex,[5] and in the same year Roger de Cantilupe was empowered to impark sixty acres of briers (brueræ) in *Badewe*, in the same forest.[5] The park of *Thieden* in the forest of Essex, belonging to John de Lessington, is recognised in the thirty-fourth of the same reign.[6] In the forty-eighth of Henry III. William de Marney had license to impark his wood of *Lire* (or *Leyre*) within the bounds of the forest of Essex;[7] and in the same year Robert de Tateshull received a license of the same kind in regard to the wood of *Little Waltham* in the same forest;[6] the

next year both William de Clovill and Richard de Tany had license to impark their woods of *Wyndeforde* and *Stapleforde Tany* in the forest of Essex.[9] In the fifty-fourth of Henry III. two licenses for enlarging parks at *Stapleforde* and *Shenefield* in the same forest were granted to Philip Bassett.[10] In the seventh of Edward I. a license was granted to John de Nevill to impark with a small foss and a low hedge or fence his wood of *Connynghall* in the forest of Essex;[11] and in the ninth of the same reign Reginald de Ginges and the Prior of Tiptre had licenses for imparking within the same forest.[12] In the thirteenth of this reign the Prior of Bickenakre had also license to impark his waste in *Woodham Ferrers* and *Danyngbury* of sixty acres of land.[13] John Filliol in the nineteenth of Edward I. received a license to impark his wood of *Wickhey*, containing eighty acres within the forest of Essex.[14] The next year a license to enlarge his park was granted to Ralph de Berners in *Rothinge Berners*, also in the forest. In the twenty-first of this reign a like license of enlargement of his park at *Copped Hall* was granted to Henry, son of Auchor;[15] *Copped Hall* or *Copt Hall*, near Waltham, in the time of Elizabeth belonged to Sir Thomas Heneage; in the third year of the reign of Richard II. it was, with Harold's Park adjoining, the property of the abbot of the Holy Cross of Waltham, who had license to enlarge it with 162 acres of his domain lands.[16] The

---

[1] Cal. Patent Rolls, p. 2.
[2] Ib. p. 32.
[3] Ib. p. 9.
[4] Ib. p. 20.
This grant was continued to Robert de Marney, in the 9th Edward III.

[5] Ib. p. 22.
[6] Ib. p. 23.
[7] Ib. p. 34.

[8] Cal. Patent Rolls, p. 35.
[9] Ib. p. 38.
[10] Ib. p. 43.
[11] Ib. p. 48.
[12] Ib. p. 56.
[13] Ib. p. 204.

[14] Ib. p. 49.
[15] Ib. p. 52.
[16] Ib. p. 54.

excellence of its pastures is commemorated in the popular rhyme :—

Lord Morleyes.   Baron parke is frutefull and fatt,
In Ley' Marney *pk.*   Howfeilde is better than that;
In Wigboro.   *Copte Hall* is beste of them all;
parcell of Peldo Hall.   Yet Hubble down may wayre
                the crowne.[1]

Harrold's Park, called in Saxton's map Harfold Park, adjoining Epping Forest, was in the possession of the Crown in the reign of Henry VIII., and the Records of the Land Revenue have preserved the following accounts with reference to it :—

' A booke concernyng money laide oute by Geffrey Gate as well for the paling of Harrold's parke, Nasing wood grene mede w'hin the same wood, and for the reddyng of the same & making of a launde there, as also making of a new standing in the same, and a newe lodge in Nasing wood, begone the vii'ᵗʰ day of August Aᵉ. xxxiii'ᵒ. and endyes at Myghelmas in ano xxxiiij'ᵗᵒ. Dᵒⁱ R. H. VIII.' ' The paling of Harroldes parke wᵗ cariage made for the same as followeth, The totall soffie of Harrold's pke afiits to xxviii'ˡˡ xi' ix'ᵈ. The paling of Nasyng wood and grove made within the same wood, xxvi'ˡˡ vii' iij'ᵈ. Cariage of posts, pales, and rayles for the same, at xxi'ᵈ by the daye, xxxviii'ˡˡ iiij' ix'ᵈ. Money paied to laborers for ridding of the grounde in grene meade for the makyng of a launde there, liii'ˡˡ xiii' vi'ᵈ. Money paied to carpenters, sawyers, and other artificers, as well for the making of a newe lodge in Nasing wood as also a new standing in Grene mede wᵗ sondrye necessaries bought for the same, xiii'ˡˡ xv'. ob.'

A license to enlarge his park of *Haringfield*, within the bounds of the Essex Forest, was granted to Hugh de Vere in the twenty-seventh of Edward I.[2] The next year John de Engaine had a license to impark at *Haselden* in the same forest.[3] In the first year of Edward II. a license to impark the wood of *Gingemounteney*, within the bounds of this forest, was granted to Edward Bacon and John his brother.[4] In the fourth of Edward II. Guido de Ferre had license to impark his wood of *Eytropp Rothinge* in this county.[5] In the seventeenth of the same reign a license was granted to Edward Earl of Arundel, and Alice his wife, to impark fifty acres of land and brushwood (brusceti) in their manor of Wolfhampton, within the bounds of the forest.[6] Robert de Bousser (Bouchier) was licensed to impark his wood of *Halsted*, in this county, in the ninth of Edward III.[7] In the thirty-fifth of Edward III. a grant of pasturage for fourteen cows is granted to the Rector of Eastwood in the King's Park at *Reilegh* ;[8] the profits of this park, in the eastern part of the county, were granted to Edward Duke of York in the fourteenth of Richard II.[9] In 1530 it appears from the Privy Purse Expenses of King Henry VIII .that 'quicke dere' were brought from the Royal park here, to replenish the Park of Greenwich ; the expense was 30*s.*

In the thirty-seventh of Edward III. Thomas Tyrell had license to impark 400 acres of pasture and wood at *Thornton* in this county ;[10] and in the fiftieth of the

[1] Norden's Survey, printed by the Camden Society, p. 8.
[2] Cal. Patent Rolls, p. 60.
[3] Ib. p. 61.
[4] Cal. Patent Rolls, p. 69.
[5] Ib. p. 72.   [8] Ib. p. 174.
[6] Ib. p. 94.   [9] Ib. p. 221.
[7] Ib. p. 122.   [10] Ib. p. 177.

same reign the Bishop of London received a like grant for 300 acres in *Wickham*, also in Essex.[1]

The same year Ralph Till was constituted keeper of the king's park of *Haveringe at Boure*, for his life.[2] And again in the thirtieth of Henry VI. John Earl of Oxford was appointed keeper of the same park, and of the whole forest of Essex.[3] The pale of the park of Havering, said to have contained one thousand acres,[4] was, before the third year of Richard II., kept in repair as far as regarded 467 perches of it (every perch of eighteen feet), by the abbot and convent of Barking, when the service was commuted for an annual payment of five marks.[5]

Adjoining to this park was *Pirgo*, a mansion and park granted by Queen Elizabeth to Sir John Grey, second son of Thomas Grey, Marquis of Dorset, and visited by Her Majesty in 1561.

Guidea or *Giddy* Hall, a little south of Pirgo, was also visited by Elizabeth in 1568; it was begun by Sir Thomas Cooke in the reign of Edward IV., and a license obtained for a park and castle at that period; it is marked as a park in Norden's Survey.

At *Thorndon*, near Brentwood, is a park mentioned in the ancient surveys, and at present containing about 735 acres, and a herd of 100 red and 550 fallow-deer; it has been long the seat of the Petre family.

At *Weald* Hall is also an extensive existing park, of three hundred acres within the pales, which appears to be marked in the ancient surveys; it contains about 200 fallow-deer; it is a beau-

tiful park, with perhaps some of the most magnificent oak timber in England.

The park of *Wanstead* in this same south-western corner of Essex, in the Elizabethan period belonged to Robert Devereux, Earl of Essex, and was very extensive; here was the celebrated seat of the Tilney family, built in 1715 and demolished in 1823. In the neighbouring forest of Waltham Sir Henry Wroth obtained a warrant from Charles II. in 1666 to enclose 1,500 acres of common in the manors of Loughton and Chigwell, 'yet so that the deer may go into the same, altho' no writ of Inquisition has been held thereon.'[6]

'*Gaines*,' an ancient disused park in the parish of Heydon Gernon, was enclosed by R. Gernon with the license of Henry III., it was then called '*Le Leyt*.' Near this was the park of '*Wyntrey*,' and to the east '*Writtle*,' the latter marked only in Saxton's Survey.

Further north is *Pleshey*; this was the ancient seat of the Bohuns, Earls of Essex, and afterwards of Thomas of Woodstock, Duke of Gloucester. 'In 1282 Humphry de Bohun, Earl of Hereford and Essex, obtained leave of Edward I. to enclose 150 acres of demesne land adjoining to his park of Waltham and Haut-Estre, called Le Plessier, to enlarge that park; which comprehended some of the land belonging to Waltham-bury, and was known by the name of Waltham Great Park in the year 1516. The two parkes called Plecy parkes, alias le Great Parks, and le little Park de Plecy, were granted to Sir

---

[1] Cal. Patent Rolls, p. 193.
[2] Ib. p. 194.
[3] Ib. p. 294.

[4] Beauties of England and Wales, Essex, p. 475.
[5] Rolls of Par. vol. vi. p. 335.
[6] S. P. O. Domestic, 1666, p. 539.

John Gates by King Edward VI.'[1] In the same parish of Great Waltham, besides the existing park of *Langleys*, was *Apchild* or *Abfield* Park, which, in 1449, belonged to Queen Margaret of Anjou.[2] The letter which Her Majesty wrote from Pleshey to the keeper of this park has been already given. She also wrote from Pleshey on the 30th of August in the same year to the keeper of Falkborne Park in this neighbourhood, desiring him to preserve the game, which the owner, Elizabeth Lady Say, had granted to the Queen ' to have our disporte in her park of Felborne.'[3]

Morant gives the following account of another extensive park in this part of Essex:—' The Manor of Warners in Great Waltham, soon after the death of Henry Warner (who died in 1556), this estate was purchased by Richard Lord Rich; that great acquirer had obtained a little before, viz. in 1536, a grant of the priory of Little Lees, &c.; these demesnes he converted into a park, about four miles in circumference, lying partly in this parish and partly in those of Little Lees and Felsted. It was called *Littley Parke*, alias *Little Hay*.'[4] This place, which has been for near two centuries disparked, was called by Dr. Walker in his Funeral sermon on the death of Charles Rich, Earl of Warwick, ' A secular Elysium, a worldly paradise, a heaven upon earth!'

New Hall, south of Lees, built in a park by Henry VII. and Henry VIII., and given by Queen Elizabeth to Thomas Radcliffe Earl of Sussex, came afterwards by purchase to George Villiers Duke of

Buckingham. It was visited by Evelyn in 1656, who remarks:—' Above all, I admired the faire avenue planted with stately lime trees in 4 rowes, for neare a mile in length; it has three descents, which is the only fault, and may be reform'd ; there is another faire walk of y[e] same at the mall and wildernesse, with a tennis-court: [the park] was well stor'd with deer and ponds.'[5] This park, like so many of the ancient parks in this county, has been long disparked; in 1691 it belonged to the Duchess of Albemarle, and was then ' well stored with deer.' At this period also (1691) I find by a letter from Mr. Abdy to Mr. Moore at Newcastle House, St. James's, that he hopes the Duchess of Albemarle will give him some deer to stock his new park at *Fœlix Hall* in this county.

In the north-western part of the county is *Audley End*, one mile from Saffron Walden, ' a nobly well-wall'd, wooded, and watered park,' wrote Evelyn in 1654; the present park contains about 143 acres, with a herd of 300 fallow-deer. Near Audley End is *Shortgrove*, where a park was enclosed in April 1835, containing 100 acres and 150 fallow-deer. To the north again, is *Chesterford* Park. ' The house was built, or begun,' says Morant, ' by William Marquis of Berkeley, the then lord of the manor, who died in 1491, a mile northward from the Town, in the middle of a park.' It afterwards belonged to the owners of Audley End, from whence Thomas Earl of Suffolk writes to his son Lord Howard of Walden, May 31, 1623, that ' he has failed to obtain an in-

---

[1] Gough's History of Pleshy, Anno 1803, p. 9.
[2] See note, p. 20.
[3] Letter of Queen Margaret of Anjou, Camden Society, 1863, pp. 100, 105.
[4] Morant's Essex, vol. ii. p. 85.
[5] Evelyn's Memoirs, vol. i. p. 292.

terview with M'. Paris, who complains of injury done to his grounds by the deer in Chesterford Park. He keeps deer éntirely for the king's pleasure and recreation; they do him more mischief than any one else, and is willing to give them up if his majesty please.'¹

Several other parks are marked in Norden's Survey of Essex, made in 1594. *Hemstead, Horeham, Henham, Maynards, Porters, Bradfield, Bell-House, Castle-Heningham,* and *Moynes* are in the north-western part of the county.

Horeham is mentioned by Leland in the following passage :—'Old Cutte married the Doughter and Heyre of one Roodes, &c. Old Cutte buildid Horeham-Haule, a very sumptuous house in Essex, by Thaxtede; and there is a goodly pond or lake by it, and faire parkes there about.'²

Bell House is said to have been enclosed by Sir Edward Bassett, knighted by James I.;³ if so, it must have been in the reign of Elizabeth, as it is marked in both Norden's and Saxton's maps.

Castle Heningham, 'a very stately howse, mounted on a hille, hauinge 3 parkes,' belonged to the Earls of Oxford, and in Elizabeth's time to Lord Burghley.⁴

In the north-eastern parts of Essex, other parks are given by Saxton; four are. marked in the neighbourhood of Col-

chester, at *Wyvenhoe, Elmsted, Grimsted,* and *Myle End;* that at *Wyvenhoe* is an existing park of 150 acres of land, with a herd of 160 fallow-deer. Four other parks appear also in Saxton's Survey, at *Wickes* or *Wykes,* or *Park Hall,* the ancient inheritance of the Bohuns in the parish of Bradfield, and at Ockley-parva, and two at Clackton.

In the south-eastern divison of Essex, besides the parks of *Rochford* and *Rayleigh* or *Raleigh,* there was one belonging to the castle of *Hadleigh* or *Hadley,* where Christopher Barton and John Trevelyan were appointed keepers in the year 1446.⁵ One at *Beches,* and at *Danbury,* once the ancient seat of the Mildmay family.

Existing Deer Parks in Essex.

1. AUDLEY END. Lord Braybroke.
2. THORNDEN . Lord Petre.
3. WYVENHOE . Mr. Gurdon-Rebow.
4. WEALD-HALL. Mr. Tower. ..
5. BELL-HOUSE . Sir Thomas Barrett Lennard, Bart.
6. EASTON . Hon. Miss Maynard.
7. HALLINGBURY Mr. Archer Houblon.
8. BRAXTED -. Mr. Ducane.
9. LANGLEYS . Mr. Tufnell.
10. BOREHAM . Sir John Tyrell, Bart.
11. SHORTGROVE . Mr. Smith.

¹ S. P. O. Dom. Cal. p. 394.
² Leland's Itin. vol. iv. p. 32, fol. 50.
³ Neale's Views of Seats, 1818, vol. i.

⁴ Norden's Description of Essex, p. 37.
⁵ Trevelyan Papers (Camden Society), p. 27.

HERTFORDSHIRE.

THREE Hertfordshire parks are found recorded in the great Domesday Survey—at *St. Albans*, *Ware*, and *Belintone.* . The park at St. Albans is described as 'parcus bestiarum silvaticarum,' and it belonged to the great Abbey at that place. The park at Ware is described in the same words, it was the property of Hugh de Grentemaisnil ; a park is marked at Ware in all the ancient maps. Belintone, the modern Benington, belonged to Peter de Valongies ; its park of 'wood or wild beasts' also occurs in the older maps of the county ; in the time of James I. it belonged to Robert Devereux, third Earl of Essex, who sold his hunting-house here with a large park of deer to Sir Julius Cæsar, knt., Master of the Rolls in the year 1615.[1]

'This shire at this day,' writes Norden in his description of Hertfordshire in 1596, 'is, and hath beene more heretofore, much repleat with parkes, woodes, and rivers.' The principal parks marked in his survey, and that of Saxton, are as follows,—at *Hatfield*, near the centre of the county, where Robert first Earl of Salisbury made two large parks, one for fallow, the other for red deer, which were united by the late Marquis of Salisbury. The present park contains 314 acres of land, with a

herd of 360 fallow-deer. In the immediate neighbourhood were the parks of *Woodhall, Brockethall, Tittenhanger, Shenley, Bedwell,* and *Punsburne.* To the east *Cheshunt* and *Theobalds* ; the latter, not marked as a park in Saxton's Survey, was the well-known favourite residence of King James I., who enclosed the park with a brick wall about ten miles in compass.[2] By a survey taken in 1650, before the destruction of the palace here, Theobalds Park contained 2,508 acres ; valued, together with six lodges, at 1,545*l.* 15*s.* 4*d.* per annum ; the deer were valued at 1,000*l.*; the rabbits at 15*l.*; the timber at 7,259*l.*, exclusive of 15,608 trees marked for the use of the navy, and others already cut down for that purpose. The park contained an avenue of a mile long, between a double row of trees. In the gallery of this beautiful palace, 120 feet by 21, were 'divers large stagges heads sett round the same, and fastened to the sayd roome, which are an excellent ornament to the same.'[3] It was in this park that Henry Cary Lord Falkland lost his life in September 1633, by breaking his leg with a fall out of a 'standing,' being there hunting with the king, 'and his leg gangrening was cut off, and his lordship died the next day died.'[4]

The park at *Cashiobury* in the south-

---

[1] Life of Sir Julius Cæsar : London, 1827, p. 32.
[2] At the distance of every mile there was fixed in the wall a square stone, with the date of the year and the number of miles. One of these, with the figure viii. and the date 1621,

still remains in a part of the old wall which forms the boundary of Mr. Russel's garden at Albury.—*Lyson's Environs,* vol. ii. p. 776, note.
[3] Lyson's Environs, vol. ii. p. 770.
[4] S. P. O. Domestic, Sept. 27, 1633.

western corner of this county, near the town of Watford, is described as between three and four miles in circumference, affording some rich scenery and noble timber.[1] Adjoining Cashiobury is 'the *Grove Park*,' and a little to the north of Watford is *Kings Langley*, where was a royal seat founded by King Henry III. The Home Park here was granted by Edward IV. to the Prior of Langley. After the dissolution it reverted to the Crown, and in 1626 'Kings Langley Park, and all the deer, marsh, grass, wood, and all trees whatsoever,' were leased to Sir Charles Morrison for 99 years, and soon afterwards passed entirely from the Crown.[2]

At *Berkhamsted* was also an ancient royal park attached to the castle there, which is mentioned as early as the twenty-first of Edward I.;[3] this, like Langley, has been for many ages disparked.

Penley Park, near Berkhamsted, was enclosed by the license of King Henry VI. in the eighteenth year of his reign.[4] It appears to have been disparked before Chauncey's time.

In the more northern part of the county, near Benington, was *Walkerne Park*, noticed in Saxton's Survey, and a little to the south of it *Knebworth*, not marked in the older maps, but which Chauncey describes as 'a large pile of brick with a fair quadrangle in the middle of it, upon a dry hill in a fair park, stocked with the best deer in the county, excellent timber, and well wooded, and from whence you may behold a most lovely prospect to the east.'

In the eastern border of the county

Saxton marks a cluster of parks near Hunsdon. Honesdon or *Hunsdon Park* is recognised as a park in the year 1124, twenty-fourth Henry I., when Richard Earl of Hertford granted to the monks of Saint Augustine of Stoke an annual gift of a doe out of his park here.[5] Henry VIII. built a palace at Hunsdon and erected it into an 'Honour,' in connection with the adjoining manors of Hansted and Joyden, the last in Essex. In the church here is a curious brass to the memory of a keeper of the park here. He is represented with his bugle-horn and broadsword levelling a cross-bow at a stag, while Death, delineated as a skeleton, is pointing a dart at his breast.[6]

In the parish of Stansted-Abbot, a little south of Hunsdon, is '*the Manor of the Rye*,' where King Henry VI. granted a license to Andrew Ogard and others to impark 50 acres of land, 11 acres of meadow, 8 acres of pasture, and 16 acres of wood.[7] This park is marked both in Saxton's and in Speed's maps, but has been very long disparked.

Saxton also marks a park near *Sabridgeworth*. A grant to impark there, and in *Thorley*, was granted by Henry VI. to John Leventhorpe, in the twenty-seventh year of his reign. The park was licensed to enclose 400 acres of land, 40 of meadow, and 40 of wood.[8]

Ancient parks appear also in Saxton's Survey at *Hondon*, *Hodham-parva*, and at *Furneaux-Pelham*. The latter place in the time of Elizabeth belonged to Lord Mount-Eagle, who sold the manor and the two disparked parks, called the Old

[1] Beauties of England and Wales.
[2] Chauncey, p. 543.
[3] Ib. p. 575.
[4] Ib. p. 394.
[5] Chauncey, p. 196.
[6] See before, p. 54, where it is engraved.
[7] Chauncey, p. 195.
[8] Ib. p. 181.

and the New Park, in the forty-second year of her reign.[1]

Parks, subsequent to the Elizabethan period, were also at the following places, as appears in Chauncey's History of the County :—At *Throcking*, the seat of Mr. Elwes, and at *Widyall* Hall, made by Richard Gulston, Esq., who died in 1686; at *Moore*, or More's place, in Hadham-magna, made by Sir Richard Atkins, Bart. ' for his conveniency,' in the time of Charles II.; at New Place, in the parish of Goldeston, where Sir Humphry Gore ' made a pretty park' in Chauncey's time;[2] at *Hamills*, where Sir John Brograve enlarged his park; at *Offley-place*, the seat of the Spencers; and at *Stagenhoe*, belonging at the same period to Sir John

Austin. Before Chauncey's time, *Gorhambury* appears to have been enclosed; the park and grounds are said[3] to include about 600 acres, well stocked with timber. *Ashridge*, near Tring and Berkhamsted, is also marked as a park in Moll's map, made in the year 1700, and engraved in Chauncey's History of Hertfordshire; but the house is in the county of Buckingham.

Existing Hertfordshire Parks.

1. HATFIELD   . The Marquis of Salisbury.
2. CASHIOBURY . Earl of Essex.
3. KNEBWORTH . Lord Lytton.
4. GORHAMBURY Earl of Verulam.
5. THE GROVE . Earl of Clarendon.
6. MOORE PARK Lord Ebury.

[1] Chauncey, p. 144.
[2] An older one is, however, here marked in Saxton.

[3] Beauties of England and Wales, vol. vii. p. 130.

G

CHAPTER IV.

NOTES ON DEER PARKS IN˙THE COUNTIES

OF

CORNWALL,   SOMERSETSHIRE,

DEVONSHIRE,   WILTSHIRE, AND

DORSETSHIRE,   HAMPSHIRE.

The ancient 'Pale Bank' or 'Deer Leap' at Hursley, in the county of Southampton.

CHAPTER IV.

CORNWALL.

ORDEN, in his survey of this county, probably written in 1584, but not published till 1728, observes, 'For matters of pleasure, the gentlemen in former times have had their parkes of fallowe-deere, whereof remayne only the vestigia; the original impaylings of manie of them, which are altogether disparked and converted to other more profitable uses for the comonwealth, by the providence of former more thriftie owners; and king Henry the 8, being therunto induced by the perswasion of some circumspecte officer of his, disparked manie parkes belonging to the Dukedome of Cornwall: the pretence that they laye so farre from the princes comon residence, they were not so apte to yelde pleasure as profit; and therefore beying disparked, were lett at an improved rent. The first parkes belonginge to the Dukedom that were disparked were *Retormell* near Lostuthiell, where yet standeth Restormell Castle, the Duke's auncient seat ; *Caribullock*, nere Devonshire ; *Liskerd* Parke near the same towne, wher the D. had also castle, now decayde; *Lenteglos* Parke, easte of Foy-haven ; and lastly, *Launceston* Parke, wher standeth *Dunhevet*, the Duke's most auncient castle. Some gentlemen there are that mayntaine their parkes, and retayne the deere, as M. Reskymer at *Merther*; M. Vivian, at *Trelawarren*, near Helston, in Kirrier hundred; M. Chawmonds at *Laucells*, in Straton hundred; M. Trevanian, lately deceased; a parke called St. Michell ; Sir Jonathan Trelawny, lately also deceased, *Poole* Park in Minhinet parishe ; M. Rowse, a parke newly erected at *Halton*, near Calstock; M. Corrington, at *Newton*; and Sir Reynold Mohuns, a parke at Boconnock.'[1]

The survey of Cornwall, by Richard Carew, of Antonie, Esq., printed in 1602, in point of time one of the first of English topographers, gives very much the same account. He tells us, ' Cornwall was stored not long since with many parkes of fallow-deere. But King Henry VIII.

being persuaded (as it is said) by Sir Richard Pollard, that those belonging to the Duke, could steed him with little pleasure in so remote a parte, and would yield him good profit if they were leased out at an improved rent, did condescend to their disparking. So foure of them tooke a fall together, to wit, *Carybullock, Liskerd, Restormel, Lanteglos*. Howbeit this good husbandrie came short of the desired promise, and the king's expectation, wherethrough the one was shent for the attempt, and the other discontented with the effect. Notwithstanding, as princes examples are ever taken for warrantable precedents to the subjects, so most of the Cornish gentlemen preferring gaine to delight, or making gaine their delights, shortly after followed the like practise, and made their deere leape over the pale to give the bullockes place. Parkes yet remaining are in East Hundred—*Poole*, Sir Jonathan Trelawneys, newly revised; *Halton*, M. Rouses, lately impaled ; and *Newton*, M. Corington's almost decayed. In West Hundred, *Boconnoch*, Sir Reginauld Mohuns. In Powder Hundred, *Caryhayes*, M. Trevanions. In Stratton, *Launcels*, M. Chamonds. In Kever Hundred, *Trelawarren*, M. Vivians; and *Merther*, M. Reskymers.'[2]

Of the five[3] Royal parks belonging to the Duchy of Cornwall :—1. *Coribullock*, or *Carbolok*, alone appears in Saxton's map of the county, engraved in 1576. It could scarcely have been reinclosed at that time, but might have retained its ancient paling; it is in East Hundred, on the confines of Devonshire, and was described by Norden as 'a fair park belonging to y[e]

---

[1] Norden's Survey of Cornwall, p. 20.
[2] Carew's Survey of Cornwall, pp. 22 *b*.

[3] Lysons mentions another at 'Hellesbury.'

Duchy, disparked in King Henry 8th's time.[1] In 1583 it is described as about two miles in compass, and disparked.[2]

2. 'The old parke at *Launston'* is named by Leland in his 'Itinerary;'[3] it is said in 1583 to have been about a mile in compass.[2]

3. *Liskard.* — Of this place, Leland says, 'about half a mile or I came to Liskard, I passed in a wood by a chapel of our lady, called *our Lady in the Park,* wher was wont to be grat pilgrimage.'[4] A park is noticed at 'Liskeard,' in the year 1446,[5] and it appears among the disparked parks in the return of 1583, three miles in compass.[2]

4. *Lanteglos,* a mile in circuit, and belonging to the queen in 1583.[2]

5. *Restormel.*— 'The park of Restormel (existing in 1446)[5] is hard by the north side of the town of Lostwithiel; Tynne workes in this parke; good woode in this parke. There is a castel on an hill in this parke, wher sumtymes the erles of Cornwal lay—a chapel of the Trinite in the parke, not far from the castelle.'[6] In 1583 it is described as about a mile in compass.[2]

In an 'extent' of the Duchy of Cornwall, 11th Edw. III., and noted by Lysons (p. clxxix.), Launceston Park is described as containing, in circuit, one league, and having then in it fifteen deer, but capable of sustaining forty. In Restormel Park were 300 deer; in Liskeard Park, 200; in the Park of Kerybollok, (containing in circuit three leagues), 150 deer; and in Trematon Park, on the north side of the castle, 42 deer.

Arranging the other ancient and existing parks of this county according to their respective hundreds, we have in East Hundred, *Poole,* in Queen Elizabeth's time belonging to Sir Jonathan Trelawney, then lately 'revived,' not marked by Saxton, and disparked before 1730.[7] *Halton,* near Colstock, then 'lately impaled,' also disparked before 1730.[7] *Newton,* in the same neighbourhood, in the Elizabethan period even 'almost decayed,' existed in 1730.[7] At *Bicton,* was 'the House of William Wraye, Esq., whereunto adjoined a parke of fallow-deere,'[8] now disparked; also, *Bradrige,* Mr. Coster's, existing in 1730.[7] In East Hundred, the return of 1583 mentions parkes at St. Melan and Mynhenett; the former belonged to Peter Coryton, the latter to Trelawny, and another, disparked, at St. Ive.

In West Hundred, *Boconnoc,* containing at present about 230 acres, much wooded, and a herd of 220 fallow-deer. In 1583 it belonged to Sir William Mohun and others, and was a mile in compass,[2] Also *Pinchley,* Lord Radnor's, in 1730,[7] existing about 1780, but since disparked. The return of 1583 mentions also a park of George Luke at 'Wartegan,' about a mile in compass.[2]

In Powder Hundred, *Caryhayes,* one mile in circuit, and in 1583 belonging to Mrs. Sibil Trevanion,[2] existing in 1730[7] and 1760, and *St. Michael,* both now disparked. Norden mentions also a park called *Trevanion,* the seat of the family of that name, 'utterly decayed' in his time, and Leland observes of a park at *Bodrugan,* 'yn this park was the house of Sr Henry Bodrugan, a man of auncient stok,

---

[1] Norden's Survey, p. 92.
[2] S. P. O. Domestic, Sept. 25, 1583.
[3] Leland's Itin. vol. vii. p. 123.
[4] Ibid. vol. iii. p. 38, fol. 19.
[5] Trevelyan Papers (Camden Society), pp. 29-31.

[6] Leland's Itin. vol. iii. p. 35, fol. 17.
[7] Mr. Tonkin, quoted by Lysons in his account of Cornwall, p. clxxix.
[8] Norden's Survey, p. 90.

88   DEER AND DEER PARKS.   CH. IV.

atteyntid for takyng part with king Richard III. agayne Henry VII.'[1]
Tregothnan, a small park of 116 acres, with a herd of 100 fallow-deer.
Penrice, near St. Austell, a small park or paddock of sixty acres, enclosed in the reign of Charles I., with a herd of from 90 to 100 fallow-deer. In Powder Hundred also was *Lansladron Park*, belonging to the Arundels, which, as Norden says, was 'the most stateliest in the shire.' It is among 'the disparked and tilled' in the return of 1583. It was in compass two miles.

In Kirrier Hundred, *Trelawarren* and *Merther*, both disparked before 1730;[2] also *Godolphin*, Lord Godolphin's ; and *Tremogh*, Mr. Worth's, imparked about 1730.[2]
Carclew Park contains about 230 acres, and 150 head of fallow-deer; it is supposed to have been enclosed more than a century.

In Pyder Hundred there yet remains a small paddock of fallow-deer, at *Prideaux-place*, the seat of C. P. Brune, Esq.; the area is but eleven acres, and the deer amount to twenty-four. Here also were *Lanhidroch*, Lord Radnor's, and *Trevaunance*, Mr. Tonkin's. *Treluddra*, in this hundred, although a park by Royal patent, as Mr. Tonkin observes, had been disparked.[2] Here also was *Pawton*, a park belonging to the Bishop of Exeter, but long disparked.

In Stratton Hundred, *Launcels*, disparked before 1730.[2]

In Lesnewth Hundred, *Trelawney Park*, not mentioned in the maps, and long disparked; and in 1583, 'a park of the Queenes, of 2 myles circuit, called Helsburye.'[3]

Of the parks enumerated by Mr. Tonkin in 1730, *Godolphin, Caryhayes* or *Carhayes*, and *Boconnoc*, were most esteemed for their venison ; and of the whole number, observes Lysons, in his account of Cornwall, 'there remained about 1760, according to Dr. Borlase in his MS. notes on Carew, *Godolphin, Tregothnan, Lanhidrock, Pinchley, Boconnoc*, and *Carhayes*. In addition to these he mentions *Pencarrow*, Sir John Molesworth's, *Tehidy*, Mr. Bassett's, *Trevathow*, Mr. Praed's, and *Werrington*, a great part of which is in Cornwall, Mr. Morice's. Since Borlase's time, the parks of *Lanhidrock, Pinchley, Pencarrow, Tehidy*, and *Trevethon*, have been disparked. There are now (1814) in the Hundred of East, the parks of Werrington and Mount Edgecumbe, a great part of both being in the county of Cornwall. In the Hundred of West, *Boconnoc*, now Lord Grenville's. In the Hundred of Powder, *Tregothnan*, Lord Falmouth's, *Carhayes*, Mr. Trevannion's, *Penrice*, Mr. Graves's, and a paddock of Sir Christopher Hawkins's at *Trewithen*. In the Hundred of Pyder, a small park at *Padstow*, Mr. Prideaux Brune's. In the Hundred of Kirrier, *Godolphin*, now belonging to the Duke of Leeds; *Carclew*, Sir William Lemon's, and a small paddock belonging to Mr. Rogers at Penrose.'

Existing Parks in Cornwall.

1. BOCONNOC	.	Hon. G. Fortescue.
2. TREGOTHNAN	.	Viscount Falmouth.
3. CARCLEW	.	Sir C. Lemon, Bart.
4. PENRICE	.	Sir C. B. G. Sawle, Bart.
5. PRIDEAUX PLACE .	}	Mr. Prideaux Brune.

---

[1] Leland's Itin. vol. iii. p. 31, fol. 14.
[2] Mr. Tonkin, quoted by Lysons in his account of Cornwall, p. clxxix.
[3] S. P. O. Domestic, Sept. 25, 1585.

DEVONSHIRE.

THE only park described as existing in Devonshire at the time of the Domesday Survey is that of *Winchelie, Winkleigh,* or *Winkley,* in Tyverton Hundred, which had been held by Brictric, and afterwards by Queen Matilda. It is described as 'parcus bestiarum,' and is not noticed, observes Lysons, in any later account.[1] The same author has extracted from the writings of Dr. Borde in the reign of Henry VIII., and those of Westcote in that of Elizabeth, a long list of parks, the greater part of which have been long disused and disparked ; though, as Westcote observes, there were in his time ' some few parks remaining of the great store our fathers could speak of.' In default of a more exact method, it may be convenient to take these lists as printed by Lysons, adding what little I am able from other authorities. Dr. Borde's list commences with—

1. *Umberley,* in the parish of Atherington. This was the seat of the Willingtons.

2. *Testock,* or *Tawstock,* near Barnstaple, abounds with beautiful scenery. It was the seat of the extinct family of the Bouchiers, Earls of Bath. This park is marked in Saxton's Survey of 1575.

3. *Mownsatro,* or Mohuns Ottery. 'Syr George Carew hath a goodly maner parke at Mohuns Otery.'[2] The park has long ago, observes Lysons, been converted into tillage.

4. *Colriche.*

5. *Chymley,* or Chulmleigh. Here, says Lysons, 'The Courtenay family had a castle and a park, converted into tillage more than 200 years.'[3]

6. *Chilitilton,* or Chittlehampton. The park of Brightleigh, or Brightley, in this parish, is probably intended, which Lysons also remarks has been converted into tillage. Brightley appears in Saxton's map.

7. *Whitchurch.*

8. *Colcombe.* This is noticed as a park by Leland, and as 'longging to the Marquise of Excester.'[4]

9. *Coliton,* or Colington.

10. *Shute,* thus also noticed by Leland: ' About a mile or I cam to Colington, I saw from an hille *Shoute,* a right goodly maner place, a mile of, on an hille-side of the Lord Marquise of Dorsete, and by it a goodly large parke.'[5] This is an existing park, containing 101 acres of land, with a herd of 150 fallow-deer. The Shute estate is held under the Crown, under the condition of at least ten head of deer being kept in the park. There is no other deer park remaining in this western part of Devonshire. The park is fenced in a singular manner, by an earthen bank ten feet high topped with alders.

11. *Wiscan, Wischcum,* or *Wiscombe.* Leland observes, ' The parkes and maner places of Wischum and Shoute, abowt

---

[1] Lyson's Devonshire, p. ccxxx.
[2] Leland's Itin. vol. iiii. p. 19, fol. 39.
[3] Lysons, p. 100.

[4] Leland's Itin. vol. iii. p. 70.
[5] Itin. vol. iii. p. 70, fol. 41.

Axminstre, in Devonshire, wer the Lord Bonevilles, and after a knightes of that name, or ever they cam to the Marquise of Dorsetes Hand.'[1]

12. *Kirklake.*

13. *Kirton,* now Crediton, which belonged to the Bishops of Exeter.

14. *Glyst,* now Clist.

15. *Tyverton,* alias *Goodbere.* — This park is marked by Saxton. Westcote speaks of two parks at Tiverton in the reign of Charles I.

16. *Ashley.*

17. *Afton,* marked in Saxton's map in the parish of West Worlington.

18. *Okington,* now Oakhampton, a large park marked in Saxton's map.

19. *Caadley,* now Calwodley. This park is marked by Saxton.

Westcote's list includes—

1. *Annery,* in the parish of Monkleigh, about four miles from Bideford and two and a half from Torrington. In the reign of Henry V. it belonged to Sir William Hankford, Chief Justice of England, of whom it is said that he was so overwhelmed by the troubles of the times that he wished for death, but not choosing to die by his own hands, he devised this extraordinary scheme to hasten his end— sending for the keeper of his park at Annery, he scolded him for not being more vigilant, and gave him strict orders to shoot any man whom he should meet with in the park at night, if he refused to answer or to give a satisfactory account of himself. Having given this charge, he walked out in his park the same night, it being then very dark, and met, as he intended, his certain destruction.[2]

2. *Inwardleigh*—belonged to the family

of Coffin, before the reign of Edward III. There were no remains of the deer park in Risdon's time.

3. *Filleigh,* Castle Hill, Lord Fortescue's, is in this parish, which perhaps is here intended.

Lysons adds the following ancient parks, not occurring in either list—

1. *Braneys,* now Bradninch, a park which belonged to the Earl of Cornwall.

2. *Hartland,* where the Abbot of Hartland had two parks.

3. *Molland,* a park belonging to the Bottreaux family.

4. *Uffculme,* the seat of the Cogans.

5. *Lyneham,* belonging to the Crockers. This is marked by Saxton, near Plimpton.

6. *King's Nympton,* belonging to the family of Pollard. This also is given by Saxton.

7. *Langtree.*—Here was a park belonging to Sir Thomas Brown.

8. *Wembury.*—Here Sergeant Hele made a park in the reign of Queen Elizabeth.

9. *Ashton,* the seat of the Chudleighs, had also a deer park.

Lysons also gives a list of parks still existing at the time he wrote (1822), most of which yet remain; they were as follows:—

1. *Werrington,* formerly belonging to the Duke of Northumberland; it is near Launceston, on the borders of Cornwall, and here Sir Francis Drake petitioned the king (Charles I.) for a license to enclose on the 28th of February, 1631. The petition sets forth 'that out of desire to increase deer and game in his lands, he has begun to inclose certain grounds which he intends for keeping deer in the parishes of Wer-

---

[1] Itin. vol. vi. p. 62, fol. 64.

[2] Lyson's, p. 353.

rington and St. Stephens near Launceston, and has increased great store of game in his other lands in the parishes of Buckland-monachorum, Yarcombe, Sempford Spiney, and Brixton, co. Devon; ill affected persons are encouraged to attempt bold practices for killing deer and game, in regard that petitioner has not a grant thereof; prays for a grant to keep the said inclosed grounds a park for deer, and that his other lands may be free-warren unto them.' [Order for the Attorney-General to prepare a Bill as prayed, Whitehall, Feb. 28, 1631.]¹ Werrington at present contains 368 acres, and a herd of about 630 fallow-deer.

2. *Castle-hill.*— The Earl Fortescue's. This is a park of 153 acres, with a herd of about 300 fallow-deer. This is said to be an old park, though not mentioned in the ancient surveys.

3. *Mount-Edgecumbe.*—The Earl of Mount-Edgecumbe's, on the sea, close to the borders of Cornwall.

4. *Heanton.*—Lord Clinton's, in the parish of Petrockstow, about seven miles from Torrington.

5. *Ugbrook.* — Lord Clifford of Chudleigh's. A park of great natural beauties.

6. *Bicton.*— Sir Robert Dennis, who lived in the reign of Elizabeth, rebuilt the old mansion here, and enclosed a deer park. It contains 100 acres, and a small herd of fallow-deer.

7. *Eggesford.*— Marked by Saxton. Hon. Newton Fellowe's. Disparked of late years.

8. *Killerton,* belonging to Sir Thomas Ackland, Bart., in the parish of Broad Clist.

9. *Poltimore.*—This park, near Exeter, is mentioned in Saxton's map. Now Lord Poltimore's.

10. *Creedy.*—Sir John Davie, Bart. Now disparked.

11. *Youlston,* in the north of Devonshire, appears in Saxton. The ancient seat of the Chichester family, in the parish of Sherwill; now disparked.

12. *Clovelly.*—Sir James Hamlyn Williams, Bart.

13. *Great Fulford.*—The very ancient seat of the venerable family of Fulford. The park is mentioned in the second year of Edward IV., when the king granted to John Staplehill in fee, both Fulford and the park of Fulford, which lately belonged to Sir Baldewin Fulford, Knight, attainted.² The park is given by Saxton; it was disparked and divided into farms about the year 1860.

14. *Little Fulford Park,* now called *Shobrooke Park.* Mr. Hippesley's, containing an area of 230 acres, and a herd of 150 fallow-deer, supposed to have been a park for two centuries.

15. *Newenham.*— Mr. Strode's, in the parish of Plympton St. Mary.

16. *Ogwell.*—Mr. Taylor's; of late years disparked.

17. *Whyddon.*—Mr. Bayley's; a park which, according to Lysons, abounds with beautiful scenery; it is in the parish of Moreton Hamstead.

18. *Powderham Castle.*—The Earl of Devon's; stands in the middle of a fine park, surrounded with walls, shaded with lofty elms, and washed by the river Ex.

Besides these lists of disused and existing Devonshire parks, there are a few others not included in the preceding which

¹ S. P. O. Domestic. Cal. p. 489.

² Cal. Pat. Rolls, p. 305.

challenge our attention. Leland mentions one at—

'*Dartington*, half a mile above Totness bridge, on the same ripe of the water that Toteness is; in this park is a great manor-place longing to the Duke of Exuster.'[1] He also notices a park and house at *Bere*, on the borders of Cornwall,[2] and tells us 'that the Bishop of Excester hath a manor-place or palace by the churchyard (of Crediton), and to this manor-place there longith a parke.'[3] This park, we are told, was conveyed 'with great reluctance' by the Bishop, to Sir Thomas Dennis, in the reign of Henry VIII.[4]

The parks in Saxton's map are not very plainly indicated, but besides those which I have already noticed, others appear to be marked at *Wolley* and *Potberidge*, near Torrington, at *Atherington* in the same neighbourhood, at *Holcombe*, near Exeter, at *Bery-Castle*, near Totness, and at *Armynton*, near Plimpton.

Existing Devonshire Parks.

1. WERRINGTON . Mr. Campbell
2. CASTLE-HILL . Earl Fortescue.
3. MOUNT EDGECUMBE, Earl of Mount Edgecumbe.
4. HEANTON . . Lord Clinton.
5. UGBROOK . . Lord Clifford.
6. BICTON . . . Lady Rolle.
7. STEVENSTONE, near TORRINGTON, Hon. Mark Rolle.
8. KILLERTON . Sir Thomas D. Acland, Bart.
9. SHUTE . . . Sir W. T. Pole, Bart.
10. POLTIMORE . . Lord Poltimore.
11. POWDERHAM . Earl of Devon.
12. HALL, near BARNSTAPLE, Mr. R. Chichester.
13. CLOVELLY . . Colonel Fane.
14. LITTLE FULFORD, or Shobrooke Park, Mr. Hippesley.
15. NEWENHAM . Mr. Strode.
16. WHYDDON . . Mr. Bayley.

DORSETSHIRE.

BLAGDEN, or *Blakeden*, an ancient royal park, formerly three miles in circuit,[5] in the precincts of Cranborne Chase, on the confines of Wiltshire, claims precedence in the list of Dorsetshire parks : it is thus noticed by Leland : 'From Craneburn I passed about 2 miles or more al by playne champain Ground, leving *Blagden*, the Kinges great park hard on the left Hand.'[6] In the reign of Edward I. the Chase of Cranborne belonged to Gilbert de Clare, Earl of Gloucester; but Blagden, as well as the chase itself, was in the possession of the Crown in the

---

[1] Itin. vol. iii. p. 49, fol. 27.
[2] Itin. vol. vii. p. 122.
[3] Itin. vol. iii. p. 68, fol. 38.
[4] Lysons, p. 145.

[5] Certificate as to Parks in Dorset, Oct. 28, 1583. S. P. O. Domestic.
[6] Itin. vol. iii. p. 87, fol. 56.

second of Edward IV.[1] Blagden has been long disparked, and was without deer in the reign of Queen Elizabeth; and the deer have now been destroyed in the chase. In the reigns of James I. and Charles I. there were but 2,000 head of fallow-deer here. In 1828, they are said to have increased to upwards of 12,000. In severe winters, it is stated in 'the Chronicles of Cranborne' (1841) that so many died, that the very earth was manured with their remains.[2]

At *St. Giles Winburne*, Leland notices a park, which, however, does not appear in the ancient maps; it then belonged to Mr. Ashley, ancestor of Lord Shaftesbury. South of Blagden is *Woodlands*, now also disparked, where Henry Hastings, second son of George, fourth Earl of Huntingdon, lived in the seventeenth century, 'in a house perfectly of the old fashion, in the midst of a large park well stocked with deer.' A curious account of this gentleman, a specimen of the country habits of the ancient nobility of a bygone age, will be found in Peck's 'Collection of Historical Pieces,' printed in 1740. In 1583 this park is described as being 'in compass one mile and better, but no deer were kept there.'[3]

Near Woodlands is *Horton*, the former seat of the Sturt family. Here there were formerly red deer,[4] but it is now disparked. It seems to be identical with Holt Park, a royal park with deer in Queen Elizabeth's time, three miles in compass.[3]

Further south is *Canford*, where two parks are marked in the surveys of Saxton (1575) and Speede (1610). One of them is recognised as belonging to Henry de Lacy, Earl of Lincoln, in the third of Edward II. They have been long disparked, and were without deer in 1583. The Great Park and the Little Park, called Lye Park, were each one mile in compass.[6]

At *Charborough*, in this neighbourhood, is a large modern park of 1,000 acres of land, containing a herd of 400 fallow and 40 red deer. It was enclosed early in the present century. There had been, however, a park at *Lichet*, belonging to Mr. Henry Trenchard in 1583, but then without deer, in compass one mile or more, not far from the present Charborough.[6]

At *Bryanstone*, near Blandford, is a small park belonging to Lord Portman, containing 100 acres and a herd of 170 fallow-deer; it was enclosed about the year 1760.

Saxton's Survey marks a park in Gillingham Forest, on the borders of Wiltshire, north of Shaftesbury, and near the village of *Motcombe*. This was a royal park, in jointure to Queen Katharine Howard, in the twenty-second of Henry VIII.[7] In 1583 it is described as containing deer, and that it was three miles in compass; Sir John Zouche, Knight, warden thereof.[6]

South-west of this we have *Sherborne Castle*, where the park is thus noticed by Leland: 'The parke of Shirborne, excepting a little aboute the logge, is enclosed

[1] West's History of Cranborne Chase, 8vo. 1816, p. 86.
[2] Another park, called *Alderholt*, is mentioned as existing, but without deer, in 1583.
[3] S. P. O. Domestic, 1583.
[4] Chafins' Anecdotes of Cranborne Chase, 8vo. 1818, p. 2.
[5] Cal. Pat. Rolls, p. 71.
[6] S. P. O. Domestic, 1583.
[7] West's Cranborne Chase, p. 88.

with a stone waulle.'[1] This park contains
340 acres, and is well-stocked with deer.[2]
In 1583, it belonged to Sir John Horsey,
and contained deer, being in compass two
miles.[3] Within the ancient forest now
called the Vale of Blackmore or Blakemore,
is *Stock*, where William de Cantilupe is
recognised as the possessor of a park in
the thirty-second of Henry III.[4] This appears to be the oldest existing park in the
county; it is an enclosure of 116 acres,
with a herd of 70 fallow-deer.

Another ancient park exists at *Melbury*,
the seat of the Earl of Ilchester, which
belonged to his ancestors in the female
line, the ancient family of Strangways. It
is thus mentioned in Leland's 'Itinerary:'
'This is a fair park hard by the manor
place of Milbyri, and yn this park is a pond,
out of the wich issueth a broketh, that with
the course of a right few miles goith into
Ivelle Ryver;'[5] and again : 'Mr. Strangways now and late began to builde richely
at his commune dwelling House in Milbyri Parke, and caussed three thousand
lode of free-stone to be fetched from
Hamden Quarre nine myles of thither.'[5]
'Thens,' continues Leland, 'a myle to
Tonmer Parke, encompasyd with a stone
waulle.' This park does not appear in
the old surveys. *Melbury Park* contains
160 acres, with a herd of about 400 fallow-
deer. It contained deer and was in circuit one mile and a half in 1583.[3]

Hooke or *Hoke Park*, now disparked, is
also noticed by Leland, 'having an auncient manor place, an it is but a mile

and ⅓ by est south est to Bemistre.'[6] In
1583, this park, containing deer, and in
compass one mile, belonged to the Marquis of Winchester.[3]

On the confines of Devonshire, not far
from Axminster, were two parks, called
Crekelade and *Marshwood*, adjoining.
They once belonged to Geoffrey de Magneville, Earl of Essex, and afterwards to
Lionel, Duke of Clarence.[7] Crekelade belonged to one Mr. Baker, in Kent, in 1583.
The park was in compass two miles or
thereabouts, but was then disparked and
converted into pasture and tillage.[3]
Marshwood, at the same period, was
the property of Sir Amias Paulet. It was
also disparked and converted into divers
tenements, and had been three miles in
circuit.[3] Near these parks, on the sea-
coast, is *Chadiocke*, where there was a
disparked park in compass a mile and
a half in 1583, belonging to Sir John
Arundel, Knight;[3] and another at Wotton,
near Cricklade, also without deer in
1583.[3]

Returning westwards, towards Dorchester, a small park at *Milton Abbey*
may be noticed. Though it was not an
ancient park, having been enclosed about
seventy years ago, it contained 90 acres
and 300 fallow-deer, and was disparked
about the year 1860.

Both Saxton and Speede recognise a
park at *Athelhampton*, or *Addlemaston*,
west of Dorchester. It was an ancient
seat of the Martin family; but no traces
or tradition of a park exist here at pre-

[1] Leland's Itin. vol. vii. p. 109, fol. 79 *b*.
[2] New Display of the Beauties of England,
vol. ii. p. 340.
[3] S. P. O. Domestic, 1583.
[4] Cal. Pat. Rolls, p. 22.

[5] Itin. vol. iii. p. 77, fol. 47 ; and vol. vi. pp.
12, 13, fol. 13.
[6] Itin. vol. iii. p. 75, fol. 45.
[7] Coker's Survey, p. 13.

sent. But neither of these surveys mark a park at *Melcombe*, a little to the north, and belonging to Sir John Horsey in 1583, containing deer, and two miles in circuit.

At *Lulworth Castle*, near the sea, there was formerly also a large park, imparked by Thomas Lord Howard in the second year of James I., who had license to enclose 1,000 acres of land in East Lulworth; the present park, if it can be so called, as there are no deer, was walled in by the late Thomas Weld, Esq., by a wall four miles in circumference.[1] Coker, in his Survey of Dorsetshire, observes of this place: 'The greatest Honor that Lulworth can boast of, is giving entertain-

ment to the King as often as he cometh the western Progresse; who chose to it to disport himselfe in the parke, as alsoe in Island of Purbeck near adjoining.'[2] In 1583, eighteen enclosures were considered as parks, though all had not deer in them, within the county of Dorset.

Existing Deer Parks in Dorsetshire.

1. STOCK . . . Mr. Yeatman.
2. MELBURY . . Earl of Ilchester.
3. SHERBORNE . Mr. Wingfield Digby.
4. BRYANSTONE . Lord Portman.
5. CHARBOROUGH, Mr. Grosvenor Erle Drax.

SOMERSETSHIRE.

A PERAMBULATION of the forest of Selwood, on the eastern frontier of this county, which was made in the year 1298, makes mention of the parks of *Witham*[3] and *Forshefe*, both probably royal parks; in the former was 'The King's Hall.'[4] This park appears to be identical with that which is marked in Saxton's Survey of 1573 as 'The Charter-House.' There was also a royal park at *Keynsham*, near Bristol, 'walled with stone,' mentioned by Leland in his 'Itinerary.'[5] Passing from the royal to the

domestic parks, we find seven parks said to be appendant to the Abbey of Glastonbury; of these the largest was *Northwood*, which, at the period of the Dissolution, 'contained in circuit four miles, the pales well repaired, the herbage very good and sweet, wherein are 800 deer, whereof there are of deer of antler 160, deer of "rascall" 640. Within this park there are 172 acres of wood of the age of 20 years, and heretofore have always been used to be felled and sold every 16 years, every acre thereof at this present survey worth 20s.

---

[1] Hutchins' Hist of Dorset, new ed. vol. i. p. 375.
[2] Coker's Survey of Dorset, p. 41.
[3] In the 35th of Henry III. Robert de Mussegros obtained leave to impark certain lands near his Park of Beyweham, within the bounds of the Forest of Selwood.
[4] Phelp's History of Somersetshire, 1839, vol. i. p. 147.
[5] Vol. vii. p. 104.

—172*l.* 10*s.* 6*d.*'[1] Northwood is thus noticed by Leland in his 'Itinerary':— 'Nordwood Park, a mile by est from Glaston; John Selwood, Abbot, builded a place there.'[2] This park was in two divisions, containing altogether 751 acres. *Sharpham*, the country-seat of the Abbot, is also noticed by Leland. 'Abbot Bere,' he says, 'made also the Manor-place at Sharpham in the park, and two miles by west from Glaston; it was afore a poore lodge.'[2] The 'Survey' before quoted informs us that 'it containeth in circuit two long miles of good mead and pasture [with two fine ponds in the same], wherein are 160 deer, whereof are of deer of antler 20, deer of "rascall" 140. Also within the park of Sharpham, there are 80 acres of wood, well set with oaks, ashes, and maples, which always have been used to be felled and sold every fourteen years, and every acre is worth at this present time 6*s.* 8*d.*; also within the same park there are 200 oaks fit for timber, every oak esteemed to be worth 11*s.*' In 1583, the Park of Sharpham belonged to Christopher Symcoxe, Esq.[3]

Wyrral Park, on the west of the town of Glastonbury, 'contained in circuit one mile and a quarter; the pales have need to be repaired, the herbage very good and fertile, with a running stream through the same; 100 deer, whereof are of deer of antler 15, deer of "rascall" 85. Within the park of Wyrral is 60 acres of fair timber, esteemed to be worth 290*l.* 10*s.*' *Pilton*, another abbatical park, six miles east from Glastonbury, contained in circuit, according

to the survey at the period of the Dissolution, 'three long miles of good pasture, the pales in good care, wherein are of deer 350, whereof there are of deer of antlers 60, deer of "rascall" 290.' This park is marked both in Saxton's and Speed's Surveys.

Leland notices two other parks in this county which had belonged to the Church: 'A mile on this syde Bathe by southe est, I saw 2 parks enclosyd with a ruinus stone waulle, now withe out Dere, one longyd to the Byshope, an other to the Prior of Bathe.'[4] The Bishop appears to have had also a park at *Welles*, enclosed by license in the third year of King John,[5] and the Prebend of Wyndescombe (*Wivellescombe?*), in the same church, obtained a license to impark his wood of that name in the fourth of Edward III.[6] The Bishop of Bath and Wells had also the right to enclose a park within his Manor of *Chedder*, near Axminster, which is alluded to in 'Smyth's Lives of the Berkeleys' (p. 130.) Thomas, Third Lord Berkeley, having been commanded by Edward III. in the 11th year of his reign, 'to repress the insolence offered by armed persons to the Bishop, who being many in number both of horse and foot, had beaten, wounded, and imprisoned, yea and robbed divers of the Bishop's servants, in his Manor of Chedder, which Manor the King had licenced him to disafforest, and to hold free in severalty, and to make a park there.' The riot above alluded to was evidently the consequence of this grant. With respect to the other ancient parks of this county, we have in the north, near Bristol,

[1] Survey quoted in Dugdale's Monasticon, vol. i. p. 10, ed. 1817.
[2] Leland's Itin. vol. iii. p. 120, fol. 86.
[3] Certificate of Parks in the County of Somerset. S. P. O. Domestic. Sept. 30, 1583.
[4] Leland's Itin. vol. vii. p. 100, fol. 14 *b.*
[5] Cal. Pat. Rolls, p. 3.
[6] Ib. p. 109.

the parks of *Wraxhall, Burton,* and *Fil-wood* (also called a Chase), all marked by Saxton. Leland says of the first, 'Here hath Syr Wylliam Gorge a meane old manor place in a valley, and on eche side of it on the hilles is a fayre Parke.'[1] Further south a park is marked at *Banwell,* near Axbridge, and near to the east between the sea and the Quantok hills is *Stowey,* of which Leland writes, 'Stowey, a poore village, standith yn a Botom, emong hilles ; here ys a goodly Manor-place of the Lorde Audeleys, standing exceding pleasantly for good pastures, and having by it a parke of redde Deere, and another of falow, and a faire brooke serving at the offices of the Manor-place.'[2] In this neighbourhood is Dunster Castle, once the seat of the Lutterells, and here were several parks of that family, which Leland also notices :—' S. Andres : In this paroche I saw a fair Park and Manor place of the Lutterelles, caullid *"Quantok Hedde,"*[3] *" Dunster Castel."* Ther is a praty park joyning to th' est part of the Castelle.' 'There was a faire park by *Minhead,* but Sir Andrew Lutterelle of late tyme destroy'd it.'[3] These parks in 1583 were each one mile in compass. A park is also marked in Saxton's Survey, at *Nettlecombe,* the ancient seat of the Trevilian family, at present containing 160 acres and 230 fallow-deer, and there was another at *Coripole,* belonging to Mr. Coles, in 1583, not noticed in that Survey, and at *Cothelston,* one mile in compass, belonging to Sir John Stawell. Nettlecombe Park, about 150 years ago, in

the time of Sir John Trevelyan, contained but 20 acres, and lay to the north of the mansion about a quarter of a mile distant. The site was altered and the park enlarged and brought nearer to the house by Sir John ; and at the same period the new park was fenced with old ship timber, bought at the seaport of Watchet, four miles distant. Some of this ancient timber still exists and does duty in the present park fence.

Petherton Park, between Bridgewater and Taunton, appears to have been the largest in the county, and was once a royal park, or forest ; a great part of it was disafforested in the 26th of Edward I. It was four miles in compass, and almost decayed in 1583. ' The whole,' observes Collinson,[4] ' is now converted into farms, and belongs to Sir Thomas Acland, Bt.' Leland writes, ' There ys a great number of Dere longyng to this park, yet hath it almost no other enclosure but Dikes to let the cattelle of the commune to cum yn : The Dere trippe over these Dikes and feede at about the Fennes, and resort to the Park agayn. There is a praty Lodge moted yn the parke.'[5] At *Huntworth* adjoining, was a park one mile in compass, which belonged to Mr. Popham in 1583. In the neighbourhood of the forest of Neroche were also several parks, of which that of *Meryfield* appears the most considerable. It belonged to Mr. Wadham in 1583, and was above one mile in circuit. *White Lackington,* near Ilminster, where in 1583 were two parks belonging to Sir George Speake[6] and

[1] Leland's Itin. vol. vii. p. 105, fol. 76 *b.*
[2] Ib. vol. ii. p. 98, fol. 60.
[3] Ib. vol. ii. pp. 101, fol. 62, 102, fol. 63.
[4] Collinson, vol. iii. pp. 56–62.

[5] Leland's Itin. vol. ii. pp. 94, 95, fol. 55, 56.
[6] S. P. O. Domestic, Sept. 30, 1583.

H

Hinton St. George, are both noticed by Leland; the latter, he remarks, had been lately made by Sir Hugh Paulet, 'not far from his House in the side of an hylle.' In 1583 it is described as two miles in circuit. It is thus noticed by Cosmo III., Grand Duke of Tuscany, in his curious travels in England, in the reign of Charles II. (1669)[1]:—'Round the house is the park, three miles in circumference, surrounded by a thick row of trees, between each of which is a terrace of turf; and where the trees begin to shoot out branches; these, intertwined together, form, along with the earth of the terraces, a fence of the strongest description. (He seems to be describing an English hedge.) In this park are six hundred deer, to which the mixture of plain, of hills, of coppice-wood, and meadow land, together with two plentiful springs of water, which are within the same enclosure, afford a most suitable abode. The deer are of two sorts, black and red; the latter, though smaller, fatten sooner than the others. They begin to' hunt them early in June, and continue it for six weeks; they hunt only the fattest, driving them with dogs into a corner of the park; they kill about one hundred annually. In winter, when the pasture fails; they give them hay and leaves of trees, particularly when snow falls (although it soon melts in these parts), making this observation, that where the moles dwell, of which there is a great abundance (and on this account they keep strict watch to prevent them spoiling the land), deer seldom resort.'

Passing to the east of the county, a large park is marked by Saxton at *Evercreech*, where the Bishop once had a park, now divided.[2] A little to the South is *Castle Carey*, where was also an ancient park, which also bore the name of *Ansford Park*, from the parish in which it was. Another is marked in the ancient surveys on the borders of Dorsetshire, near *Cucklington*, which perhaps is identical with ' Master Carente's House and Park,' which Leland left on his left hand as he rode from Stourton to Stapleford (Stalbridge) in Dorsetshire.[3] At *Farley Castle*, the venerable seat of the Hungerfords, near Bradford, on the confines of this county and Wiltshire, there was also a park existing in 1654,[4] and which is described in an old survey printed in Sir R. C. Hoare's 'Hungerfordiana' (p. 100), as 2 miles and 3 quarters in circuit, 'A very fayre and parkly grounde, replenished with 26 deer of antler, and 44 of rascall.'

I find licenses for imparking granted by Edward III. in the second year of his reign, to Sir Richard Dammory (D'Amori), Knight, at Ubbelegh (*Ubley*), in the north-eastern part of Somersetshire, and by Henry IV., in the thirteenth year of his reign, to Sir Thomas Beauchamp, Knight, comprehending 250 acres in 'le Shand,' in his Manor of *Ashill*, close to Neroche forest, in the south of the county.[5]

The present parks in Somersetshire are *Pixton*, belonging to the Earl of Carnarvon, near Dulverton, on the borders of Devonshire, a park of about 140 acres,

---

[1] 4to. (London, 1821).
[2] Gough's Camden, vol. i. p. 109.
[3] Leland's Itin. vol. vii. p. 108, fol. 79 *a*.

[4] Will of Anthony Hungerford, of Black Bourton, county of Oxford, Esquire.
[5] Cal. of Patent Rolls, pp. 103, 259.

with a herd of 200 fallow-deer ; *St. An-dries,* near Bridgewater, where there are both red and fallow-deer ; *Alfoxton* and *Halsewell,* near the Quantock hills ; *Sandhill,* near Taunton ; *Ammerdown,* near Bath ; *Long Ashton* and *Leigh Court,* near Bristol. In the latter, said to have been a deer-park from time immemorial, there were also wild cattle till the year 1806, when they became so savage that the owner was obliged to have them all shot.[1]

Existing Parks in Somersetshire.

1. DUNSTER CASTLE, Mr. Luttrell.

2. NETTLECOMBE COURT, Sir Walter Calverley Trevelyan, Bart.

3. PIXTON . . . . The Earl of Carnarvon.

4. ST. ANDRIES . . Sir Alexander Hood, Bart.

5. ALFOXTON . . . Mr. St. Albyn.

6. HALSEWELL . . Colonel Tynte.

7. SANDHILL . . . Sir John Lethbridge, Bart.

8. AMMERDOWN . . The Rev. Mr. Joliffe.

9. LONG ASHTON . Sir J. Greville Smyth, Bart.

10. LEIGH COURT . Sir W. Miles, Bart.

WILTSHIRE.

THE royal park of *Clarendon,* near Salisbury, sometimes called 'The forest of Pancett,' with its twenty groves, each of them a mile in compass,[2] is probably one of the oldest, as it was also the largest, park in this county. Here were two royal palaces, called 'The King's Manor,' and 'The Queen's Lodge,' the scene of the famous 'Constitutions' in the reign of Henry II. In the forty-fifth of Edward III. a commission was issued by the Crown, to enquire concerning the existing defects in the Manor and Park of Clarendon ;[3] and in the fiftieth of the same reign, the king confirmed to the Prior of Ivy Church[4] pasture for forty oxen and cows within the same. Leland observes, 'The parke of Clarington is a very large thing, and

hath many kepers yn it.'[5] In the time of Charles I. it was still in the hands of the Crown, and a warrant passed, dated August 21, 1635, to pay to Philip Earl of Pembroke and Montgomery, Warden of the Forest of Pancett, alias Clarendon Park, 30*l.* per annum for provision of hay for maintenance of deer in winter.[6] In 1583 it was in the keeping of the Earl of Pembroke, and was seven miles in compass.[7]

To the north-east of Salisbury is the forest of Chute, and the ancient royal castle and park of *Ludgarshall,* also called the Park of *Collingbourne,* from the adjoining village of that name. In the fortieth of Henry III. it was held by William de Valence, the brother of the king. In 1404 it was granted by Edward IV. to

---

[1] Information of Sir W. Miles, Bart.
[2] Magna Britannia, 1731, vol. vi. p. 51.
[3] Cal. Pat. Rolls, p. 187.
[4] Mons. Ederosus.

[5] Itin. vol. iii. p. 98, fol. 69.
[6] S. P. O. Domestic, 1635.
[7] Note of Parks in the County of Wilts. Sept. 24, 1583. S. P. O. Domestic.

H 2

George Duke of Clarence, with a park of 200 acres at Collingbourne.[1] 'The castell stoode in a parke, now clene down,' says Leland in his 'Itinerary,'[2] written in the reign of Henry VIII. In 1583, Lurgatshall belonged to Lady Bridges, and was two miles in circuit. In the immediate neighbourhood is *Everleigh,* where a park once also existed, as appears by a return of parks granted by lease within the Duchy of Lancaster.[3] Still more to the north is *Savernake* Forest and Park, in the neighbourhood of which were two other ancient parks, *Tottenham* and *Sudden,* which in 1583 were the inheritance of the Earl of Hertford. Savernake at this period is described as nearly six miles in circuit, Tottenham three miles, and Sudden two miles.[4] It was at Tottenham Park, in July 1620, where Mr. Chamberlain, in one of his gossiping letters to Sir Dudley Carleton, mentions 'the death of a young gentleman of good sort, one Waldron, who was killed by the rise or bound of a buck in the king's presence.'[5] Tottenham is described by Aubrey in his 'Wiltshire Collections,' as 'a most *parkely* ground and *romancy* pleasant place, with several walkes of great length of trees planted.'

Ramsbury, north of Savernake, was the Park of the Bishop of Salisbury. It is thus noticed by Leland, 'There is a right fayre and large parke hangynge upon the clyffe of an highe hille, welle wooddyd over Kenet, hard on the south syde of the place.'[6] In 1383 it is described as four miles in circuit, being the inheritance of the Earl of Pembroke.[4]

Littlecote Park, adjoining, is not noticed in the park return of 1583; but is laid down in Saxton's map of this county of the year 1576. Evelyn calls it, in 1654, 'a noble seate park and river.'[7] There was also, according to the return of 1583, a park at *Clatford,* near Marlborough, belonging to Mr. Goddarde, and nearly three miles in circuit;[4] it is not marked in the old surveys.

At *Wotton Basset,* on the borders of Braden Forest, were two ancient parks. Of these the most remarkable was the great park of *Fasterne,* or Vasterne, as it was sometimes called. One park here was enclosed by Philip Basset in the thirty-first of Henry III.,[8] and at the death of Aliva (Basset) Lady Despencer, in the ninth of Edward I., it contained 789 acres, of which 616 were arable and 173 pasture. In the twenty-first and twenty-eighth of the same reign, Hugh Despencer obtained letters patent to enlarge it;[8] and again, in the thirteenth of Edward II., it was further increased by taking 300 acres of wood, then included under Braden. Despencer also appears to have added to it by means less regular, and in the 'Wiltshire Archæological Magazine' (vol. iii. p. 247), is the account of a forcible entry made upon his manor by the adherents of the parties whom he had injured. Leland (Collect. vol. iv. p. 248) says, 'a little before Lady-day 1489, King Henry VII. roade into Wiltshire on hunting: and slew his gres (buck) in three places in that shire. He first hunted in the forest of Savernake, the second in the good Parke of Fastern, the

---

[1] Aubrey's South Wilts, printed in 1862, p. 359.
[2] Vol. vii. p. 11, fol. 22.
[3] Cotton MS., Titus, b. iv. fo. 297.
[4] Note of Parks in the County of Wilts,

Sept. 24, 1583.   S. P. O. Domestic.
[5] Court and Times of James I. vol. ii. p. 209.
[6] Itin. vol. vii. p. 83, fol. 65 *b.*
[7] Diary, June 6, 1654.
[8] Cal. Pat. Rolls, pp. 40–56.

third in Blackmore Forest, and so returned to Windsor. Also he was at
Ramsbury with the Bishop of Salisbury.'
Fastern was granted by patent, in 1555-6,
to Sir Francis Englefield, who presently
turned 'the great park' into enclosures,
leaving about 100 acres, called Wotton's
Lawn, to be used as common, &c.[1] In
1583 'the little park of Vasterne,' belonging to Her Majesty, is estimated as two
miles in compass, and was in the keeping
of Sir Henry Knyvett.[2]

In 1583 there was a park at *Liddiard
Tregose*, belonging to Nicholas St. John,
Esq.,[2] and another at *Burdrope*, near Swin-
don, belonging to Thomas Stevens, Esq.[2]

A very ancient park existed at *Elcombe*,
in this neighbourhood, which belonged, in
the reign of Edward I., to the Lords
Lovell, of Titchmarsh. Sir Thomas
Wroughton owned also a park at *Odehill*,
or Over-Wroughton, one mile in compass,
as appears by the return of 1583.

At *Dantsey*, to the west of Wotton Basset, was 'a stately park with admirable
oakes,' in 1583, the property of Sir John
Danvers, and four miles in circuit.[2]

To the north again, near Malmesbury,
were the parks of *Okesey* and *Charleton*.
The former was a Royal park, but of
limited extent, being but one mile in circuit; in 1583 it was in the keeping of Sir
Giles Poole. Aubrey describes it 'as
admirably well wooded; the best oakes
in the county.'

Charleton Park was two miles in circuit, and belonged to Sir Henry Knyvett
in 1583.[2]

Pinckney is a small existing park in
this neighbourhood, containing 100 acres
and a herd of 70 fallow-deer.

Cole Park, which is given in Saxton's
Survey, but not represented as impaled,
belonged to the Abbot of Malmesbury.
Another ancient disused park was at
Somerford-Mauduit in this vicinity, which
had belonged to the Hungerfords of Farley Castle.[3] 'There is a parke by Farley Castle,' writes Leland in his 'Itinerary' (vol. ii. p. 60, fol. 32), besides the
park of *Stoke* near Bradford, a small park
belonging to Anthony Hungerford in
1583.[2]

Draycot Park, between Malmesbury
and Chippenham, is not given by Saxton,
but is thus mentioned in Leland's 'Itinerary,' 'Draicote, where Sir Henry Long
hath a fair manor place, and a park about
a mile from Avon streeme.'[4] It is represented as three miles in circuit in the
return of 1583.

The Abbot of Cirencester had a park
at *Stanton St. Quinton*, near Draycot,
which appears to have been disparked at
the period of the Reformation; it is thus
described by Aubrey, writing about 1659,
'The parke, very large, comes to the
house. Yet is remaining part of the wall
of it, built with mortar, and overgrown
with ivy; the highest that I know to any
park, likely of old here were kept stagges.
Martens in the parke in my grandfather
Lyte's remembrance.'[5]

At *Castle Combe*, on the borders of
Gloucestershire, there was also an ancient
park, as appears by the Court Rolls of

---

[1] Aubrey's Collections, pp. 204-216.
[2] Note of Parks in the County of Wilts,
Sept. 24, 1583. S. P. O. Domestic.
[3] I find the park in Little Somerford, called

Maraditch Park, mentioned in the will of
Anthony Hungerford, Esq., in 1654.
[4] Itin. vol. ii. pp. 54, 55, fol. 29.
[5] Aubrey's Collections, p. 288.

that manor, as early as the year 1377, when a fine of 100 shillings was imposed for stealing a deer. In 1436, it appears also by the Court Roll that there were in the park one hundred deer of all kinds.[1] 'On the hills in the park here, were in 1645, felled many a gallant oak,' observes Aubrey in his ' Wiltshire Collections.'

At *Cosham*, or *Corsham*, on the confines of Pewsham Forest, a park is marked by Saxton; and here Richard Plantagenet, Earl of Cornwall, second son of King John, mentions 'his parks' in his grant to the tenants there, printed in the ' Collectanea Topographica et Genealogica' (vol. ii. p. 317). ' This park was wont,' says Leland, ' to be in dower to the Queens of England.' Two parks, called *Holme Park* and *West Park*, are recognised in Corsham in the ' Return of Parks within the Duchy of Lancaster' (Cotton MS. Titus, B. iv. fol. 236).

Between the forests of Pewsham and Blakemore were the parks of *Bowden*, *Spye*, and *Bromham*.

Of *Bowden*, Aubrey writes, ' Here hath been a parke, and till about 1660, the pales stood about it.' It was three miles in circuit, and the freehold of the Lady Sherrington, in 1583.[2]

Spye Park is said to be a very ancient, and is still occupied by deer; it is an area of 370 acres, with a herd of 300 deer.

Bromham belonged to the Baynton family, and was in 1583 a park of two miles in circumference.

The comparatively modern park of *Bowood* occupies part of the Royal forest of Pewsham, disafforested in the time of

James II. It contains 150 acres, and a herd of 280 fallow-deer.

At *Melksham* there was, in the Elizabethan period, a park in 1583, the inheritance of William Brunker, Esq., and here I find a license for imparking, granted to Hugh le Despencer in the thirty-third of Edward I.[3]

There was a Royal park at *Devizes*, at a very early period; it is noticed by Leland, and in 1583 was held under the Crown by Sir Henry Knyvett, being estimated at three miles in compass.

Near Devizes is *Roundway*, a park of 160 acres, with a herd of 200 fallow-deer.

Earlstoke Park, in the same neighbourhood, contains about 136 acres, and a herd of 324 fallow-deer. It is believed to have been enclosed in the early part of the eighteenth century.

At *Broke*, near Westbury, a park is marked in the ancient surveys, which is thus noticed by Leland: ' There is a fayre parke, but no great large thynge. In it be a great nomber of very fayre and fyne greyned okes apte to sele howses.'[4] This place gives the title of Baron to the Lords Willoughby de Broke.

Saxton marks a small park at *Corsley*, near *Longleat*, the latter at present the most considerable park in the county; it is 576 acres in extent. There is a herd of 740 fallow-deer. Longleat was imparked by John Thynne, Esq., before the year 1576; but the exact date is unknown.

Of *Stourton*, on the borders of Somersetshire and Dorsetshire, Leland tells us, ' There is a parke emonge hilles yoining on the manor-place. The ryver of Stoure

---

[1] Scrope's History of Castle Combe, 4to. 1852, pp. 163–240.
[2] Note of Parks in the County of Wilts,

Sept. 24, 1583. S. P. O. Domestic.
[3] Cal. Pat. Rolls, p. 64.
[4] Leland's Itin. vol. vii. pp. 86, 87, fol. 67.

risith ther of 6 fountaines or springes, whereof 3 be on the northe side of the parke, harde withyn the pale; the other 3 be north also, but without the parke. The Lord Stourton gyvith these 6 fountaynes yn his armes.'[1] Aubrey adds, 'The park is large, but bald for timber trees, only some old stagge-headed trees remayning. This tract of country was heretofore all horrid and woody; it bordereth on the forests of Bruton and Gillingham.'[2] Stourton was imparked by license granted to John Stourton, Esq., in the sixth of Henry VI.; the grant comprehended a thousand acres of land.[3]

The Royal park of *Meere*, adjoining Gillingham Forest, was in 1583 in the keeping of Sir John Zouche. The rent to Lord North, the lessee of the Crown, being 5l. per annum, 'sufficient pasture and feeding for the deer in the same park, as well in winter as in summer,' being reserved. Lord North assigned his interest in this park to George Blythe, gentleman, in the sixteenth year of Elizabeth.[4]

The park of *Fonthill*, not given in Saxton's map, belonged in 1583 to Sir James Mervyn, Knight, and was two miles in circuit. At *Wardour* Castle there were two parks, described in 1583 as respectively two miles and three miles in circumference.

Returning towards Salisbury, from whence we commenced the notices of the parks in this county, the park at *Wilton* requires some observation. Although neither marked in the surveys of Saxton or Speed, or in the general return of

parks in the year 1583, there is yet evidence that it was enclosed for deer as early as November 22, 1578. This appears by a letter from Henry Earl of Pembroke, to Sir Edward Stradling, in which he requests him 'to bestow upon him some deer towards the storing of his new park;'[5] the letter is written from Salisbury, and could only refer to Wilton. Sir Edward Stradling's park was at St. Donate's Castle, in the county of Glamorgan. The present park at Wilton contains 256 acres, and is stocked with a herd of 200 fallow-deer.

A small park at *Compton*, in this neighbourhood (of 90 acres), with a herd of about 170 fallow-deer, is said to have existed from time immemorial, and is mentioned in the third of Edward I. (1274).[6] On the other side of Salisbury is the little park or paddock of deer at *Brickworth*, with its herd of 50 head of fallow-deer; the extent is not more than twenty-five acres and a half. The date of this miniature park is unknown, but it has existed for more than a century.

Existing Parks in Wiltshire.

1. TOTTENHAM . Marquis of Ailesbury.
2. CHARLETON . Earl of Suffolk.
3. PINCKNEY . . Mr. Creswell.
4. SPYE . . . Mr. Spicer.
5. BOWOOD . . Marq. of Lansdowne.
6. ROUNDWAY . Mr. Colston.
7. ERLESTOKE . Mr. Watson Taylor.
8. LONGLEAT . . Marquis of Bath.
9. WILTON . . Earl of Pembroke.
10. COMPTON . . Mr. Penruddock.
11. BRICKWORTH . D[r]. Countess Nelson.

[1] Leland's Itin. vol. vii. p. 107, fol. 78 b.
[2] Aubrey's Wiltshire Collections, p. 389.
[3] Cal. Pat. Rolls, p. 274. In the 25th of the same reign the king granted to this gentleman the office of supervisor of all the parks and woods, &c. in the county, at the annual rent of 3s. 4d. per annum.—*Ib.*
[4] Original indenture *penes* Baroness North.
[5] Stradling Correspondence, 8vo. 1840, p. 71.
[6] Information of the owner, Mr. Penruddock.

HAMPSHIRE.

TWO parks only are mentioned in the Domesday Survey within the county of Southampton, viz. that at *Waltham*, afterwards called Bishop's Waltham, belonging to the Bishop of Winchester ; and at or near *Watingewelle*, now Watchingwell or Watchingwood, in the Isle of Wight, which was the property of the King. The park at *Waltham*, in the Survey 'parcus bestiarum,' translated by Warner, 'a pound for cattle !' adjoined the forest of East-Bere ; in Leland's time, 'welle replenished with deere;' it is reported to have contained a thousand acres, but has been long converted into farms.[1] It is marked as a park in the surveys of Saxton and Speed.

Watchingwood is in the parish of Shalfleet, between Colbourn and the Forest of Parkhurst, and to this Royal Forest the park appears to have been attached, being, as I conclude, the park alluded to in the following letter from Sir John Dingley to the Earl of Pembroke, written in 1642 : 'There is a park alsoe belonging to the Captaine (of Carisbrook Castle), which is 3 miles about ; and there is alsoe a common for the whole country to put in horse and beast without stint, which is called by the name of Parkhurst Chase ; the King, and consequently the Captaine,

hath fallow-deere in it, and doth keepe a keeper and a rainger to keep them and to looke unto them, that they do not lie in men's grounds, which hath bin very much abus'd, by suffering the deere to ly out, and soe they are almost quite destróyed ; and in my time the country hath quite destroyed the woods and bushes ; and alsoe some have made encroachment, and have taken in some of the common for private use.'[2] The Great Park of Parkhurst was in the parish of St. Nicholas. There were also the New and Little Parks, in Carisbrook parish. The deer have been long destroyed in all of them, as well as in the Forest of Parkhurst.

There were other Royal parks in Hampshire ; at *Lyndhurst*, in the New Forest, attached to the King's house there, and marked in Saxton's map ; and at *Freemantel*,[3] near Kingsclere,[4] in the north of the county, the custody of which park was granted to William de la Pole, Earl of Suffolk, by King Henry VI. in the twenty-first year of his reign,[5] at *Odiham*, in the north-eastern part of Hampshire, was also a Royal park, in which Richard de Rokelande was constituted keeper of the young game, 'pullanorum,' in the fourteenth year of Edward III.,[6] and William Warbleton, keeper, in the thirty-fifth of Henry VI.[7]

---

[1] Warner's Collections for the History of Hampshire, p. 269.
[2] Worsley's Isle of Wight (1781), p. 11.
[3] 'Where King John much hunted' (query John of Gaunt?) Warner Collections for Hamp. p. 167.
[4] In the 53rd of Henry III., William de

Wintreshull had license to impark his wood of Frollebury within the bounds of the *forest* of Fraidmantell (Cal. Pat. Rolls, p. 42). Could this be the origin of this park ?
[5] Cal. Pat. Rolls, p. 285.
[6] Ib. p. 136.
[7] Ib. p. 297.

The Bishops of Winchester, besides their Domesday park at Waltham, had another at *Hursley*, near Winchester, which is probably as ancient, though it is not noticed in the Conqueror's Survey, which indeed omits the parish of Hursley altogether. It is thus noticed by Leland in his 'Itinerary:' 'Ther is a park 3 miles out of Winchester, almost by south, caullyd Hursley, longging to the Bishop of Winchester, and by this park was a castelle caullid Merden, whereof some smaul ruines or tokens yet remayne.'[1] Hursley Park has been long dissevered from the see of Winchester, having been for many generations the seat of the Heathcotes, baronets of that place. The present park contains altogether 440 acres, of which the house and gardens occupy about 18. There is a herd of 220 fallow-deer. The old park-bank, of enormous height and size, extends far beyond the bounds of the present park, and includes part of Ampfield wood, and the meadows to the south of the house. A free-bord of 18 feet in width can still be traced, here called 'a deer-leap;' an evidence probably of that ancient right (saltatorium) with which the bishops of Winchester were no doubt invested. [See page 85, where it is engraved.]

There were many other ancient deer parks in this county (though but four now remain); these shall be noticed in order. Beginning with those in the north-eastern part of the county, we have *Beaurepaire*, near the forest of Pembury, or Pamber, on the borders of Berkshire. This park appears to have been enclosed by Sir Bernard Brocas, Knight, by the Royal license, in the forty-second year of Edward III., and comprehended ' 121 acres of land and 30 acres of wood in Sherbourne St. John, not within the bounds of the forest, and 22 acres of land in Bromley, which were within the bounds of the Forest of Pembury.'[2] Adjoining ' Beaurepaire' is ' The Vyne,' the ancient seat of the Sandys family. A park is marked here in Saxton's map, though Warner tells us in his Hampshire collections that ' no traces of a park are to be found here.' The Vyne is in the parish of Sherbourne St. John, where John de St. John had license to impark 100 acres of wood in his manor of *Sherbourne*, within the bounds of the Forest of Pembury,[3] in the twentieth of Edward I.; and in 1306, the thirty-fifth of the same reign, John de St. John prays to be allowed to continue his park within this manor, which was enclosed by John his father. The answer which he received was, that all such parks made since the disafforesting of forests were to be disparked.[4] Three parks are marked near *Basing*, in Saxton's Survey; and a fourth called ' *Preu Park*,' by Speed. Queen Elizabeth hunted here during her progress in 1601. It was then the residence of the Marquis of Winchester. Upon the destruction of that noble seat during the rebellion in the seventeenth century, the family removed to *Hackwood*, a corruption, as it is said of Hawkingwood, originally the lodge in the park belonging to Basing-house, with which it was connected by avenues of chesnuts two miles in length. The present park of Hackwood contains

1 Itin. vol. iii. p. 105, fol. 74.
2 Cal. Pat. Rolls, p. 183. It was enlarged also by license in the 12th of Richard II.

3 Cal. Pat. Rolls, p. 55.
4 Rolls of Parl. vol. i. p. 201.

about 800 acres of land, with a herd of 250 fallow-deer. License for imparking the wood of Haywood, within the Forest of Pembury and Eversley, was granted to William de Brayboes in the sixth of Edward I.[1] A park at Eversley is marked in Saxton's map, the same, no doubt, with that at *Bramshill*, the well-known scene of Archbishop Abbot's mishap, in 1621, and which is noticed in Speed's Survey. And in that period, at *Dogmansfield*, the seat of the Mildmay family, there was an ancient park, though the deer have been removed; the same fate has befallen the park at *Elvatham*, or Elvesham, where Queen Elizabeth was entertained by the Earl of Hertford, in 1591. A little south of Dogmansfield is *Itchel Park*, which appears in Saxton's, but not in Speed's, map, to the west of which was *Kemshot*, a park also long disparked; and in the north-west, on the borders of Berkshire, a park is marked near *Iclere* or *Higholere*, the present seat of the Earl of Carnarvon.

The Patent Rolls show that a park was licensed to William de Valence, in the thirty-fifth of Henry III. at *Newton*, and at *Colingbury* in the forty-first of the same reign. These parks were within the bounds of the Forest of Southampton, if the New Forest is not intended; we may suppose that Pembury is meant, and that Newtown on the borders of Berkshire, just above Highclere, is the park which is given by Saxton.

The park of *Hurseborne* or *Hurstbourne*, to the north-east of Andover, occurs in the ancient surveys, and is undoubtedly an ancient park. It contains an area of 563 acres, with a herd of 700 fallow-deer.

Between the forests of Buckholt and West Bere, west of Winchester, a park is marked at *King's Samborne* in Saxton's Survey, which I find noted as a park belonging to the Duchy of Lancaster in the reign of Queen Elizabeth,[2] and another at *Michelmarsh*, a little south of it, which I suppose to be that enclosed by license by the Prior of Swithin's, at Winchester, in the sixth of Edward III. Between Badsley and Chilworth, south of Hursley, a park is given by Saxton which does not appear in Speed's map, and another at ' Wade,' near the New Forest, which Speed denominates *Poltons*. He marks also a park a little north of Redbridge, called *Grove Place*; at *Rockborn*, on the borders of Wiltshire, another is given by both authorities. Near this is an existing park, called *Hale Park*, which appears to be ancient; it is on the borders of the New Forest, and a park is marked near the site in Speed's Survey. Hale Park contains about 60 acres of land, and a herd of about 40 spotted, or menell deer. Near Lymington another park is given by Speed, which he calls *Park house*. On the eastern side of the Itchin there was a park at *Merwell*, and there were two near *Tichfield*; one of these, at that period, belonging to Mr. Wriothesley, is thus noticed by Leland, ' There is also a parke, the ground whereof is somewhat hethy and baren.'[3]

Speed also marks a park at *Southwick*, the present seat of the Thistlethwayte family; there were deer here, according to ' Kip's Views of Seats,' in 1714. Southwick was disparked about the year 1808. Two parks are marked by Speed near *Havant*

[1] Cal. Pat. Rolls, p. 48.
[4] Cotton MSS., Titus B. iv. fol. 297.

[3] Itin. vol. iii. fol. 79.

on the borders of Sussex ; one only is given by Saxton. Near *Hambledon* both maps mark another, as well as one between Eastmean and Petersfield, and others near *Alresford*[1] and *East Tistead*, the latter called *Rotherfield* by Speed.

In the Isle of Wight, besides the Royal Forest and Park of Parkhurst, there was a good park at *Appuldurcombe*, the chief seat of the Worsley family, ' well stocked with deer,' in 1781.[2]

In the nineteenth of Henry VI., Lewis

Meux, Esq. and Alice his wife, had license to impark 300 acres of wood and pasture in the parishes of Shorwell and Kingston in this Island.[3]

Existing Parks in Hampshire.

1. HURSLEY . . Sir William Heathcote, Bart.
2. HACKWOOD . Lord Bolton.
3. HURSTBOURNE The Earl of Portsmouth.
4. HALE PARK . Mr. Goff.

---

[1] Omitted by Speed.
[2] Worsley's Isle of Wight, p. 218.

[3] Cal. Pat. Rolls, p. 283.

CHAPTER V.

NOTES ON DEER PARKS IN THE COUNTIES

OF

CAMBRIDGE,   NORFOLK, AND

HUNTINGDON,   SUFFOLK.

Queen Elizabeth's Oak at Huntingfield, in Suffolk, from a Photograph, in 1866.

CHAPTER V.

CAMBRIDGESHIRE.

THE county of Cambridge, from the marshy nature of a great part of its soil, is but ill adapted for deer parks, and there seem consequently to have been but few at any time within its bounds, but among them there are two which appear in the Domesday Survey, one of which till the end of the last century remained an existing park. I allude to *Kirtling*, commonly called Catlige or Catlage, not far from Newmarket, on the confines of Suffolk. From the reign of Henry VIII. it was the seat of the North family ; at the period of the Conquest *Chertelinge* belonged to the Countess Judith, widow of Waltheof Earl of Northumberland, and the park of wild beasts *(parc̄ bestiarū silvaticarū)* is particularly recorded in the great Domesday Survey. A plan of the manor made in 1646 marks two parks at Kirtling, the scene of those frequent Buckhuntings which are described in the lives of the Norths[1] during the period preceding

[1] Ed. 1826, vol. i. p. 47.

the Restoration of Charles II. in 1660. Not far from Kirtling is the *Burch* of Domesday, now *Borough* or Borough-Green, a park also recorded in Domesday, in the very same words as in the former instance. Before the Conquest this manor belonged to Editha, Queen Consort of Edward the Confessor ; after that event it was granted to Alan Earl of Brittany ; it afterwards came to a family who took their name from hence. The Patent Rolls show that Thomas de Burgh obtained license to impark his wood of *Burgh* or *Borough*, in the fourth year of Edward III. But the park is not marked in Saxton's Survey dated in 1576. It gives, however, a park on the very borders of the county near Wratting, which appears to be the present *Wratting Park.* Near this is *Horsheath*, the ancient seat of the Audleys and afterwards of the Allingtons, who were settled here in the reign of Henry V. William Allington, Esq. is said to have had the King's license to impark here in 1448.[1] This park is also marked by Saxton ; it was visited by Evelyn in 1670, being then in the possession of the Lord Allington, and he dwells upon 'the sweet prospect and stately avenue.' After the extinction of the Allington family this place was sold in 1775, and the park let to farm.[2]

Wimpole, or Wimple, near Caxton, once the seat of the Earl of Radnor, but since

1740 that of the Earls of Hardwicke. There were deer here in 1714 ;[3] the park is said to contain 250 acres.[4]

At *Downham*, in the more northern part of the county, in the Isle of Ely, was a park which belonged to the Bishops of Ely, and is marked as a park in Saxton's Survey ; it appears to have been disparked before 1691.[5]

Between Downham and Whittlesea is *Doddington*, an ancient estate of the See of Ely, but also for a long period the seat of the now extinct family of Peyton. Although no park is marked in the old maps, there probably was one here, as would appear by the following extract from a letter from Lord Chancellor Clarendon to Secretary (Morrice ?) ; it is dated August 4, 1666. 'The king since his Restoration, made the elder son of Dr. Peyton, of the Isle of Ely, a loyal man, *who had given him deer to restock his parks*, a baronet ; as he died without issue His Majesty has regranted the baronetcy to Algernon, the second son ; but lest he should die issueless, it would be well to put the other sons into the patent, the family being noble, ancient, and worth 3,000*l.* a year in land.[6]

Existing Park in Cambridgeshire.

WIMPOLE   .   Earl of Hardwicke.

[1] Lysons, p. 216.
[2] Topograph. vol. ii. p. 378.
[3] Kip's Views of Seats.

[4] Lysons, p, 287.
[5] Lysons' Cambridgeshire, p. 178.
[6] S. P O. Domestic.

HUNTINGDONSHIRE.

'HUNTINGDONSHIRE in old times,' writes Leland in his Itinerary, 'was much more woddy than it is now; and the dere resortid to the Fennes; and part of the redde (deer) of this forest of later times kept Thornay fennys.'¹ Leland appears to use the term *forest* here generally in the sense of woodlands, though 'Wabridge Forest,' marked as an impaled park, appears in the surveys of both Saxton in 1576, and Speed in 1610. It is near Huntingdon, and at Alkimonbury, or *Ankenbury,* in this neighbourhood, John de Segrave obtained license to impark a wood within the bounds of the forest of Wenbergh (or Wabridge), in the fourth year of Edward II.² The Patent Rolls preserve a notice of a much earlier license in this county for a park at *Glatton,* on the borders of Northamptonshire, granted to Fulk, of Newcastle, in the 26th of Henry III.³

The parks marked by Saxton are the following, all now long disparked:—

1. *Somersham,* on the confines of Cambridgeshire. This was anciently a park belonging to the bishoprick of Ely, and enlarged by license the 14th of Richard II., and afterwards a Royal park. I find it included in 'A Breviate of the woods, ᵽkes, and closes, &c. belonging to his Majesty, 18 Jan. 1608.'⁴ It was part of the jointure of Queen Henrietta Maria,

and afterwards seized by the Parliament during the Interregnum.

2. *Sapley Park,* near Huntingdon.

3. A park near Abbots Ripton, called '*Ripton Park*' in Speed's map.

4. A park at *Buckden* or *Bugden,* the ancient seat of the Bishops of Lincoln.

5. A park a little south of 'Pirrye,' or Perry.

6. A park marked near *Buckworth,* which in Speed's map is called 'Buckworth Grove.'

7. A small park marked at *Elton,* near Fotheringhay, on the borders of Northamptonshire. This was the seat of the ancient family of Sapcott.

The present parks in this county are Kimbolton and Cunnington:—

1. *Kimbolton,* supposed to have been enclosed at an early period; 150 acres are fenced off for deer, but the park is much larger. There is at present a herd of 260 fallow-deer.

2. *Cunnington.* A small park or paddock of 46 acres, enclosed before the year 1800, with a herd of from 80 to 90 fallow-deer.

Existing Parks in Huntingdonshire.

1. KIMBOLTON . . The Duke of Manchester.

2. CUNNINGTON . Mr. Heathcote.

---

¹ Leland's Itin. vol. iv. p. 31, fol. 48.
² Cal. Patent Rolls, p. 71.
³ Ib. p. 19.

⁴ Printed in the Appendix to the 11th Report of Commissioners on the Woods, &c., p. 701.

NORFOLK.

ALTHOUGH this flat and comparatively uninteresting county is not particularly well-adapted for deer parks, yet several have existed within its extensive limits from the very earliest topographical information which we possess. One at least is mentioned in the Domesday Survey, at *Coteseia*, the modern *Costessey* or *Cossey*, the old Jerningham seat near Norwich ; at the time of the Conquest the property of Alan Earl of Moretaine, and which had belonged to ' *Guert*,' in the Confessor's days. Here, ' one park with beasts,' occurs among the profits of the manor. Cossey has been long disparked, but it remained a park in the Elizabethan period, ' in circuit two miles or thereabouts,' in the possession of the Lady Jerningham, as appears by the Return of ' the Names of Parks keeping deer within the County of Norfolk,' dated in April 1581, and preserved in the State Paper Office.[1] The Royal parks at this period were *Dereham* and *Shipdham*, in the hundred of Mitforde, each two miles in circuit, and *Heningeham*, in that of Holt, but one mile in circumference. Shipdham had formerly belonged to the See of Ely. The old park called *Little Haw*, and the new park called *West Haw*, are mentioned as early as 1277. In the 3rd of Elizabeth, and again in the 26th of the same reign, this park was granted to the Wodehouse family, ' *with the deer in the park*,' and about 1585 it was conveyed to Sir Thomas Gaudy.[2]

Taking a topographical view of the parks of this county, we have to the east of Norwich the hundreds of Tunsted, Happing, West and East Elegg, Blofeld, Claveringe, and Loddon. No ancient parks appear in this district; but there were deer at *Langley*, in the hundred of Loddon, the seat of Sir Thomas Beauchamp Proctor, Bart., in 1781, and there is a small modern park at *Rackheath*, a few miles to the east of Norwich, belonging to Sir Henry Stracey, Bart., enclosed about the year 1854.

To the north of the county town are the hundreds of Holt, North and South Erpingham, Hayneford, and Taverham. In the first of these divisions is the large park of *Melton-Constable*, the ancient seat of the Astleys, now Lords Hastings. It is a park of 700 acres, with herds of 80 red-deer and 180 fallow. This park is said to be ancient, though not included in the Return of 1581.

At *Thornage* in the same hundred, there was, however, at that period a park, now long disused, belonging to Sir William Butts, Knight, one mile and a half in circuit ; and at *Bayfield*, the seat of Mr. Joddrell, a park is mentioned as existing in 1781.[3] In the hundred of North Erpingham, is *Felbrigg*, once the seat of the Windham family, one of the most beautiful situations in Norfolk. There were deer here in 1781, and it occurs among the parks of the county in 1581. It then be-

[1] S. P. O. Domestic, Eliz. vol. cxlviii. No. 63.

[2] History and Antiquities of Norfolk, 1781, vol. viii. p. 60.
[3] Hist. of Norfolk, vol. vii. p. 8.

longed to Roger Windham, Esq., and was one mile in circuit; near this is the modern park of *Gunton*, enclosed in 1825 : it is a park of 600 acres, with a herd of 150 fallow-deer.

In South Erpingham, there was a park at *Baconsthorpe* in 1581, belonging to William Haydon, Esq., two miles in circumference; and there had been one at *Blickling*, near Aylsham, which once belonged to the Bishops of Norwich (but was disparked before 1581); it afterwards belonged to the Hobert family. The park at Blickling is at present one of the largest in this county, containing about 620 acres, of which 145 are wood, and 26 water; there is a herd of 270 fallow-deer. There appear also to have been once deer parks at *Buxton* and *Oxnead*, ancient seats of the Pastons, Earls of Yarmouth.

To the south of Norwich are the hundreds of Humliarde, Hensed, Depward, Erisham, and Diss. In that of Humliarde was *Brakonask* or *Brakenash* Park, belonging in 1581 to Thomas Townshend, Esq., one mile in circuit; it has been long disparked. In Depward Hundred is *Shelton*, once the seat and park of an ancient family of that name : it is noticed among the Norfolk parks in 1581, when it belonged to Thomas Shelton, Esq., and was one mile in circuit. It was sold by the Shelton family and disparked early in the seventeenth century.[1] There was a park at *Erisham* or *Earsham*, in the hundred of the same name, attached to the castle of Bungay in Suffolk, which in 1307 was returned as well stocked,[2] and which in 1581 belonged to the Earl of Arundel, 'one mile and a half in compass;' and another

at *Hanworth.*, in the same hundred, belonging to the same nobleman, which, however, it is stated in the list already referred to, was without deer in 1581. The Earl of Arundel possessed also in 1581 another park in the hundred of Diss, at *Winfarthing*, estimated at one mile in circumference. *Winfarthing* was a very ancient park; in 1259 it belonged to Sir William Munchensy, and was then well stocked with deer; it afterwards was the property of the Lords Grey of Ruthyn, when it is also stated to have been well stocked with deer : 'all which (parks) were nothing worth above their outgoings and repairs.' Two parks are mentioned here in the reign of Queen Elizabeth. In 1604 this park was full of deer, and Sir Bassingbourne Gawdy, of West Horling, Knight, had every year a fee doe and buck, and liberty of hunting them in the park, which was then Lord Arundel's.[3]

In the south-western parts of Norfolk lie the hundreds of Guiltcross, Shropham, Wayland, Grimshoe, South Greenhoe, and Clackhouse. In the first-named of these, at *Kenninghall*, the Earls of Arundel, and afterwards the Howards Dukes of Norfolk, had an ancient seat, situated in the midst of a large park, which contained 700 acres, well stocked with deer; the house was pulled down about 1650.[4] In 1581 this park is said to have been two miles and a half in circuit. There was also a park in the adjoining manor of *Lopham*, belonging to Richard Bigot, in 1301. This also was the property of the Earl of Arundel, in 1581; it was then said to be three miles and a half in circuit. At Old Buckenham (in the hundred of Shro-

---

[1] History, &c. of Norfolk, vol. ii. p. 136.
[2] Suckling's Suffolk, vol. i. p. 136.
[3] History and Antiquities of Norfolk, 1781,

vol. ii. pp. 187, 194.
[4] History of Norfolk, vol. vi. p. 90.

pham), the name of which is supposed to allude to deer, an ancient park certainly existed, as it is mentioned in the charter of foundation of the Monastery here, by William de Albini,' Earl of Arundel, in the time of King Stephen;[1] and in 1242 the king sent his writ to the keepers of the lands of Hugh de Albany, Earl of Arundel, that they should deliver to Robert de Tateshale two bucks of his gift, out of the park lately belonging to the said Hugh, in his town of Buckenham.[2] At *Attleborough*, in the same hundred, the Earl of Sussex owned a park in 1581, three miles in circuit. And at *Weeting St. Mary*, in the hundred of Grimshoe, a modern park is said to have been enclosed by the Earl of Montrath, about the year 1781.[3] Another is said to have been enclosed by Mr. Vincent, at Buckenham-Toft, in this same district, in the reign of Charles II.

Returning towards Norwich, and the midland districts of Norfolk, we have the hundreds of Forehowe, Mitford, and Laundich. The Domesday Park of Cossey in Forehowe, has been already noticed. In the same hundred is *Kimberley*, the ancient seat of the Wodehouse family, and derived by them by inheritance from the old Norfolk House of Fastolf. Here has been for a very long period an ancient park, though it is not recognised in the 'Government Return of 1581 : at present it contains 180 acres, and a herd of 120 fallow-deer.[4]

In the hundred of Mitford was the ancient park of *Whinbergh* or *Whinborough*. In the thirty-eighth year of Henry III., William, Lord Bardolph, impleaded Thomas le Parker for entering his park here, and taking his beasts, &c. The Sheriff returned that it was in the liberty of the Bishop of Ely and Hereford : a *non omittas* was awarded. The park at this time is said to have contained 500 acres of land.[5] In 1581 this park, which has been long disused, was in the possession of Robert Southwell, Esq. ; it is described 'as two miles or thereabouts in circuit.' At the same period there were parks at *Hockering* and *Woodrising*, in this same hundred ; the first belonging to Lord Morley, and being one mile in circuit, the latter to Robert Southwell, Esq., of double that extent : these also have been long disparked.

In the hundred of Laundich, the venerable park of *Elmham*, called North Elmham, to distinguish it from South Elmham, in Suffolk, claims precedence. Elmham, situated on the south-west side of the river Wensum, was a castle of the Bishops of Norwich, but exchanged with the Crown in the reign of Henry VIII. There was a noble demesne and park near Brisley, which is mentioned in the time of John de Grey, Bishop of Norwich, in the reign of King John.[6] In that of Queen Elizabeth, in 1602, this ancient park became the property of the Cokes of

---

[1] Dugdale's Monasticon, ed. 1830, vol. vi. p. 418.
[2] History of Norfolk, vol. viii. p. 76.
[3] Ib. p. 125.
[4] Sir John Wodehouse, knighted by Henry IV., married the sole daughter and heir of Sir Thomas Fastolf of Kimberley, thus noticed in a curious pedigree of the family :—'being

matched to Fastolf's heir, he had enlarged his elbow room ; and it was he who made the moated hall and tower within the park at the east end of the town, of more remark than the old one in the west disparked long since.'— *Neale's Views of Seats*, 1820, vol. iii.
[5] History of Norfolk, vol. viii. p. 90.
[6] Ib. pp. 42, 54.

Holkham, whose heirs are now Earls of Leicester : it is now, however, disparked, the deer being removed to Holkham in 1844.

Lord Sondes has a modern park also at *Elmham,* enclosed about the beginning of the present century : it contains 140 acres and a herd of about 100 fallow-deer. In this hundred ancient parks are said to have existed, both at *Mileham,* belonging to the Cokes in 1600, and in the parish of Swanton-Morley, called *Bywick Park,* the property of the Morleys, and afterwards to their heirs and descendants, the Parkers, Lords Morley.[1]

The western district of Norfolk, surrounded on two sides by the sea, is divided into the hundreds of North-Greenhoe, Brothercross, Smithdon, Gallow, and Frebridge. In the first-named is the extensive domain of Holkham, enclosed by the first Earl of Leicester of the Coke family between the years 1735 and 1759. It then contained about 840 acres of land.[2] The deer were removed here, as has been already stated, in 1844, from the ancient Episcopal park of Elmham : the present park at Holkham contains 595 acres and a herd of 450 fallow-deer.

At *Hunstanton,* the venerable seat of the L'Estrange family, at the very northwestern corner of Norfolk, in Smithdon Hundred, was an extensive park, now without deer ; and at *Rainham,* the seat of the Marquis Townshend, is also a large

park, in the same condition, but which was 'well stocked with deer' in 1776.[3] But at *Houghton,* once the residence of Sir Robert Walpole, and now of his descendant the Marquis of Cholmondeley, the deer still remain. The park is said to have been enclosed by Sir Robert Walpole about the year 1722 : it is an area of 450 acres, with a herd of 210 fallow-deer.

At Castle-Rising, in the hundred of Frebridge, was a famous royal chase for deer, now long broken up and disused. But in its near neighbourhood a Royal park has very lately been reestablished at *Sandringham,* by H. R. H. the Prince of Wales ; deer being brought hither from Windsor, in the autumn of 1863. This notice of the only Royal, as well as the most modern park in this county, may fitly conclude these notes on the ancient and modern parks of Norfolk.

Existing Parks in Norfolk.

1. BLICKLING . Marquis of Lothian.
2. HOUGHTON . Marquis of Cholmondeley.
3. KIMBERLEY . Earl of Kimberley.
4. MELTON-CONSTABLE, Lord Hastings.
5. ELMHAM . . Lord Sondys.
6. GUNTON . . Lord Suffield.
7. HOLKHAM . Earl of Leicester.
8. RACKHEATH . Sir Henry Stracey, Bart.
9. SANDRINGHAM, H. R. H. the Prince of Wales.

---

[1] History of Norfolk, 1781, vol. viii. pp. 119, 152.
[2] Ib. vol. vi. p. 32.

[3] Beauties of England, 3rd ed. 1776, vol. ii. p. 36.

SUFFOLK.

SUFFOLK, like Norfolk, can claim one Domesday Park, that at *Eiam*, the modern *Eye*, in the hundred of Hartismerc. It had been in the tenure of Edric, but was granted to Robert Malet at the Conquest. Saxton's Survey of this county (which bears date in 1575) marks four parks in this hundred, at *Redgrave*, one near *Burgate*, at *Westhorp*, and near *Thwaite*; the first was the seat of the Bacons, the last of the family of Reeve. Westhorp was the noble seat of Charles Brandon, Duke of Suffolk, and was demolished about the middle of the eighteenth century. At Thornham, the seat of Lord Henniker, there was at one time a park, disparked by Sir John Major, the great-great-grandfather of the present lord.[1]

There were also deer at *Broome Hall,* the seat of the Cornwallis family, as appears by 'Kip's Views of Seats,' engraved in 1714.

In the adjoining hundred of Hoxne, ancient parks were recognised by Saxton at *Wingfield, Denham,* near *Monks-Soham,* not far from Framlingham, and at *Kelsall,* an ancient seat of the Dukes of Norfolk. The park at Wingfield was originally enclosed by license granted to the De la Poles, Earls of Suffolk,[2] in the fifteenth century the most important family in this county : it has, with the others here mentioned, been long disparked.

The park at *Framlingham* (the well-known castle of the Howards, Dukes of Norfolk), which is in the hundred of Loes, may be considered the most interesting within this county, though it belongs to former times and not to the present day. A very curious account of it, from a Roll dated in the seventh of Henry VIII., has been already given in the Second Chapter of this work. The Roll gives a minute account of the number of the deer which were killed and how they were distributed. The number altogether was so great (96 bucks are said to have been killed in one year) that the park was probably at that time larger than Loder, in his History of Framlingham, represents it to have been, namely, about 600 acres, and three miles in circumference.[3] The same author has preserved, among the Customs of the Manor, the following rules relating to the privileges of this great park :—' The reparation of the Park-pales, where standing, was done by certain tenants, who were freely to take timber for that purpose out of Oldfrith wood. All Trees growing without the Park-pales, and not above sixteen foot distant from them, belong to the Lords of this Manor, and the pasture thereof to the Tenants of the respective lands adjacent to those pales, which breadth of xvi foot the Lords had to walk and ride without about the pales ; no ways or passages for carts, &c. lead thro' the

---

[1] Information of Lord Henniker, 1866.
[2] Beauties of England (Suffolk), vol. xiv. p. 313 ; and Cox's Magna Brittannia, vol. v.

p. 217.
[3] Loder's History of Framlingham, 1798, p. 329.

Park, but for the Lords and their Tenants only.'¹ The latest date referred to in these customs is the twelfth of Charles I.

Saxton marks also a park at *Kenton*, the old seat of the Garneys family, in the hundred of Loes.

At *Letheringham*, the ancient seat of the Wingfields, and afterwards of the Naunton family, in the same hundred of Loes, there was also a park, given in Saxton's Survey, but which, together with everything else of interest at this place, has been long destroyed.

At *Glemham*, between Framlingham and Saxmundham, there was, until very lately, an existing park of dark deer, belonging to the Earl of Guilford, and another remains at *Campsea-Ashe*, in the same neighbourhood.

In Blithing Hundred were the parks of *Henham, Bliborough, Huntingfield*, and *Heveningham*.

Huntingfield belonged in the time of Elizabeth to Lord Hunsdon, and here the Queen visited him, and is said to have shot a buck with her own hand, from a venerable tree in the park, still known as ' *Queen Elizabeth's Oak*,' a tree described about 1773 as ' in some degree of vigor, tho' most of its branches are broken off, and those which remain are approaching to a total decay, as well as its vast trunk.'² A beautiful etching of this celebrated oak is given by Strutt in his Silva Brittanica (1824), and it is engraved from a photograph taken in 1866 in the present work.³ Of the adjoining park of *Heveningham* a notice has already been given (p. 34), where the annual grant of a buck and

doe, conceded by Sir John Heveningham and Dame Alice his wife, and Anthony his son and heir in 1533, to Nicholas Bohun, Esq., is given at length. More than a century later, 50 head of deer were begged from this park, at that time belonging to the regicide William Heveningham, by Sir Henry Wood, for ' his own little park at *Lowdham*, which he has re-inclosed, the pales being broken down, and the deer sold during the Usurpation.'⁴ Lowdham is in the hundred of Wilford, near Woodbridge, but is not marked in Saxton's Survey of 1575, or in that of Speed in 1610.

In the north-eastern part of Suffolk, near Beccles, is *Barsham*, an ancient seat of the Echinghams, Blennerhassets, and Sucklings. ' The meadows around the hall, which formed a park as early as the fourteenth century, are now divided into small enclosures ; but stags' horns are occasionally found where new ditches and drains are dug.'⁵

Stow Park is in the Duke of Norfolk's manor of Bungay Soke. At an Inquisition taken at Ipswich, on the 11th of January, 1307 (35th Edward I.), when Roger Bigot died, it was said : 'Item est ibidem Parcus cum feris, qui vocatur Stowe Park, et valet herbagium p : an : vᵉ. viiiᵈ. et sub-bosco ibid nihil.' It appears from deeds that the Duke of Norfolk claimed Stow Park as his freehold, and as a park belonging to the manor of Bungay Soke at a much later period ; and it is recognised in the accounts of the bailiffs of the manor in the thirty-eighth of Henry VIII. It is not however given by Saxton.

---

¹ Loder's Framlingham, p. 390.
² Suckling's Suffolk, vol. ii. p. 411.
³ See page 111.

⁴ S. P. O. Domestic, Nov. 1660.
⁵ Suckling's Suffolk, vol. i. p. 46.

There is a park of fallow-deer at *Somer-leyton*, in the north-eastern angle of the county. In this neighbourhood is *Flixton*, erected about the year 1616, by Sir John Tasburgh, in the centre of an extensive park.

A little to the south is *South Elmham*, from the year 1094 a residence of the Bishops of Norwich. ' The Park Farm ' still points out the site of the ancient Episcopal park here, and which is described in an Indenture of June 22, third of Elizabeth (1561), 'between Edward Lord North of the one partye and John Laurence of South-Elmham in the county of Suffolk, yeoman, of the other partye,' witnessing that, for the consideration of 1000*l.*, Lord North, who was in possession of this estate (and of much more ecclesiastical plunder), sold to the said John Laurence, 'all those the grounde and soyle called the newe Parke, as it is now enclosed with a pale, in the parish of Saint James in South Elmham, and all the soyle betwene the pale of the said parke, and the dyche without the same pale, together with the soyle of the said dyche, and also all his dere, his woods, and tymber growing or being within the same parke, or within the lymites of the said dyche without the said pale, or between the same pale and the said dyche.'[1] This deed proves the ancient right of Freebord already referred to (see p. 118), and gives the probable date of the destruction of this ancient park, which is not likely to have been continued after its sale to the Suffolk yeoman.

Helmingham, in the central parts of Suffolk, midway between Needham and Framlingham, has been, from the Elizabethan period, the venerable seat of the Talmache family, though not marked in Saxton's Survey. It is at present a park of 396 acres, with herds of 30 red, and 450 fallow-deer, and is celebrated for the beauty of its fine oak timber. A more modern park exists at *Shrubland*, the seat of Sir G. B. Middleton, Bart.

In the more southern districts of Suffolk Saxton marks a park at *Nettlested*, in the hundred of Cleydon ; and another near *Hadley*, in that of Cosford. The latter is perhaps identical with that park enclosed by license at Hadlegh in com. Suffolk, in the forty-third year of Edward III., granted to Helminges Le-Gette, Esq., comprehending 300 acres of land, 20 acres of meadow, 180 acres of pasture, and 139 acres of wood. There is an existing park at *Polstead* about five miles south of Hadley.

In this neighbourhood, a few miles south of Ipswich, on the western bank of the Orwell, is *Woolverstone* Park, containing 380 acres, and a herd of about 300 fallow-deer of the menell or spotted variety. This park appears to have been enclosed about the time of the erection of the mansion, which was in 1776.

On the opposite bank of the *Orwell* is a smaller park which takes its name from the river. It is an area of less than 200 acres, with about that number of fallow-deer. *Orwell* Park appears to have been enclosed by Lord Orwell, before 1764. At *Brightwell*, near Ipswich, there was also a park belonging to Sir Samuel Barnadiston, Bart., in 1714 ;[2] and there is an

---

[1] Original Deed *penes* the Baroness North, 1566.

[2] Kip's Views of Seats.

existing park at *Christ Church*, near the county town.

Near Sudbury, in Babergh Hundred, bordering on the county of Essex, three ancient parks are given by Saxton ; at *Chilton, Small Bridge*, an ancient Waldgrave seat, and at *Gifford Hall*, in the parish of Stoke-Neyland, a very old seat of the Mannocks family. A group of three more parks is also marked by him near *Lavenham*, in the northen part of the same hundred (the ancient inheritance of the Veres Earls of Oxford), and one also at *Cavendish* on the borders of Essex. At *Long Milford*, in this neighbourhood, the seat of the Parker family, there were deer within the last twenty years.

In Risbridge Hundred, Saxton marks three contiguous parks near Straddishall. These appear to have been the parks called *Great Park, Estry Park*, and *Broxley Park*, granted to Sir John Cheke, in the third of Edward VI., as parcel of the possessions of Stoke-Clare,[1] once belonging to Lionel Duke of Clarence.

One park only is given by Saxton in the hundred of Thingoe, at *Chevington* in the immediate neighbourhood of *Hengrave*, the well-known beautiful seat of the Gage family. It appears from ' a Book of Accompt of all kinds of deere put into Hengrave pke,' that it was finished and licensed at Michaelmas 1587. The new park contained 300 acres, belonging to Sir Thomas Kitson the younger, and was stocked as follows :—

' Deere of all kinds taken owte of Chev-

ington pke in the beginning of the last year ix** xiii.

' Rec^d· and also put into Hengrave pke, viz. : out of Lopham Parke xiiii. ; out of Westrop Parke, xxvi. ; out of Wetherden Pke, iii. Rec^d· as given by Mr. Clement Higham being tame and whight, i. Rec^o· out of Mr. Jernegan[2] his Pke one whight doe, i. Rec^d· out of Mr. Crane[3] his Pke viii. Remayned in the yere ended as before, lxx. (cccxvi.)

' Whereof killed and spent in the House in Chrysmas, ii. Given unto Mr. Clement Higham, ii. Morts with one lost, xi. Killed and sent unto London of bucks, ii. Given unto Mr. Seckford, i. Stolen, i.(xix.)

' And so, Remayns of bucks, xviii. Sores, xx. Sorrels, xlviii. Pryketts, xxv. Does and fawnes, ix**vi. (cciiij**xvii.)

' In 1712, the extent of both Great and Little Park at Hengrave was 500 acres ; the present park is but 230 acres.'[4]

At *Little Saxham* in this hundred, the seat of the family of Croftes, there was a park in 1638, as appears by a plan of the manor given by Mr. Gage in his admirable ' History of Thingoe.' The Croftes family had also a manor and park at *Bardwell*, in the adjoining hundred of Blackbourn, as we find by the will of Sir John Croftes, dated 21st of January, 1557.[5] Adjoining Little Saxham is Ickworth. '*Ickworth Park*,' says Gage, ' which is well stocked with deer, is very extensive, containing with the woods, above 1,900 acres, lying in Ickworth, Chevington, Little-Saxham, and Horningsherth.'[6]

---

[1] Kirby's Suffolk Traveller, 2nd ed. p. 250.
[2] Mr. Jernegan's Park, Somerley, in the hundred of Lothing.
[3] Mr. Crane's Park, Chilton, in the hundred of Babergh.

[4] History and Antiquities of Hengrave, p. 4.
[5] Gage's Thingoe, p. 135.
[6] Ib. p. 303.

Chevington has been already noticed as a park recognised by Saxton in 1575. It was an ancient seat of the Abbots of St. Edmund, and from its retired situation in a woody undulating country, it soon became a favourite retreat. There was a park here, adds Gage, well stocked with deer. Upon the Dissolution, the Manor and Park of Chevington were granted to Sir Thomas Kytson, whose son appears to have transferred the deer to Hengrave in 1587.

That there was a park also at *Hawsted*, the ancient seat of the Drury family, in this vicinity, there is no doubt; both great and little park occur on the old plan of the estate, engraved in the ' History of Thingoe,' and in the reign of Queen Elizabeth, the rector received a buck and doe in lieu of tithe for the demesne lands.[2]

At *Livermere*, near Culford, is a modern and existing park, praised by Mr. Young for its beauty.

Euston, on the borders of Norfolk, the seat of the Duke of Grafton, is the largest park in this county, though it is at present without deer, having been disparked by the father of the present Duke. It contained, according to Neale in his ' Views of Seats' (1821), 1,450 acres ; it was the theme of Blomfield's ' Farmer's Boy.'

Where smiling Euston boasts her good Fitzroy,
Lord of pure alms, and gifts that wide extend;
The farmer's patron, and the poor man's friend.

In 1671, Euston belonged to Lord Arlington ; and 'here,' observes Evelyn, ' my lord was pleased to advise with me about

ordering his plantations of firs, elms, limes, &c., up his parke, and in all other places and avenues. I persuaded him to bring his parke so neare as to comprehend his house within it, which he resolved upon, it being now near a mile to it.'[3] In another place, this delightful and most gentlemanlike author observes, 'Anno 1677, August 29. We hunted in the park [at Euston], and killed a very fat buck.' ' The park pale 9 miles in compass, and the best for riding and meeting the game that ever I saw ; there were now of red and fallow-deere almost a thousand, with good covert, but the soil barren and flying sand, in which nothing will grow kindly ; the tufts of firs, and much of the other wood, were planted by my direction some years before.'[4]

Existing Deer Parks in Suffolk.

1. HEVENINGHAM . Lord Huntingfield.
2. HELMINGHAM . Mr. Tollemache.
3. HENGRAVE . Sir Thomas Gage, Bart.
4. REDGRAVE . . Mr. Wilson.
5. ICKWORTH . . Marquis of Bristol
6. FLIXTON . . Sir R.Shafto Adair, Bart.
7. WOOLVERSTONE Mr. Berners.
8. ORWELL . . Mr. Tomline.
9. CHRIST-CHURCH Mr. Fonnereau.
10. LIVERMERE . Late Sir W. Middleton, Bart.
11. SOMERLEYTON . Sir Francis Crossley, Bart.
12. POLSTEAD . . Mr. Tyrell.
13. SHRUBLAND . Sir G. Brooke Middleton, Bart.
14. CAMPSEA-ASHE. Mr. Sheppard.

[1] Gage's Thingoe, p. 440.
[2] Ib. p. 447.
[3] Evelyn's Memoirs, 4to ed. vol. i. p. 426.
[4] Ib. p. 462.

CHAPTER VI.

NOTES ON DEER PARKS IN THE COUNTIES

OF

BEDFORDSHIRE,	BERKSHIRE, AND
BUCKINGHAMSHIRE,	OXFORDSHIRE.

Death of the Buck—Henry Prince of Wales and Robert Devereux, third Earl of Essex
Copied from the Original Picture by Lucas de Heere, at Hampton Court.

CHAPTER VI.

BEDFORDSHIRE.

UGH DE BELCAMP (Beauchamp) is recorded in the Domesday Survey to have possessed a park of wild beasts (parchus ferarum silvaticarum) within his manor of Stachedene (Stagsden) in the western confines of this county : no further notice appears to have been preserved of this park.

The parks which were attached to the manor and castle of Ampthill, early in the sixteenth century, in the hands of the Crown, and erected into an ' Honour ' by Act of Parliament, may perhaps next claim our attention. No less than eight cluster round the town of Ampthill, according to Saxton's Map of Bedfordshire, engraved in 1576. Besides *Ampthill Great Park*, there were the parks of *Houghton*, or *Houghton-Conquest, Broknoro*, or *Brogborough Park, Beckering Park*, and a park near *Flitwick.* Here there is still a small park or paddock, belonging to Mr. Brooks.

The Great Park of *Ampthill* was held under the Crown by various persons until it was granted by Charles II. to Mr. John Ashburnham ; it afterwards came by pur-

chase to Viscount Fitzwilliam, and again to the Earls of Upper Ossory. The custody of the park appears to have been held by the noble family of Bruce.[1] There is in the State Paper Office a petition from Robert, Earl of Elgin, to the King (Charles II.), for a grant of 100 trees growing in Ampthill Park, in order to enclose some part of it for red-deer ; a warrant was granted for this purpose on the 11th of May, 1664.[2] The Park of Ampthill was surveyed by order of Parliament in 1653.

The park at *Houghton-Conquest* was also called Dame Ellensbury Park. Like Ampthill, it was formerly held under the Crown, and was granted in fee to Lord Bruce in 1630.[3] In 1738 it passed by purchase to the Bedford family.

Brogborough and *Beckerings Parks* are in the parish of Ridgmont. Both appear to have been in possession of the Crown previous to the Usurpation. After the Restoration, both were granted by Charles II. to the family of Ashburnham, and came afterwards by purchase to the Radcliffes : they have been for ages disparked.

In the north-western part of the county,

[1] Lysons' Bedfordshire, p. 38.
[2] S. P. O. Domestic.
[3] Nichols's Progresses of King James I.,

vol. i. p. 521 note ; and Lysons' Bedfordshire, p. 96.

on the borders of Buckinghamshire, is *Turvey*, for many centuries the chief house of the great family of Mordaunt. Here, in 1297, William Mordaunt had the king's license to enclose a park,[1] which is given in Saxton's Survey : it has been for a long period disparked.

A little more to the north is *Carlton*, where, and in *Harold* adjoining, John de Pabenham had in 1313 license to impark his woods, being within the king's forest.[2] Harold afterwards belonged to the noble family of Grey. The park at this place is marked both in Saxton's and Speed's Surveys.

In the north of the county are *Bletsoe* and *Melchbourn Parks*, seats of the ancient family of St. John, but neither of them marked as parks in either Saxton's or Speed's maps.

South-east of Ampthill is *Wrest Park*, in the parish of Flitton, the ancestral seat of the Greys, but not, it would seem, an ancient park, being undistinguished as such in the older maps of the county already referred to.

To the south again is *Toddington*, where a park is marked by Speed. This was the seat of the Cheneys, and afterwards of the Wentworths, by whom, probably, the park was made.

Adjoining Toddington is *Chalgrave*. Here Sir Nigel or Neal Loring, one of the founders of the Order of the Garter, retired to spend his latter days ; and here, in the year 1365, he had the royal license to enclose a park.[3]

In the south-eastern corner of the county, on the confines of Hertfordshire, is Luton and the park of *Luton Hoo*. 300 acres here were enclosed by Sir Robert Napier in the early part of the seventeenth century. 'The park,' writes Lysons, 'was enlarged by the late Lord Bute to 1,200 acres, and it now (1806) contains about 1,500.'[4]

West of Luton and Dunstable, on the edge of Buckinghamshire, is *Eaton Bray*, successively the manor of the families of Bray and Sandys. Here a park is given by Saxton, now long disparked.

It remains to mention the park of *Woburn*, the chief seat of the Duke of Bedford, though it appears to have no claims to great antiquity, and is not found marked as a park in the ancient surveys. Woburn Park is very extensive, and is surrounded by a wall eight feet in height. There are here both red and fallow-deer : the doe venison is said to be remarkably good.

Existing Deer Parks in Bedfordshire.

1. WREST PARK . Countess Cowper.
2. WOBURN . . . Duke of Bedford.
3. FLITWICK . . Mr. Brooks.

---

[1] Collins's Peerage, Bridges' ed. vol. iii. p. 310.
[2] Pat. 6 Ed. II.

[3] Cart. 39–40 Ed. III. quoted by Lysons.
[4] Lysons' Bedfordshire, p. 108.

BUCKINGHAMSHIRE.

NOTICES of two parks in this county occur in the Domesday Survey. The one, at *Oakley*, the Saxon Acleia or Acklai, signifying oak trees and a plain, and exactly descriptive of its situation in the ancient Bernwode Forest, in Tickesell Hundred (now part of Ashendon Hundred) about six miles WNW. of the River Thames; the other at *Crendon*, the Credendone of the Survey, in the same hundred, and south-eastern verge of the same forest.[1]

The park at Oakley belonged to the king, but no further notice of it occurs.

Crendon was granted to Walter Giffard, and here a park for beasts of the chase, 'parcus bestiarum silvaticarum,' is expressly mentioned, but, like Oakley, no further mention of it is recorded.

Saxton's Survey of this county, which was made in 1574, marks a park near Chilton, at a spot still called *Chilton Park*, midway between these ancient parks.

At *Doddershall*, in the parish of Quainton, in the same hundred of Ashendon, the seat of the ancient family of Pigot, was a park existing in the seventeenth century, as appears by a plan of that date engraved in Lipscomb's Buckinghamshire (p. 51.) This park was converted into arable and meadow, and the keeper's lodge demolished about the year 1789.[2]

A park also appears to have existed at *Over-Winchendon*, the seat of Philip Lord Wharton, in the reign of Charles II.

In the hundred of Buckingham, to the north-west of that of Ashendon, and in the north-western angle of the county, Saxton gives two parks; the one near *Edgcott* and in the parish of Twyford, which appears to have been a park of the Wenman family,[3] and of which I find no further account, and the other at *Thornton*, on the borders of the county of Northampton. Here was the seat of the Tyrrells, and here Queen Elizabeth, in the first year of her reign, licensed George Tyrrell, Esq., to impark 500 acres of meadow and wood, and enclose the same with pales or fence, at his discretion, and make a park there, &c.[4] Thornton has been long disparked. At *Stockholt*, in this neighbourhood, Thomas Linford, Esq. had license to enclose 'quendam jampnum,' certain furze-land, and a certain wood adjacent to his park, in the thirteenth of Henry IV.[5] The beginning of the great park at *Stowe* must be ascribed to Sir Peter Temple, who, about the year 1651, enclosed a park here on the disparking of Wicken Park, in the county of Northampton, by the Lord Spencer, the deer of which he bought.[6] There appear, however, to have been ancient parks in this parish and in Westbury adjoining at a very early date, as we find from the

---

[1] Lipscomb's History of the County of Buckingham, vol. i. pp. 198, 350.
[2] Ib. vol. i. p. 411.
[3] Willis's Hundred of Buckingham, p. 333, A.D. 1755.

[4] From a translation of the Grant *penes* the Hon. Richard Cavendish, the present proprietor.
[5] Cal. Pat. Rolls, p. 259.
[6] Willis, p. 276.

conveyance of Sir John Chastillon in 1414, mentioning the woods in the parishes of Stow and Westbury, with the parks called *Royes* or *Royesia's Park,* and *Makelines* or *Malcolm's Park,* &c.[1]

Stowe, said to contain nearly 1,500 acres, was disparked after the celebrated sale at this place in 1848, but of late years, under the careful management of the present Duke of Buckingham, it has been restocked, deer being brought from Langley Park and Blenheim.

At *Lenborough,* two miles south of Buckingham, was an old seat of the Ingolsby family. Sir Richard Ingolsby, about 1617, enclosed this lordship, and made a park, which his grandson disparked about 1673.[2]

Adjoining to the hundreds of Ashendon and Buckingham is that of Cotteslow, in the north of which is Whaddon Chase. There were in old times two parks here, granted by the Crown, with the Chase, to the custody of various persons. In the reign of James I. they were in the possession of George Villiers, Duke of Buckingham, and afterwards came to the family of Mr. Selby-Lowndes, the present proprietor. This Chase was supposed sufficient to feed one thousand head of deer. The Giffards were its hereditary keepers under the De Burghs, Earls of Ulster, in the time of the three first Edwards.[3] In the centre of this same hundred of Cotteslow is *Wing,* once the seat of the Dormers, Earls of Carnarvon. Here was a park noticed in Saxton's Survey, which appears to have been dis-

parked and the timber cut down by Sir William Stanhope about the year 1727.[4]

At *Burstone* or *Birdstane,* a little south of -Wing, was a park also noticed by Saxton, and which in the reign of Elizabeth belonged to Sir Henry Lee, K.G. It has been long disparked. The following mention of it is from Leland's 'Itinerary':—'Birdsteine, in the Vale of Aylesbury, where Mr. Leigh hath a goodly house with orchards and a parke. This Birdsteine is almost in the middle of the Vale of Aylesbury.'[5]

The large park of *Ashridge* occupies the south-eastern extremity of this hundred; it is about five miles in circumference, and has been celebrated for its great variety of ground, and fine plantations of oak, beech, and ash: it was anciently in two divisions, one of them stocked with fallow and the other with red-deer.[6]

In Newport Hundred, occupying the most northern part of the county, bordering on Northamptonshire and Bedfordshire, there was an ancient park, near Olney and Lavendon, on the borders of Bedfordshire: it is given by Saxton, and is thus alluded to in Leland's 'Itinerary':— '*Castel Parke,* a mile from Laundon Abbey, and Laundon, is withyn a myle of Olney; this parke longgid to the Souches, but now lately sold to the Lord Mordant."[7] This might have been identical with that which was imparked by Ralph Basset, of Drayton, in the forty-eighth year of Edward III., as appears

---

[1] Willis, p. 296.
[2] Ib. pp. 35–36.
[3] Lipscomb's Bucks, vol. iii. p. 498.
[4] Ib. vol. iii. p. 525.
[5] Itin. vol. iv. p. 127, fol. 191 *b.*

[6] Lipscomb's Bucks, vol. iii. p. 447.
[7] Itin. vol. vii. p. 2, fol. 3. In the third of Elizabeth it belonged to the Crown, and was let to J. Marshe for 21 years. Cotton MSS., Titus, B. iv. fo. 297.

by the license for 310 acres granted at that time.[1]

At *Gayhurst,* anciently written *Gote-hurst,* the well-known seat of the Digbys, in the same hundred, a park is also noticed by Saxton, and another at *Moulsoe,* or *Mulshoe,* near Newport Pagnell. ' Park-wood ' and ' Park-farm ' still attest its site. .

The southern part of the county is divided into the hundreds of Aylesbury, Desborough, Burnham, and Stoke.

At *Bradenham,* in the hundred of Desborough, was the seat and residence of the Lords Windsor, and the site of an ancient park existing in the early part of the seventeenth century, and marked in the ancient maps. A small existing park is at *Turville,* on the borders of Oxfordshire, and closely adjoining Stonor, in that county.

The hundred of Burnham is remarkable for the site of an ancient park, at *the Vache,* in the parish of Chalfont St. Giles, the seat of a family who took their name from hence, and flourished in the fourteenth century. This park is given in Saxton's Survey.

On the very edge of the county adjoining Bedfordshire is *Cheniés.* This was the seat of the Russells, and here were two parks in the time of Leland ; one is marked in Saxton's map ; but as neither are given by Speed, we may suppose they were disparked before the reign of James I.

In the hundred of Stoke, which is the most southern part of the county, we have to notice the parks of *Bulstrode, Langley,* and *Ditton.*

Bulstrode Park is in the parish of Hedgerley, by which name it is distin- guished in Saxton's Survey : it contains about 800 acres, is well wooded, and stocked with a great number of deer.[2]

Langley was a Royal park, and there is extant a grant from Richard III. of its custody, dated in the year 1483.[3] In 1523 Henry VIII. appointed Henry Norres, Esq., Keeper of the king's woods in the county, Plaunte, or new park of Langley. In 1540 it is called ' The Park of Plaunt in Langley,' and in the second year of Edward VI. the Princess, afterwards Queen Elizabeth, received from her brother a grant of this park, with bucks and does therein.[4] Norden, Surveyor of the Woods to King James I., thus describes it :—' Langley Parke, lying within Buckinghamshire, whereof M. Edmond Kederminster is Keper, hath about 140 fallow deere, about 35 of antler, about 14 buckes. This parke is divided into two parkes by a new erected pale. The groundes also differing in nature. The upper grounde heath, and full of bogges, unprofitable, and impassable. The lower grounds reduced to a better use, for the game, and more delightful to hunte in, by reason of the faire artificial lawns latelie made and leveled with manie convenient and pleasant standinges.'[5]

At present Langley Park comprehends about 300 acres, with a herd of 220 fallow and a few red-deer.

Stoke-Poges was the principal seat of the noble family of Molins, though they had property in other parts of the county. Sir John de Molins obtained license from Edward III., to impark his woods in

---

[1] Cal. Pat. Rolls, p. 189.
[2] Lipscomb's Bucks, vol. iv. p. 507.
[3] Grimaldi's Origines Genealogicæ, p. 179.

[4] Lipscomb's Bucks, vol. iv. p. 532.
[5] MS. Brit. Mus. quoted by Lipscomb, vol. iv. p. 533 note.

K

Ilmere, in the hundred of Ashendon, in 1337, and in 1340, the woods of *Sywardeshull* and *Wynard*, in this county, with 300 acres adjoining, and to fortify his manor-houses of Stoke-Poges and Ditton with walls of stone.[1] '*Ditton Park*,' writes Norden in the MS. Survey already alluded to, 'hath about 220 deere, about 50 of antler, and 20 buckes. The circuit of this parke is 2¼ miles ; little timber. It containeth in quantitie about 195 akers good grounde.'

Existing Deer Parks in Buckinghamshire.

1. STOWE   . The Duke of Buckingham.
2. ASHRIDGE . Earl Brownlow.
3. TURVILLE . Mr. Butlin.
4. BULSTRODE The Duke of Somerset.
5. LANGLEY   . Mr. Harvey.

BERKSHIRE.

OF the Royal parks of *Windsor*, which naturally claim our first attention in the consideration of the parks of Berkshire, so much has been collected in ' The Annals of Windsor,' by Messrs. Tighe and Davis, and also by Mr. Menzies, in his magnificent work on ' The Great Park of Windsor,' that it may be sufficient to observe that the earliest notice of a park here is in the thirty-first of Henry III., when a payment of 30*s.* 5*d.* occurs in the accounts of William Fitz-Walter to the park-keepers, and 5*s.* for the keep of birds in the park.[2]

From this period we find constant reference to Windsor parks in the Originalia and other rolls. Thus in the forty-fifth of Henry III., the Constable of the Castle was ordered to sell wood in Windsor Park, and out of the proceeds to enclose it.[3] In the fiftieth of Edward III., we first hear of the New Park of Windsor called *Wythemere*, which then appears to have been enclosed.[4] Commissions had been previously appointed to enquire into the state and condition of Windsor, and of the manor, forest, and park, there.[5] Two hundred acres were enclosed by Edward IV. in the sixth year of his reign, adjoining to the town of New Windsor. This was a considerable addition to, if not the origin of, what is now the *Home Park*, called in 1509 the *Lytle Park*, and the scene of the hunting of Henry VII. and Philip King of Castile, where after dinner ' eyche of the kyngs kylled certene deare, to theire owne hands, with their crosbowes.'[6] Norden, in his map and survey,[7] made at the beginning of the reign of James I., in the year 1607, tells us that the Little Park at this period contained about 280 acres of good ground, with a herd of ' 240 fallow-

---

[1] Lipscomb's Bucks, vol. iv. pp. 545, 546.
[2] Annals of Windsor, vol. i. p. 30.
[3] Ib. p. 81.
[4] Ib. p. 178.

[5] Annals of Windsor, p. 134.
[6] Ib. p. 440.
[7] Given in Annals of Windsor, vol. ii. p. 31, from Harl. MSS. 3749.

deer, of antler 68, buckes 30, by supposition.' 'It paleth 3⅜ mile, and of itself hath small meanes.'

The Great Park at the same period (1607) was stated at 3,650 acres, and it was estimated to contain 1,800 fallow-deer. The red-deer were all in the forest outside. The extent of the Great Park is now (1864) about 1,000 acres less than in 1607 ; the number of deer the same as in that year, but the land that has been turned to other purposes was the poorest, and much better has been added.[1]

In the time of Queen Anne, according to the Duchess of Marlborough's celebrated ' Account of her Conduct ' (printed in 1742), in order to answer the Crown warrants for deer in the Windsor Great Park, it was necessary to keep up four or five thousand head of deer in the park, for which the allowance was but 500*l.* a year. The ranger was also obliged to be at the expense of making and sometimes of buying hay for the deer ; the keepers' wages were payable out of this allowance, with several other expenses, which (her Grace added) in parks belonging to the Crown are much greater than in others.[2]

Stowe, referring to Windsor Castle, speaks of ' the pleasant pastime arising out of the forest, chace, and fourteen parkes that waite upon it.'[3] In this enumeration he probably intended the Great and Little Parks of *Windsor, Moate Park, Sunning-hill Park.Follie-John Park,* and *Easthamstead Park,* all in Berkshire ; *Guilford Park, Henley Park, Woking Park, Chobham Park, Byfleet Park,* and *Bagshot Park,* in Surrey; and the parks of

Langley and *Ditton,* in Buckinghamshire. In Norden's curious survey of the Honor of Windsor, the extent of all these parks, besides that of the ' Rayles,' or enclosed parts of the forest, which were not properly ' Parks,' is given ; the whole drawn upon vellum and accurately coloured. The ' Rayles ' included in this account were those of Swinley, Bagshot, and Cranbourne. A copy of the general map of this survey is given in the ' Annals of Windsor.' A plan of the Great Park, on a larger scale, is given in Mr. Menzies's volume, as well as a survey of the same at the present period.

The *Moate Park* lay between the Great Park and Clewer, and, observes Mr. Menzies, ' with the exception of the small purchases made at Fyfields, preserves its ancient boundaries.' In 1650 a survey was made of it, when it was stated to contain 603 acres, 17 perches, and valued at 204*l.* ;[4] it was sold during the Usurpation with other Royal property, but repurchased by the Crown in 1684, and now forms part of the Great Park.

Sunning-hill Park is farther from Windsor, beyond Cranbourne Chase, and nearer to what is now called Virginia Water. ' This park,' we are informed,[5] ' possesses the privilege of being tithe-free as long as sixteen head of deer are kept in it.' Sunning-hill Park is supposed to have been granted by King Charles I. to the family of Cary.[6]

The Park of *Foli-John,* in New Lodge Walk of the Forest of Windsor, about two miles south of Bray, appears to have been enclosed by Oliver de Bordeaux, in

[1] Menzies's History of Windsor Great Park, fo. 1864, p. 9.
[2] Duchess of Marlborough's Account, &c., p. 292.
[3] Annals, p. 143, ed. 1631.
[4] Menzies, p. 14.
[5] Neale's Views of Seats, 1818, vol. i.
[6] Lysons' Berks, p. 382.

1316, by the license of the King (Edward II.) ; and in the same year the King granted to him in fee all the land and tenements of Foli-John at Hyermere, within the bounds of the forest. But this park and lands were subsequently reunited to the Castle and Manor of Windsor, by Edward III., in the thirty-third year of his reign.[1] From this period the park of Foli-John belonged to the Crown, and the names of its keepers often figure among the grants preserved in the Patent Rolls. In 1630 it passed from the Crown, having been granted to Henry Hene, Esq., created a baronet in 1642.[2]

The Park of *Easthamstead* is recognised as a Royal park in the thirty-ninth of Edward III.;[3] it was for many years a Royal residence. Here, according to Holingshed, Richard II. resorted for hunting, in August 1381. In 1531 it was the residence of Queen Catherine, when the Lords of the Council were sent hither to persuade her to be conformable to the King's will and consent to a divorce. It was enlarged by James I. in 1615; 250*l.* having been paid by his Majesty for that purpose.[4] It was granted by Charles I. to William Trumbull, Esq., whose son petitioned Charles II. in 1661, setting forth that 'the grant was on condition of his keeping 200 deer for his Majesty's recreation: the deer there,' he adds, ' have been universally destroyed, and it is almost impossible to procure any.'[5]

There appear to have been several other parks within the precincts of Windsor Forest, as we find by the licenses in the Patent Rolls. Thus, in the fortieth of Henry

III., Henry de Haia had license to assart and impark 240 acres of his domain lands of *Hexington* within the Forest of Windsor. And in the tenth of Edward I. the Priory of Ankerwyke was allowed to impark 100 acres of the waste of the Abbey of Chertsey, in *Egware*, within the bounds of the same forest. Again in the fourteenth of Edward II. John de Foxley was licensed to impark certain lands in Bray, within the forest of Windsor, called ' *Pokemere* ' (Puckmere, near Foxleyfarm, in Bray). In the eleventh of the following reign the King restored to the Bishop of Salisbury and his successors free chase of Bishopsbeere (Billingbere, near Maidenhead), in Windsor Forest.

The Bishops of Salisbury had also a palace and park at *Sunning*, near Reading, which is alluded to by Leland in his ' Itinerary ;' it was exchanged with Queen Elizabeth in 1574.[6] Near Reading also was *Whitley Park*, which is laid down in Saxton's map of 1574. This, before the Reformation, belonged to the Abbot of Reading, and is also noticed by Leland. It was granted by Queen Elizabeth to Sir Francis Knollys.[7] At *Stratfield Mortimer*, seven miles to the south-west of Reading, on the borders of Hampshire, were two parks which originally belonged to the Mortimers Earls of March, and afterwards became vested in the Crown: they were with the Manor granted by Queen Elizabeth, in 1564, to Henry Lord Hunsdon.[8] Another ancient and still existing park in this neighbourhood is at *Aldermarston*, for a long period the seat of the Forster family. It is noticed in Saxton's

[1] Annals of Windsor, vol. i. pp. 130, 187.
[2] Lysons' Magna Brittannia, Berks, p. 436.
[3] Annals of Windsor, vol. i. p. 178.
[4] Original papers *penes* the Baroness North.
[5] Cal. State Papers, 1661, Aug. 20.
[6] Lysons, p. 379.
[7] Ib. p. 341.
[8] Ib. p. 375.

Survey, and is remarkable for its fine old oak trees. At present it contains 120 acres and a herd of 100 fallow-deer. A more modern and still existing park is at *Hall Place*, in the parish of Henley, five miles from Maidenhead and four from Henley-on-Thames. It belongs to Sir Gilbert East, Bart., and is a park of 150 acres, with a herd of about 100 fallow-deer.

There is also a park at *Englefield*, the seat of Mr. Benyon, which is said to have existed in the reign of Queen Elizabeth, when it belonged to Sir Francis Walsingham, having been forfeited by Sir Francis Englefield. It contains about 350 acres, and about 300 fallow-deer. Either this park, or one at Bradfield, in the adjoining parish, is marked in Saxton's Survey.

Saxton's Survey also gives us a park at *Yattendon*, about eight miles to the northeast of Newbury, and eleven miles west of Reading. Here, in 1447, Sir John Norris, Master of the Great Wardrobe to King Henry VI., and ancestor of Lord Norris, of Rycot, had a license to embattle the manor house, and to impark 600 acres of land.[1]

In the parish of Spen, or Spene, there appears also to have been a park noticed in Saxton's Survey, which was given by Sir William Essex to King Henry VIII. in 1542.[2]

Saxton also notices parks at *Hamstead-Marshall*, and at *Hungerford*, in the south-western angle of the county : the former was, since the early part of the seventeenth century, a principal seat of the Craven family, and there were deer here, as appears by the view of the place, in Kip's ' Views of Seats,' in 1714.

At *Welford*, six miles north-west of Newbury, is an existing park of 100 acres, with the same number of fallow-deer.

Farther north, towards Wantage, is *Wolley* Park, containing under 100 acres, with a herd of 180 fallow-deer. This park was enclosed about the end of the last century. A small park exists also at *Buckland*, on the borders of Oxfordshire, near Faringdon, belonging to Sir William Throckmorton.

It remains to notice an ancient park which once existed at *Radley*, between Abingdon and Oxford, which was disparked, as Leland informs us, ' by reason that the scollars of Oxford muche resortyd thither to hunt.'[3] This was an old complaint against the Oxford scholars, and even attracted the notice of the Legislature, inasmuch as an Act of Parliament was passed in the ninth of Henry V. (A.D. 1421), which enacted that 'scholars of Oxford hunting disorderly in parks in the counties of Oxford, Berks, and Bucks, shall be banished the University.'[4]

Existing Deer Parks in Berkshire.

1. WINDSOR . . Her Majesty the Queen.
2. SUNNING-HILL, Mr. Crutchley.
3. ALDERMARSTON, Mr. Higford Burr.
4. ENGLEFIELD . Mr. Benyon.
5. HALL-PLACE . Sir Gilbert East, Bt.
6. HAMSTEAD-MARSHALL, Earl of Craven.
7. WELFORD . . Mr. Eyre.
8. WOLLEY . . . Mr. Wroughton.
9. BUCKLAND . . Sir William Throckmorton, Bart.

---

[1] Lysons, p. 445.
[2] Ib., p. 373.

[3] Leland's Itin. vol. vii. p. 75, fol. 64.
[4] Rolls of Parliament, vol. iv. p. 131.

OXFORDSHIRE.

THE Royal Park of *Woodstock*, according to Rous, in his ' History of the Kings of England,' was founded in the fourteenth year of Henry I. (A.D. 1113–1114), and was the oldest in England : its claim to be considered the oldest park in this country cannot, however, be maintained ;[1] but it has been supposed that it might have been the first park enclosed with a wall, a permanent fence, which the great plenty of stones in the neighbourhood would naturally suggest. Rous adds, but it is doubtful whether he had any authority for doing so, that many villages were destroyed in its completion, and that it was seven English miles in circuit.

Of this favourite seat of Royalty it will be sufficient here to observe, that it was granted by Queen Anne to the Duke of Marlborough in 1705, and the name changed to *Blenheim*. In 1666, as appears by a warrant in the State Papers, the keepers were paid an annual sum of 40*l.* as wages, and a like amount allowed for provision of hay for the deer.[2] At present it contains 2,800 acres, of which about 1,150 are open to the deer: there is a herd of about 770 fallow and 64 red-deer.

The following curious service has reference to this ancient and Royal park. The Manor of Stanton-Harcourt in this county was held of the Crown ' by the

service of finding four *brousers, i. e.* men to cut the brushwood, in Woodstock Park in winter time, when the snow shall happen to fall, and tarry and lie and abide be the space of two days, and so to find the said brousers there brousing, so long as the same doth lye, every brouser to have to his lodging every night, one billet of wood, the length of his axe halve, and that to carry to his lodgings upon the edge of his axe ; and the king's bailiffs of the demesnes, or of the Hundred of Wootton, coming to give warning for the said brousers, shall blow his horn at the gate of the Manor of Stanton-Harcourt, and there the said bailiff to have a loaf of bread, a gallon of ale, and a piece of beef of the said Lord of Stanton-Harcourt ; and the said lord to have of custom yearly out of the said park, one buck in summer and one doe in winter ; and also the Lord of Stanton-Harcourt must fell, make, rear, and carry all the grass growing in one meadow within the park of Woodstock, called Stanton and Southley Mead, and the fellers and the makers thereof have used to have of custom of the king's majesty's charge sixpence in money and two gallons of ale.'[3]

Cornbury, another ancient Royal park, long alienated from the Crown, lies to the west of Woodstock : it is recognised as a park as early as the thirteenth of Edward III., when John de Solers was appointed

---

[1] See p. 13.
[2] S. P. Dom., May 16, 1666.

[3] Skelton's Oxfordshire, Wootton Hund., p. 18.

keeper of the king's horses in his park at Cornbury during pleasure.[1]

At the same period Joan, widow of Thomas de Musgrave, held certain lands in Blechingdon by the service of carrying one shield of brawn, price twopence-halfpenny, to the king whenever he should hunt in this park of Cornbury, it being understood that one shield of brawn so carried to the king on his first day of hunting should suffice during the whole of his stay at his manor of Woodstock.[2]

Cornbury remained in the Crown till after the Restoration, when it was granted by Charles II. to the great Lord Chancellor Clarendon, who took his second title of Viscount Cornbury from this beautiful park and place. Plot, in his 'History of Oxfordshire,' makes some remarks upon the deer in this park having dwarf and irregular heads, the result, as he contends, of a part of it having been turned into a coney warren before the Restoration; 'but as soon,' he adds, 'as the warren was destroyed, they came again to have as fair branched heads as any deer whatever in the adjoining forest'[3] (of Whichwood). Evelyn records a visit here in October, 1664 :—' I went,' he says, ' with my Lord Viscount Cornbury to Cornbury, to assist him in the planting of the park, and beare him company, a house lately built by the Erle of Denbigh in the middle of a sweet park, walled with a dry wall ; the parke well stock'd.'[4] At present there are about 450 acres open to the deer, of the old forest breed ; the number does not exceed 140.

Still more surrounded by the forest of Whichwood, of which, like Cornbury, it was an adjunct, was the Royal seat and park of *Langley* : it is said to have been occasionally used by the Court till the reign of Charles I. King James I. was here in progress in August, 1605.[5] It remained in the Crown, though long disparked, till the recent enclosure of Whichwood Forest.

South of the forest near Witney is *Minster Lovel*, where Sir William· Lovel had license to impark certain lands in the eighteenth of Henry VI.[6]

North of Woodstock are the parks of *Ditchley* and *Glympton.* The former contains 330 acres, and 200 fallow-deer, the latter 72 acres and 60 fallow-deer. Neither of these parks is marked in the Surveys of this county by Saxton in 1574, by Speed in 1605, or by Plot in 1676. There appears also to have been a park at *Broughton* Castle, the seat of the Lords Say and Sele. The name is preserved in the '*Buck Park,*' and in the Records of the Corporation of Banbury, 'The Lord Sayes Buck,' is incidentally mentioned.

At *Hook-Norton,* in the north of the county, on the borders of Warwickshire, Leland notices an ancient park, long disused and forgotten. He describes it as ' a fayre Park and an old Manor-Place. It longed to Chaucer, then to the Poles, Dukes of Suffolk by marriage, now from Brandon to the kynge by exchange.'[7]

If the map in Plot's ' History of Oxfordshire ' may be taken as an authority, there were in 1676 parks at *Hanwell,* the seat

---

[1] Cal. Pat. Rolls, p. 135.
[2] Kennett, vol. ii. pp. 73, 74.
[3] Plot's History of Oxfordshire, 2nd ed. p. 194.
[4] Evelyn's Memoirs, vol. i. p. 350.

[a] Nichols's Progresses of James I., vol. i. p. 529.
[6] Cal. Pat. Rolls, p. 281.
[7] Leland's Itinerary, vol. vii. pp. 72-3. Fol. 63.

of the Copes ; at *Blechingdon*, belonging
to the Annesleys Earls. of Anglesea, and
at *Yarnton*, near Oxford, belonging to the
Spencers. At *Beckley*, on the borders of
Otmoor, about five miles north-east from
Oxford, was undoubtedly an ancient park,
for which a Charter was obtained by
Hugh de Spencer, in 1312. It afterwards
reverted to the Crown, and in 1457 King
Henry VI. presented Archbishop Chichele
with twelve trees from his park at Beckley
towards building All Souls College.[1] It
is marked in all the ancient maps, although
long disparked : a farm called ' Park-
House ' still attests the site.

License to enclose a park in the neighbouring village of *Elsfield,* three miles and
a half from Oxford, was granted to Gilbert de Elsfield in the first year of Edward III.[2] This park, if it ever existed,
has been long destroyed, but an ancient
one remains at *Holton,* five miles east of
Oxford, once the seat of the Bardolfs.
The date of the park is unknown, but if
we may judge from the size of the oaks,
one of which measures twenty-seven feet
in circumference at five feet from the
ground, it must be of great antiquity.
Holton Park contains about 200 acres,
and 100 fallow-deer.

Before noticing the parks south of Oxford, the *Park or Paddock in the College
of St. Mary Magdalen* in the University
itself, claims a brief description. Of this
beautiful, and may it not be called unique

park, Dr. Bloxam writes :—' My impression
is that deer were first introduced into a
portion of the space behind the new
buildings (then a bowling-green and gardens) about the beginning of the last century, and that, as they increased, more
space was given to them till the whole was
at last absorbed into what is now called
" The Grove ; " but no historical account,
or even tradition of them, is extant.'[3]

The extent of this miniature park is
eleven acres, and there is a herd of forty
fallow-deer.

Nuneham-Courtenay, the seat of the
Harcourt family, was purchased by Simon Lord Harcourt in 1710, and the
beautiful park probably enclosed by his
lordship subsequently : it is said to contain 1,200 acres, six miles and a half in
circumference.

At *Ricot,* near Thame, the ancient seat
of the Lords Norreys, and afterwards of
the Berties Earls of Abingdon, was a park
which is marked in all the old maps, and
which has been disparked within the
present century. Kip's view of this place,
taken in 1714, notices ' The East India
Deere Parke,' besides another and larger
park.

Thame Park, containing at present 250
acres, and 180 fallow-deer, can lay claim
to great antiquity, the abbey here being
refounded by Alexander, Bishop of Lincoln, in 1138, in the park[4] of Thame,
which had before belonged to the Bishop.[5]

---

[1] Guide to Architectural Antiquities in the
Neighbourhood of Oxford, p. 209, &c.
[2] Cal. Pat. Rolls, p. 100.
[3] In 1707 there is a charge in the Liber
Computi, ' Damas in arbusti interficientibus.'
At the same time, and afterwards, it was found
necessary to purchase venison for the gaudy ;
the deer had increased sufficiently when George
III. visited the College in 1786 to attract his

attention. No deer are represented in Magdalen Grove in 1731, as appears by the view
in the Oxford Almanack of that year, but they
are engraved in the view of the College in
1787, in the same Almanack.
[4] Query whether the word *parcus* here ought
not to be translated inclosure ?
[5] Dugdale's Monasticon, new ed., vol. v.
p. 404.

It occurs in all the ancient maps, and has long been the seat of the Wenman and Wickham families.

South of Thame, and on the very verge of the county of Buckingham, is *Stonor.* Here is a · fayre Parke,' noticed by Leland, although not appearing in Saxton's Surveys. ' This Park is nearly three miles in circumference, and contains a considerable portion of beech woodland, the mast produced by which, and the thyme and other fragrant herbs with which the pasture abounds, are said to contribute much to the flavour of the venison and to have been the cause of its celebrity.'[1] Another park, then belonging to the Stonor family, is marked by Plot in the adjoining parish of *Watlington.*

The Royal Manor and Honor of *Ewelme,* which once belonged to the De la Poles Dukes of Suffolk, a little to the south of Watlington, formerly boasted a 'right fair parke,'[2] of which the following notices have been preserved:—On the 9th of May, 1536, King Henry VIII. appointed Edward Ashfield to the office of keeper of the Manor of Ewelme, with the garden there, as also keeper of the Park of Ewelme and master of the wild beasts there, with the herbage and pannage of the said park, and the browse and windfalls there, &c. ; and again, in 1551-2, King Edward VI. conveyed the Manor and Park of Ewelme to his sister, the Princess Elizabeth, for her life. In a survey of this manor, taken in 1609, it is stated that Lord William Knollys was then keeper of the park, and master of the wild beasts in the same, in which park there was a house or lodge in

good repair, and that the same park contained in circuit 3,000 paces. On the 21st of March, 1627, King Charles I., by Letters Patent, conveyed to Sir Christopher Nevil, K.B., and Sir Edmund Sawyer, their heirs and assigns for ever, in consideration of the sum of 4,300*l.*, all that park called Ewelme Park, containing 895 acres, which was part of the manor of Ewelme ; also six acres, four of which were in a place called Haseley, and two in a place called Ellesmere, the keeper of the park having heretofore been accustomed to save the hay thereof for the deer and wild beasts in the said park, to be held subject to a rent of 60*l.* per annum.[3] Ewelme Park was probably disparked at this period: it does not appear in Plot's Survey of the year 1676, although marked in the older maps, together with a smaller park in the adjoining village of *Bensington,* or *Benson.*

In the neighbourhood of Henley are two existing parks, *Greys-Court* and *Crowsley* : the former is an ancient park, noticed by Leland, in the Elizabethan period, the seat of the House of Knollys : at present it is reduced to thirty acres, with 90 head of fallow-deer. Formerly, as appears by the ancient surveys, it must have been of much larger extent. *Crowsley Park* is thought to have been enclosed in the time of James II., when the present mansion was built. It has an area of about 200 acres, with a herd of 190 fallow-deer.

Both Saxton and Speed concur in marking a park at *Maple-Durham,* the ancient seat of the Blounts ; and it would appear by the map in Plot's ' Oxfordshire '

[1] Neale's Views of Seats, 1818, vol. iii.
[2] Leland's Itin. vol. ii. p. 34, fol. 7.
[3] Historical Notices of Swyncomb and Ewelme, by the Hon. and Rev. Alfred Napier, 4to. Oxford, 1858, pp. 204, 207, 212, 217.

that there was in 1676 a park at *Caver-.*
sham, at that time belonging to the Craven
family.

Existing Parks in Oxfordshire.

1. BLENHEIM . . The Duke of Marlborough.
2. CORNBURY . . Lord Churchill.
3. DITCHLEY . . Viscount Dillon.
4. GLYMPTON . . Mr. Barnett.

5. HOLTON . . . Mr. Biscoe.
6. COLLEGE OF ST. MARY MAGDALEN,
Oxford.
7. NUNEHAM-COURTENAY, The Rev.
William Harcourt.
8. THAME PARK. . Lady Wenman.
9. STONOR . . . Lord Camoys.
10. GREYS-COURT . Hon. and Rev. Sir
Francis Staple-
ton, Bart.
11. CROWSLEY PARK, Mr. Baskerville.

CHAPTER VII.

NOTES ON DEER PARKS IN THE COUNTIES

OF

LEICESTERSHIRE,	WARWICKSHIRE,
RUTLANDSHIRE,	AND
NORTHAMPTONSHIRE,	WORCESTERSHIRE.

The Keeper's Lodge, in the Great Park, at Staunton-Harold, Leicestershire, 1840.

CHAPTER VII.

LEICESTERSHIRE.

URTON in his 'Description of Leicestershire,' printed in 1622, observes of the parks in this county : 'This shire hath bene reasonable well stored with places for vert and venison, but now not so well furnished ; the ancient Forest of Charn-wood, commonly called Loughborough Forest, by reason of the vicinity, hath long ago been disafforested,[1] of which I shall speake hereafter in his place. The Chase of Leicester is now well replenished with game. It did anciently belong to the Earles of Leicester, who had many parkes also neere adjoyning. It now be-longs to the Dutchie of Lancaster.' Bur-ton proceeds to give a list of 'the parks now in use.' But perhaps the most con-venient arrangement will be to notice those ancient parks first, which were in the immediate neighbourhood of Leices-ter ; next, those in the vicinity of Charn-wood Forest, and afterwards those in other parts of the county; premising that,

[1] It passed from the Crown to the Lords of Manors in the time of Henry II.

as there is no notice in Domesday Book of any park or hay in this county, the deer were probably confined to their primæval haunts—the forests of Leicester and Charnwood, before the Norman Conquest. Four parks are marked by Saxton in the precincts of Leicester Forest. These, according to Leland in his 'Itinerary,'[1] were :—

1. '*The parke* by *S. Mary Abbey*. (The Frith park sumtyme a mighty large thyng, now partely disparkid, and partely bering the name of the new parke, welle palid).'[1] The park of St. Mary Abbey was granted by Henry Duke of Lancaster to the new college at Leicester, called the Newark.[2]

2. '*Bellemont's Leye*, sometyme a great park by Leicester, but now (writes Leland) converted to pasture.'

3. *Barne Park*, also called Baron Park, belonged, as the former did, to the Earls of Leicester. 'Standing upon the side of Leicester Forest, near unto Kirby, was, in 1647, the Inheritance of Sir Henry Hastings, of Braunston, knight.'[2]

4. *Tooley Park*, 'sometime belonging to the Castle at Earle Shilton, now (writes Burton) part of the Dutchy of Lancaster.' 'All these,' adds Leland, 'be the king's,' and all have been for many generations disparked.[3]

The *Frith Park, Bird's Nest* or *New Park*, claims a more particular notice. In 1279 it was found by inquisition that Ed-

mund Earl of Leicester had at Shilton, 'boscum et liberam chaceam et *parcum* qui vocatur *Tholowd*.'[4]

In 1297 it was found that the same Edmund Earl of Leicester and Lancaster, the King's brother, at the time of his death, held Frith Park, in the Forest of Leicester.[5] In the marriage-settlement of King Henry VI., in 1444, he gives to his intended consort, *inter alia*, the Honour of Leicester, including several manors in and about the forest, *cum agistamento parci de la Frith*.[6]

In 1571 William Lord Cobham was cited, to show by what title he held Frith Park otherwise called *the New Park of Byrdesnest* ;[7] and in 1606, a survey was made with a view to this park being offered for sale ; the whole number of acres, 815a. 2r. 30p., worth by the year 407*l*. 11*s*. 11*d*.[8]

In the precincts of Leicester Forest also are *Kirby* and *Desford*, at both of which were ancient parks ; Kirby, imparked by William Lord Hastings by license, in 1474, now, says Burton, the inheritance of Sir Henry Hastings ; and *Desford*, which he includes among the disparked parks, belonging to the ancient Earls of Leicester, now part of the Dutchy of Lancaster. '*Newhall Park*, belonging to Mr. Turvile of Thurleston ' in this neighbourhood, is found in the same list, as well as '*Hinkley* sometime belonging to the Barony of Hinkley.'[9]

---

[1] Leland's Itin. vol. i. p. 21.

[2] Nichols's Leicestershire, vol. iv. pp. 782–3, taken from Burton's corrected copy of his History in 1641.

[3] I find Tooley Park included in the list of Parks, &c. belonging to his Majesty in 1608. See Appendix to the 11th Report of Commissioners on Woods, &c., p. 701.

[4] Nichols's Leicestershire, vol. iv. p. 774.

[5] Esch. 25. Edw. I., No. 51, Leicr.

[6] Rot. Pat. 27 Hen. VI., vol. v. p. 118.

[7] Trin. Rec. 14 Eliz. rot. 24.

[8] Original document *penes* W. Herrick, of Beaumanor, Esq., quoted by Nichols in the History of Leicestershire.

[9] Burton's Description of Leicestershire, p. 6.

Kirkby-Malory, near Tooley Park, was a large park, very well wooded and stored with deer, and set in the lifetime of Sir Thomas Noel, Baronet, since deceased (1696), for several years (deer excepted) at 100*l.* per annum, and the running of six horses,[1] &c.

'A belt of parks almost wholly encircled Charnwood,' writes Potter in his history of that forest, 'to which indeed they owed their origin, either as affording facilities for more free hunting than the thick woodland permitted, or as furnishing additional protection to the forest itself. This belt was formed by the parks of *Groby*, of which there were four, extending altogether several miles on the southern borders, and of *Bardon, Whitwick, Gracedieu, Garendon, Burleigh, Loughborough*, two parks, *Beaumanor, Quorndon, Swithland*, and *Bradgate*.'[2]

It was found by inquisition in the year 1279, that the Lord William de Ferrers held the manor of *Groby*, and had in his domain four parks. In 1287 the pasture and pannage were worth per annum 66*s.* 8*d.*, and the underwood of the said parks 6*s.* 8*d.* per annum. In Leland's time, Groby was the inheritance of the Marquis of Dorset; he observes, 'there is a fine large parke by the place a vi miles in compase.'[3] Groby was disparked before 1622, but is marked as a park in all the older maps.

Bardon Park, originally 1,225 acres, imparked previously to the year 1300; a considerable portion was originally *infra forestam*. It belonged to Roger Quincy

Earl of Winchester,[4] and afterwards to the Earls of Oxford, according to Burton, who places it among the disparked parks in 1622.

Whitwick originally belonged to Hugh de Grentesmaisnell. Queen Elizabeth, in 1569, granted it to Sir Henry Hastings, Knight and Henry Cutler, Gentleman. It is included in Burton's list of disused parks in 1622.

Gracedieu, adjoining Whitwick, but not found marked as a park in the ancient surveys.

Garendon Park is included in Burton's list of 'parks which are now in use,' and as belonging to the Earl of Rutland in 1622. I conclude it was afterwards disparked, as the present park of Garendon, containing about 1,500 acres, of which somewhat less than 500 are occupied by a herd of 300 fallow-deer, was enclosed by Sir Ambrose Phillipps in the latter part of the reign of Charles II.

Burleigh or *Burley* was a park in use in 1622, when it belonged to the Earl of Huntingdon.

Loughborough Park was imparked by Hugh le Despencer, and disparked in the year 1630,[5] according to Burton's corrected copy of his history in 1641. Leland observes of it, 'Lughborow parke a mile from Lughborow toune. This parke cam to the Marquise of Dorset by exchange of landes with the kinge.'[6]

Beaumanor.—Henry, first Lord Beaumont, who died in 1340, according to Camden, is said to have enclosed the park here with a stone wall. It is thus

---

[1] Nichols's Leicestershire, vol. iv. p. 767.
[2] Potter's Charnwood Forest, 4to. London, 1842, p. 117.
[3] Itin. vol. i. p. 19.

[4] Potter's Charnwood Forest, p. 160.
[5] Nichols's Leicestershire, vol. iv. p. 782.
[6] Itinerary, vol. i. p. 20.

noticed by Leland in his ' Itinerary;'[1] ' riding a little farther I left the Parke of Bewmaner, closid with a stone walle, and a pratie logye yn it, longging a late to Beaumont.' It was disparked before 1622.[2]

Quorndon, supposed to be the same as Barrow Park, which belonged to the Earls of Chester, and which existed as early as the reign of Henry I.[3]

Swithland is not found marked as a park in Saxton's or Speed's Surveys. It is near Bradgate.

Bradgate Park was imparked before the year 1247, as appears by the very curious agreement between Roger de Quincy, Earl of Winchester, and Roger de Somery, Baron of Dudley, about their mutual hunting in Charnwood Forest and Bradgate Park, dated in that year, and which I have given at length in a former part of this work. In its present state, this celebrated and historical park is about seven miles in circumference, and formed into several divisions by means of stone walls, the materials for which are found on the spot ; it is mostly covered with the common fern or brakes, and the projecting bare and abrupt rocks rising out here and there, with a few scattered gnarled and shivered oaks, in their last stage of decay, present a scene of wildness and desolation, highly contrasted with some of the beautiful adjoining valleys and fertile country. There were about 500 deer, chiefly fallow, some

years ago ; the venison is esteemed some of the finest in the kingdom, arising from the peculiar wild verdure of the park, but numbers perish every winter from the severity of the cold and little shelter that it affords them.[4] 'At Bradegate there is a fair parke,' says Leland, 'a vi miles compace, and a lodge lately buildid there by the Lord Thomas Grey, Marquise of Dorset, father to Henry that is now Marquise.'[5]

There appears to have been another old park in this district, called *Acle*, or *Ackley* or *Okeley Park*, in the parish of Sheepsted. It was of considerable extent, and was given by one of the Earls of Leicester to the Abbey of St. Mary de Pratis. Among other privileges the abbot and convent had the right shoulder of every wild beast (*cujuslibet feræ*) taken in the park of Acle.[6]

At *Ashby de la Zouche* were two parks, belonging, in Burton's days, to the Earl of Huntingdon. ' One of which parkes, called the Old Park, was belonging to the Baron Zouch of Ashby, the other imparked by William Lord Hastings, by license of K. Edward IV. (14th E. IV.).' The smaller of these is marked in Saxton's map as ' *Prestop Park.*'

Donington Park, the seat of the Marquis of Hastings, is also noticed by Burton as a park belonging to the Earl of Huntingdon. Leland observes, ' Dunnington Castelle is in the border of the Forest of Charley towards Darbyshire, and hath

---

[1] Itin. vol. i. p. 20.

[2] In the Compotus of John Kyrkeby, bailiff of Elizabeth Lady Beaumont for Beaumanor, 3 & 4 Hen. VI. is this item :—' in vad' Rob'ti Chalous cementar' custod' mur' lapid' parci et laund' ib'm viijs. ;' which I understand to imply that this mason had a yearly fee of 8s. for keeping the stone wall of the park in

repair. At the view of Frankpledge, 22 Edward IV. Ralph Shirley was steward of Beaumanor ; Radulpho Shirley, senescallo.

[3] Nichols's Leicestershire, vol. iii. p. 120.

[4] See Bloxam's Description of Bradgate Park, 12mo. Leicester, note 3.

[5] Itin. vol. i. p. 19.

[6] Potter's Charnwood Forest, p. 174.

thereby a park. As I remember it is an 8 miles from Leicester, it longgid as I herd sumtyme to the Erles of Leycester, now it is the kinges.'[1] Here is a herd both of fallow and red-deer.

At *Coleorton* in this neighbourhood was an ancient park, imparked by John de Maureward, in the reign of Edward I.[2]

Staunton-Harold, the ancient seat of the Shirleys Earls Ferrers, is marked as a park in all the older maps, but it is not known when it was first enclosed. There were two parks here : the great park, towards Bredon on the hill, was disparked by Sir Henry Shirley, Bart., in 1623. The smaller park by the house remains to this day. It was in the former that Francis Shirley, Esq., who died in 1571, is recorded to have passed most of his time, ' with his horses, hounds, and deere in his parke at Staunton, wherein he had great delight.'[3] The great park is still so called, though divided into farms. Within its precincts stands ' The Lodge,' an ancient house moated round, formerly the residence of the keeper, and which I have caused to be engraved as an appropriate illustration to this work.[4] The present park of Staunton-Harold contains about 129 acres, with a herd of 230 fallow-deer.

Bagworth Park, reimparked by William Lord Hastings in the year 1474, appears, says Nichols, to have been of old times very large and extensive. He estimates the extent at 400 acres of land. In 1325 the abbot and convent of St. Mary de Pratis applied to the king in Parliament for the tithes of Bagworth Park,[5] which in

1622 was the inheritance of Sir Robert Banaster, Knight, and was then ' in use,' but has been long disparked.

Bosworth Park contains 400 acres of land, and a herd of about 250 fallow-deer, all black. This park must be comparatively modern, not being marked either in Saxton's or Speed's maps.

Gopsall Park appears also to be modern, though said to have existed two hundred years. It is a park of 500 acres, with 264 fallow and 15 red-deer.

On the borders of this county and Northamptonshire is *Holt*, or *Hoult* as Burton writes it, where was, in his time, a disused park, enclosed by Thomas Palmer, Esq., by license granted twenty-sixth of Henry VI. North of this is *Laund*, where was an ancient park marked in Saxton's Survey, which appears to have been granted by charter in the thirty-second year of Henry III., and which grant was confirmed to the prior there, by King Edward II., in the twenty-second year of his reign.[6]

Further north is *Cold-Overton*, where John de Segrave obtained license to make a deer-leap (saltatorium), ' in parco suo de Cold-Overton,' in the fourteenth year of Edward III.

In the hundred of Framland, in the northeastern angle of this county, is *Croxton Park*, belonging to the Duke of Rutland. It contains 570 acres, exclusive of plantations and water, and a herd of 350 fallow-deer ; and is enclosed with a stone wall. Although not marked as a park in the old maps, it has been supposed from an

---

[1] Lel. Itin. vol. i. p. 23, fol. 24.
[2] Nichols's Leicestershire, vol. iv. p. 782.
[3] Stemmata Shirleiana, p. 50.
[4] See p. 37 for the grant of ' Parkerrhippe,'

granted by George Shirley, Esq., in 1584.
[5] Nichols's Leicestershire, vol. iv. p. 989.
[6] Cal. Pat. Rolls, p. 326.

L

expression in the register of the Abbey of Croxton (infra ambitum muri) to have been a park enclosed with a wall as early as the year 1162. From a careful examination of the passage however of the register, as printed by Dugdale, it appears to me that the expression *parci de Croxton* probably refers to the enclosure there, as distinguished from the open lands, in the same sense as that in which it is constantly used in the North of England and in Scotland and Ireland. The present park, I suspect therefore, from its not appearing in the lists of Saxton, Speed, or Burton, was not enclosed till

after the middle of the seventeenth century.

Existing Deer Parks in Leicestershire.

1. BRADGATE .	. Earl of Stamford and Warrington.
2. GARENDON .	. Mr. Phillipps, now called De Lisle.
3. DONINGTON .	. Marquis of Hastings.
4. STAUNTON-HAROLD, The Earl Ferrers.	
5. BOSWORTH .	. Sir A. Dixie, Bart.
6. GOPSALL .	. The Earl Howe.
7. CROXTON .	. The Duke of Rutland.

RUTLAND.

A CONSIDERABLE portion of the little county of Rutland was in former days occupied by the Royal Forest, which went by the same name, traces of which appear in the numerous enclosed woods with which Speed's map of the county is studded. Rutland Forest was also called 'Lee-fielde,' and to the north of it was the ancient park or wood of Okeham, called 'Fliteris,' enclosed by Richard Earl of Cornwall, by license, in the thirtieth year of Henry III.[2] In Saxton's map it is engraved 'Flyttern Parke:' it is mentioned as Okeham Park, from whence it is not far distant, in the forty-seventh of Edward III., when William Gambion was appointed keeper during pleasure.[3]

Ridlington Park, in the southern dis-

trict of this forest, is recognised as a park in the thirty-ninth of Henry III., when it was the subject of an inquest on the part of Peter de Montfort;[4] it afterwards belonged to the Harringtons, and is marked as a park both in the Surveys of Saxton (1576) and Speed (about 1610).

South of Ridlington the Bishops of Lincoln had a park marked in the ancient surveys at *Liddington*, which the Patent Rolls show to have been increased by license in the fifth of Edward III. with sixty acres of land, and to have been enclosed with a stone wall.[5]

Near Burley-on-the-Hill, in the centre of the county, Saxton marks a park, called '*Barnsdale.*'

At *Burley* was 'a princely park and

---

[1] Monasticon, vol. vi. pt. 2, p. 872, ed. 1830.
[2] Cal. Pat. Rolls, p. 23.

[3] Cal. Pat. Rolls, p. 47.
[4] Ib. p. 27.
[5] Ib. p. 111.

woods adjoining,' purchased from the Harringtons of Exton, by the celebrated George Villiers Duke of Buckingham, 'who made it one of the finest seats in these parts of England.'[1] Among the State Papers is a warrant, dated December 30, 1634, to advance to John Scandaren 100*l.*, for bringing 40 red-deer alive from Hatfield Chase, Yorkshire, to this park, no doubt a present from the King to the Duke.[2] Evelyn visited it in 1654, and observes, 'Next by Burleigh House, belonging to the Duke of Buckingham, and worthily reckon'd among the noblest seates in England, situate on the brow of a hill, built *a la moderne*, near a park wall'd in, and a fine wood at the descent.'[3] Near Burley is *Exton Park*, enclosed by license of Charles I. about the fifteenth

year of his reign. It is a noble existing park of 800 acres, with a herd of 400 fallow-deer.

One other park remains in this county, at *Normanton*, a little to the south of Exton : it contains 700 acres, 400 of which are appropriated to a herd of about 500 fallow-deer. The date of its enclosure is uncertain.

In Speed's map, it may be added, a park is marked at *Uppingham*, and others are given in the map attached to 'Wright's Rutlandshire' (1684) at *Martinsthorp*, Lord Denbigh's, and at the Priory at *Brooke.*

Existing Parks in the County of Rutland.

1. EXTON . . Earl of Gainsborough.
2. NORMANTON. Lord Aveland.

NORTHAMPTONSHIRE.

MORTON, in his 'Natural History of Northamptonshire,' printed in 1712, observes that there are more parks in this county than in any other county in England, and proceeds to add, that although some of them, particularly those which bear that name in the older maps of the county, are now disused, and retain only the name; yet the number is rather enlarged than diminished, and that there are now above twenty parks that have deer in them, and they all lie at a convenient distance from the houses of

the owners, whereas some of the older ones, now disparked, were remote.[4]

The Forest of Rockingham, spread over the northern districts of this county, on the borders of Rutlandshire, appears to have been from the earliest times studded with a number of parks, besides several '*Lawns, in the nature of parks*,' as we find from the 'Reports on Woods and Forests and Land Revenue of the Crown,' submitted to Parliament in 1792.[5] There were in this forest at this period 'the Lawn of Benefield, 384 acres, in the

---

[1] Wright's Rutlandshire, 1684, p. 30.
[2] S. P. O. Domestic, p. 423.
[3] Evelyn's Memoirs, 4to. ed., vol. i. p. 276.

[4] Morton's History, p. 12.
[5] 9th Report, p. 549.

tenure of Mr. Hatton; the Lawn of Farming-Woods, 200 acres, in the tenure of Lord Ossory; the Lawn of Moorhay, 316 acres; and the Lawn of Sulehay, 51 acres, in the tenure of Lord Westmoreland. Of the first of these lawns it is reported that 'it is a tract of pasture land, in the nature of a park, enclosed, and set apart for the feeding of the deer, granted by Queen Elizabeth in the twenty-fifth year of her reign to Sir Christopher Hatton.'[1] The Patent Rolls preserve the names of several ancient parks licensed within the forest verge, of which the following may be taken as examples. In the first of Edward I. the manor of *Brigstock*, with the park, was assigned to Queen Eleanor in dowry. In the eighteenth of the same reign, Walter de Langton had license to impark his wood of *Ashley* in the same forest, and two years later a further license to increase it. In the thirty-fifth of Edward I. the Abbot of Peterborough was licensed to impark certain woods within the bounds of this forest, and in the ninth of the next reign Humphry de Bassingburne had another license of the same description. The Park of *Drayton*, near Thrapston, a little south of the forest, was imparked in the second year of Edward III. by a license granted to Simon de Drayton, the extent originally being but 30 acres, increased by another license in the fourth of the same reign. A license was in the second of Edward III. granted to Robert Wivill, clerk, to impark his wood of Littlehawe, near Loveden (*Liveden?*) in this county. The manor of Liveden, which was for a long period the seat of the Tresham family, is probably intended,

and here a park appears marked in Saxton's map of the county, dated in 1576. The Park of *Haringworth*, within the forest, the principal seat of the Zouches, is recognised in the third of Edward III., and a license granted to William la Zouche to make a deer-leap within that manor. In the seventeenth and twenty-second of this reign Simon Simeon was licensed to enclose and impark his wood of *Gratton* or *Gretton*, in the adjoining parish, 'parvo fossato et bassa haiâ.'

Frequent notices also occur in the Patent Rolls with relation to the Royal parks of *Clyff*, or *King's Cliff*, or *Clive*, and *Brigstock*, within the forest; the latter has been already mentioned, and appears to have been a favourite Royal Preserve, on the edge of the Forest of Rockingham. Leland, in his 'Itinerary,' with the accustomed accuracy of the old topographer, notices that there were not red but fallow-deer in Rockingham Forest, and 'divers lodges for the kepers of the falow dere yn it.' He observed also, 'the fair Lodge' in Haringworth Park, 'long tyme in the Souches' handes,' and of Clyff Park, that 'it is partely waullid with stone and partely palid.'[2]

Besides Brigstock, Liveden, Haringworth, and Clyff, Saxton's Survey records parks at *Colly-Weston, Fotheringhay,* and near *Pipwell,* and at *Gedington,* the last known as *Gedington Chase,* in 1712, belonging to the Duke of Montague; at this latter period, as we learn from the map in Morton's 'History of Northamptonshire,' many changes had taken place and many new parks had been enclosed; near Stamford the Park of *Burghley,* Lord Exeter's;

[1] 9th Report, p. 539.

[2] Leland's Itin. vol. i. pp. 14, 24, and vol. v. p. 107.

near *Rockingham* Lord Rockingham's; and at *Deane* Lord Cardigan's: the latter at present is a park of 700 acres, with about 400 fallow and a few red-deer.

A little to the north of Deane is *Blatherwick*, an existing park of 566 acres, with a herd of 450 fallow-deer; it does not appear to have been enclosed in 1712.

South of Gedington is the Park of *Boughton,* the former seat of the Dukes of Montague, and now of their descendant the Duke of Buccleuch: it contains about 300 acres, and 440 fallow-deer. At *Hemington*, on the borders of Huntingdonshire, was a more ancient park, noticed by Saxton, and which also belonged to the Montague family.

At *Carlton* Hall, the seat of the Palmer family, is an existing park; and at *Dingley*, near Harborough, was also a deer park very recently existing.

Passing further south, and towards the midland districts of Northamptonshire, a park should be noticed at *Cottesbrooke*, belonging to Sir John Langham, which is not, however, given in Morton's Survey in 1712: it contains at present 83 acres, and 170 fallow-deer. The same survey marks a park however at *Lamport*, in this neighbourhood, the seat of the Isham family.

About five miles directly south of Lamport, and two miles north of Northampton, is the interesting park of *Moulton*, noticed by Leland. 'It is,' writes Baker, 'an extra-parochial estate of about 450 acres, walled round; in early records indifferently called Moulton Park, and Northampton Park, being locally connected with the former and a feudal appendage of the latter. There is direct evi-

dence of the existence of this park as early as Henry II.' Baker gives extracts from many records from the seventh of Henry III. (1222) till 1634, regarding Moulton Park, and the repair of the park wall, by which it appears that the men of certain villages were bound to repair it, and that each village had an allotted portion. An interesting relic of feudalism still remains in the names of the villages of Clipston, Crick, Deene, Draughton, Trafford in Byfield, &c., which are cut in the inside of the wall to point out their respective quotas of murage. When it was disparked is uncertain, but evidently not until after the twenty-third Henry VIII. (1531), in which year Sir John Mordaunt, Surveyor-general of the woods and forests, was required by Royal mandate to write to the officers of our forest of Saucey and of our park of 'Moulton,' commanding them to deliver to John Hartwell, Esq., and Richard Wale, Gent., 'such and as many oaks convenable for posts and rayles, with the lops, tops, and bark of the same, as shall be sufficient for enlarging the park at Hartwell and making a new lodge there.'[1]

Overston Park adjoining, originated in a license obtained in the thirty-ninth Henry III.(1254), by Gilbert de Millers to convert his wood at Overton into a park. In 1830 it contained nearly 800 acres.[2] It is not given in Saxton's Survey, and is now disparked.

West of Moulton are the manors of *Harleston, Althorp,* and *Holdenby.* The first is described by Baker as an eminently beautiful park, containing about 160 acres, and well stocked with deer.[3]

---

[1] Baker's History of Northamptonshire, vol. i. p. 52.

[2] Baker's Northamptonshire, vol. i. p. 58.
[3] Ib. p. 170.

Althorp, the well-known seat of the Spencers, was imparked by license, fourth Henry VIII. (1512), by Sir John Spencer, then John Spencer, Esq., '300 acres of land, 100 acres of wood, and 40 acres of water, in Old Thorpe,' with free warren there, and in Great Brington.[1] The park in the whole extent contains 543 acres, and there were at one time 800 head of fallow-deer kept in it. The herd at present is reduced to about 140, and the park to 124 acres. Upon the death of the grandfather of the present Lord Spencer, his uncle, better known as Lord Althorp, gave the entire herd to King William IV. They were all caught, the bucks' horns being sawn off, and removed in vans to the Royal parks. The park was restocked from Dingley Park in this county by the late lord. In this park is a hunting or hawking-stand, erected by the first Lord Spencer in 1613, on the occasion of the visit of King James I. The interior was formerly ornamented with curious paintings representing hunting scenes, which are now destroyed. Althorp was visited by John Evelyn in 1675 and 1688. He describes it as 'very finely watered, and flanqued with stately woods and groves,' and 'the park walled in with hewn stone, planted with rows and walles of trees, canals, and fish-ponds, and stored with game.' The park of Althorp was considerably enlarged by Charles Earl of Sunderland, its then possessor, between the years 1729 and 1733.

The Royal Park of *Holdenby* was licensed to be imparked in 1578, Sir Christopher Hatton being the owner at that time—'300 acres of land, 200 acres of meadow, and 70 acres of pastures in Holdenby, Church-Brampton, and Chapel-Brampton.'[2] It appears to have been 'impaled' about the year 1608, 109*l.* 10*s.* 6*d.* being allowed in the 'extraordinary' accounts of King James I. at that period.[3] 'A parke of fallowe-deare' is mentioned in Norden's Survey of Northamptonshire,[4] and there were upwards of 200 deer of different kinds at the destruction and sale of this Royal palace in 1650, besides a herd of wild cattle valued at 42*l.*[5]

South-west of Althorp, and near Daventry, is *Norton,* a modern park of about 246 acres and a herd of 100 fallow-deer, enclosed about the year 1845.

Fawsley, the ancient seat of the Knightley family, lies about four miles south of Daventry. Here is an existing, ancient, and very beautiful park, extending with Badby Wood to nearly 700 acres. The part open to deer is about 300 ; the herd of fallow-deer numbers 326. The new park, now incorporated with the old one, was enclosed in the reign of Elizabeth.[6]

Near Fawsley is *Litchborough,* where there is a small existing park belonging to Mr. Grant.

A small walled park existed at *Catesby,* on the borders of Warwickshire, which is marked in Morton's map of the county in 1712.

At *Canons-Ashby,* still further south, there is an existing park of 37 acres, with a herd of about 100 spotted fallow-deer. It is not known when the park was enclosed, but the beginning of the sixteenth century has been supposed to be the date ; it

---

[1] Baker's History of Northamptonshire, vol. i. p. 110.
[2] Ib. p. 200.
[3] Original papers *penes* the Baroness North, 1566.
[4] Antiquarian Rep. vol. ii. p. 48.
[5] Baker's Northamptonshire, vol. i. p. 197.
[6] Ib. p. 384.

is not however marked as a park in the Survey of 1712.

The same Survey, however, recognises the park at *Aynhoe*, in the south-western angle of the county, which still exists. It contains about 170 acres, and a herd of fallow-deer, which formerly numbered 200, now reduced to 50.

The forest of Whittlebury or Whittle-wood and the adjoining, Salcey or Sacy Forest, occupied the southern limits of Northamptonshire. The former, before it was disafforested in 1850, comprehended 4,111 acres, and there were between 1,700 and 1,800 deer of all sorts. In the year 1792, it is stated, that about 138 bucks and 100 does were here annually killed. In Salcey Forest there were no deer.[1]

In the neighbourhood of these forests there were several parks, of which the following may be mentioned in, and adjoining Whittlebury :—

Easton-Neston, near Toucester.—Sir Richard Empson, in the fourteenth of Henry VII. (1499), obtained a license to impark 400 acres of land and 30 acres of wood here, and permission to embattle his manor-house.[2]

At *Paulerspury* adjoining, the park, now disparked, stretched along the side of Whittlebury Forest, from Wakefield Lawn to Shelbrook Lawn. In the thirty-eighth of Edward III. (1363), it was found by inquisition that it would not be to the damage of the king if he granted license to John Pavely to convert his woods called Ottewood and Farnsted, containing 175 acres, into a park ; and in the tenth of

Henry IV. (1409), Sir John St. John had license to enlarge his two parks called the Old and the New Park.[3]

Astwell Park, in the parish of Wappenham, was imparked by Thomas Lovett, Esq., in 1564, and disparked probably early in the eighteenth century. (For the history of its formation, see the Second Chapter of this work, p. 35.)

Potterspury Park.—William de Ferrers, Earl of Derby, had a license in the fourteenth of Henry III. (1230) to enclose his wood of Pyrie, and converted it into a park. In the twenty-ninth of Edward I. (1300), Matilda Countess of Warwick died seized of the manor of Potters Pyrie and an enclosed park, with beasts of chase, underwood, and herbage. It is recognised as a park so late as the first of Henry VII. (1485).[4]

Wykehamon or *Wicken Park.*—John Fitzallen de Wolverton had license in the eighteenth of Edward I. (1289) to enclose his park of Wyke-hamon, within the forest of Whittlewood. In the fourth of Henry VIII. (1512) John Spencer, Esq., had a confirmation of a free park of 300 acres in Wyke-hamon, with free warren; but his descendant Robert, second Earl of Sunderland, disparked it about 1651, when Sir Peter Temple, Bart., ancestor of the Duke of Buckingham and Chandos, purchased the deer, and enclosed the celebrated park at Stowe in Buckinghamshire.[5]

Plumpton Park.—In the second of Edward III. (1328) Richard Damary had license to impark his woods of Ubleigh in Somersetshire, and Plumpton Pury in

---

[1] 8th Report of Commissioners of Woods and Forests, &c., p. 471 ; and Select Committee on Woods, &c., 1848–9..
[2] Baker's Northamptonshire, vol. ii. p. 334.

[3] Baker's Northamptonshire, vol. ii. p. 204.
[4] Ib. p. 220.
[5] Ib. p. 252.

Northamptonshire. The name is retained
in a small public-house, called '*Plumb
Parker Corner,*' and between 80 and 90
acres adjoining, the property of Sir C.
Mordaunt, Bart., still retain the name of
The Park.[1]
Stoke Park contains about 400 acres.
In the fifty-fourth of Henry III. (1270)
Pagan de Chaworth had license to enclose
his wood of Stoke in Northamptonshire.
In the first of Charles I. (1629) the king
granted to Sir Francis Crane, Knight, the
park of *Stoke Brewerne*, with all lands
known by the name of the park, and all
deer, and free warren.[2]

Hanley Park, or Hanley Free Hay, as
it was usually called whilst within the
precincts of Whittlebury Forest ; it was,
in fact, part of the forest, and was included
in it in the perambulation of Whittlewood
Forest, in the twenty-seventh of Edward I.
(1299).[3]

But the most important of all the parks
in this forest district, was the Royal Park
of *Grafton*, an ancient appendage to the
Manor-house or Palace of Grafton-Regis,
containing about 995 acres, one-third
in Grafton parish, another in Potters-
pury and Yardley-Gobion, and the remainder in Alderton and Paulerspury
parishes. It was subdivided into two
parks, commonly called Grafton Park
and Pury Park. There were two lodges
for keepers. The two parks occupied the
entire intervening space between Grafton
and Watling-Street, or Chester Road,
and communicated with Whittlebury
Forest near the Gullet. It was stocked
with deer, and intersected by rectilinear

avenues of noble oaks. These have long
since been sacrificed to agricultural im-
provements, and the whole converted into
farms, but an old inhabitant of Grafton
remembered (writes Baker) portions of
the park paling reaching almost to the
village.

Grafton was erected into 'an Honor'
by Act of Parliament, in the thirty-third
of Henry VIII. (1541). In the sixteenth
of Charles I. (1640-1) the king granted to
Thomas Marsham, of London, Esq., and
Ferdinand Marsham, Gent., the office of
custos of the parks ' called Grafton Parke
and Potters-pury Parke,' part of the honor
of Grafton for life, with a stipend of 2*d*.
per diem for each park, with the herbage
and pannage of the parks, and the browsing wood, windfall wood, and dead wood,
and the reversion of the offices to Edward Earl of Dorset, Chamberlain of
Queen Henrietta, for life. Three years
after, the king, subject to the above grant,
in consideration of 7,000*l*. conveyed ' all
that park or parks called Grafton Park,
with liberty to dispark the same, to Sir
George Strode, of Westerham in Kent,
and Arthur Duck, of Chiswick in Middlesex, in fee.'[4]

Midway between the forests of Whittlebury and Salcey was the park of *Hartwell,* containing 320 acres, with the lodges
and houses, 'disparked for ever as well
from vert and hunting as from all other
things to a park incident or belonging,'
granted for 2,100*l*. to Endymion Porter,
Esq., in the fifth of Charles I. (1629-30).[5]

At *Gayton,* on the confines of Salcey
Forest, was an ancient park which Ingel-

[1] Baker's Northamptonshire, vol. ii. p. 213.
[2] Ib. p. 241.
[3] Ib. p. 340.

[4] Baker's Northamptonshire, vol. ii. p. 114, &c.
[5] Ib. p. 184.

ran de Fiennes had license to enclose in the forty-third of Henry III. (1258), 'with a good strong ditch and hay, so as to prevent the Royal beasts of chase from entering, and convert it into a park;' and in the fifth of Henry IV. (1403) John Trussell had license to make a park of 300 acres of meadow, pasture, and wood in Gayton. This park has long since been disparked and converted into fields, but about 20 acres of wood remain.[1]

To the north of Salcey Forest, and between it and Yardley Chase, a park is marked at *Horton* in the ancient surveys. This was the seat in the time of Henry VIII., of William Parr, created Lord Parr of Horton.

Near *Higham Ferrers*, bordering on the county of Bedford, was an extensive park, for which I find, among 'divers extraordinaries accrued and paid since the first

of May 1608,' the sum of 1,500*l*. was paid to the Lord Stanhope by King James I.[2]

Existing Deer Parks in Northamptonshire.

1. BURGHLEY	.	Marquis of Exeter.
2. ROCKINGHAM	.	Mr. Watson.
3. DEANE	.	Earl of Cardigan.
4. BLATHERWICK		Mr. Stafford O'Brien.
5. BOUGHTON	.	Duke of Buccleuch.
6. CARLTON	.	Sir G. Palmer, Bt.
7. COTTESBROOKE	.	Sir J. Langham, Bt.
8. ALTHORP	.	Earl Spencer.
9. NORTON	.	Mrs. A. Seymour.
10. FAWSLEY	.	Sir R. Knightley, Bart.
11. LITCHBOROUGH.		Mr. Grant.
12. CANONS-ASHBY.		Sir H. Dryden, Bt.
13. AYNHOE	.	Mr. Cartwright.
14. WHITTLEBURY	.	Lord Southampton.

WARWICKSHIRE.

DONNELIE, which Dugdale supposes to be the modern *Beldesert*, 'a hilly tract, bordered with deep vallies,'[3] near Henley-in-Arden, may perhaps lay claim to be the spot which as far as we know is earlier connected with the chase than any other place in the county of Warwick—not that there was any park there, strictly speaking, at the period of the Domesday Survey—but the Earl of Mellent is there recorded

to have been possessed of the 'Hay' at Donnelie, containing half a mile in length and as much in breadth. This Hay is remarkable among the number which are mentioned in Domesday, from having its size particularised. It was formerly worth twenty, and at the time of the survey thirty shillings. Beldesert at a very early period became the principal seat of the great family of Montfort, who were very

---

[1] Baker's Northamptonshire, vol. ii. p. 278.
[2] Original Account *penes* the Baroness North.
[3] Dugdale's Warwickshire, Thomas's ed.

vol. ii. p. 798. From this second edition all the references are made.

nearly connected with Henry de New-burgh, the first Earl of Warwick of the Norman line, brother of the Earl of Mellent ; and here their chief castle, called from its pleasant situation Belde-sert, was erected. Two parks, occupying probably the site of the ancient 'Hay,' are mentioned in connection with the manor in the first year of Edward VI. In Dugdale's time 'the castle with the park wherein it stood' is recorded, but it is not found in Saxton's map, and I con-clude had really been disparked soon after the extinction of the principal branch of the Montfort family in the latter half of the fourteenth century.

The ancient parks of *Wedgenock, Hase-ley,* and *Grove* should next engage our attention ; these parks from a very early period were attached to the castle of Warwick, and are noticed in Leland's 'Itinerary,' and in the ancient maps of the county. Wedgenock is expressly mentioned by John Rous, the antiquary, in his ' History of the Kings of England,' as having been made by Henry de New-burgh, Earl of Warwick, after the example of the park of Woodstock, imparked by King Henry the First.[1] It still exists, though greatly reduced in size,[2] containing at present but 45 acres, with a herd of 70 fallow-deer, and is the property of the Earl of Warwick. During the middle ages, in consequence of the frequent forfeitures of this earldom, Wedgenock was often at the disposal of the Crown. In the twenty-first year of Richard II. it was granted to Thomas Earl of Kent, on the attainder

of the Earl of Warwick. In the first year of Edward VI. it was granted to John Dudley Earl of Warwick, on whose attainder it came again to the Crown. The following notices respecting it are derived from original evidences in posses-sion of Lord Willoughby de Broke. It was eventually granted to the Greville family, the ancestor of the present Earl of Warwick, in the fourteenth year of Queen Elizabeth.[3]

Indenture of the 20th of October, 1st Elizabeth, 'between Richard Dennys of Cold-Aston in the county of Gloucester, Esq., and Sr Richard Verney, Knt,' being a lease of 'the herbage and pannage of the Queen's Majestie's Park of Wedge-nock in the County of Warwick, and of the fishery, and also the herbage and pan-nage of the Queen's wood called Ferne-hill, adjoining to the said park, and also the deputy-keepership of the Queen's Majestie's Manor-House or Lordship of Goodrest in the park of Wedgenock ; and also the said Richard Dennys to be paler or walker of the said park, and to be keeper and woodwarde of all the woods, &c.' The house called Goodrest, observes Dugdale, 'was built by Thomas Beau-champ, Earl of Warwick, in part of Ed-ward III. and Richard II.'s time. I sup-pose it was so called in respect that some of the Countesses of Warwick, to avoyd much concourse of people, retired hither when they were near the time of child-birth ; for it is plain that many of their children were born here.'

Indenture of the 22nd of December,

[1] Joannis Rossi Hist. Reg. Angliæ, 2nd ed., 8vo. Oxon, 1745, p. 138.
[2] In the 26th of Edward I. it contained, however, but twenty acres ; but it was enlarged by Thomas Beauchamp, Earl of Warwick,

with certain woods called Wedgenock Donele, in the parish of Hatton. Can this be the Donnelie of Domesday which Dugdale fixes at Beldesert ?
[3] Dugdale's Warwickshire, vol. i. p. 272.

2nd Elizabeth, 'between Sʳ Richard Verney and Thomas Fisher, of Warwick,
Esqʳ,' being a lease of the park of Wedgenock, excepting 'the going within the said
park of haulf a dozen or not exceeding
haulf a score of geldings or nagges of
Sʳ Richard Verney, or such of his friends
as may come with him at all tymes of his
coming *gestwyse* to the said park, and
during their abode there *guestwyse*, so
that it exceed not four dayes and four
nights at any one time.'

Agreement of the 4th of January, 2nd
Elizabeth, between Sir Richard Verney
and Thomas Fisher, Esq., whereby Fisher
engaged 'to build a house in the park of
Wedgenock, of three bayes, near unto the
forde leading out of the new railes into
the old park, and in the same to make
one loft or lodging for a keeper to lye as
occasion may serve for the better preservation of game.' Tithes of pannage and
venison from Wedgenock Park were
granted by Margery, Countess of Warwick in Henry III.'s time, to the Hos-
pital of St. Michael at Warwick, and in
after times a buck and doe were given
annually to the vicars of Kenilworth,
Budbrook, and Hatton, in lieu of tithes,
now commuted into money. A fat buck,
however, is still given to the wardsmen of
Thomas Oken's Charity at Warwick.

The Park of *Haseley* is not mentioned
by Dugdale, and although marked in
Speed's map, was probably disparked before the end of the sixteenth century, when
it had ceased to belong to the earldom of
Warwick. *Grove*, on the contrary, in the
parish of Budbroke, is still stocked with

deer, although in October, 1822, part of
the deer were sold,[1] some few escaped,
and there is now a herd of about 80
fallow-deer. This place, long the seat of
the Dormers, was an ancient park of the
Beauchamps Earls of Warwick, the lodge
here having been built by Thomas Earl of
Warwick, in the seventeenth of Richard II.[2]

Besides their parks at *Wedgenock*,
Haseley, and *Grove*, the Earls of Warwick
had a park or chase at *Sutton* and at
Studley, in the northern and western parts
of this county.

Sutton Park, or Chase, is of considerable size, and was called before the reign
of Henry I. a forest. The Domesday
Survey makes the woods here to extend
to two miles in length and one in width.
Henry I. granted it to Roger Earl of
Warwick, and it long remained attached
to the earldom of Warwick. The park,
which the Lord Basset of Drayton erected
at Drayton-Basset, about the beginning of
King John's time, was within the limits of
this chase, and hence the agreement entered into between Waleran, Earl of Warwick, and the Lord Basset in the third of
John, the earl recognising the park on the
annual receipt of two good bucks, and a
provision that the fence of the park should
be kept up, and preserved 'sine buke-
stall,'[3] without a buck-stal, that is, as
Cowel defines it, 'a deer hay, toil, or
great net, to catch deer with, which by
the statute of the 19th of Henry VII. is
not to be kept by any man that hath not
a park of his own, under pain of 40l.'
Many other remarkable grants and licenses connected with this chase may

[1] One half to Mr. Geast for 36s. a head,
the other half to Lord Anson for 38s. a head.
MS. note of the late H. E. Landor, Esq.

[2] Dugdale's Warwickshire, vol. ii. p. 660.
[3] Ib. p. 909.

be seen in Dugdale's 'History of Warwickshire.'

Studley was also a park of the Earl of
Warwick in the twenty-fourth year of Edward I., as appears by a commission issued out to certain persons to enquire who
those were that had entered therein and
killed his deer. In more ancient times
the park here had belonged to the Montforts.[1]

But by far the largest and most remarkable of the parks of this county were
those which in the time of Queen Elizabeth belonged to the Earl of Leicester and
his magnificent castle of *Kenilworth*, of
which Dugdale writes that 'he has heard
some who were the servants of the great
Robert Dudley Earl of Leicester say,
that the charge he bestowed on this castle,
with the parks and chase thereto belonging, was no less than sixty thousand
pounds.' It appears by the survey taken
of Kenilworth in the reign of James I.
that 'there lyeth about the same castle in
chases and parks 1200*l.* per an., 900*l.*
whereof are grounds for pleasure ; the rest
in meadow and pasture thereto adjoining.
There joineth upon this ground a park-
like ground called the king's-wood, with
xv several copices lying altogether, containing 789 acres within the same, which
in the Earl of Leicester's time were
stored with red-deer, since which the deer
strayed, but the ground in no sort blem-
ished, having great store of timber and
other trees of much value upon the same.'
'The circuit of the castle, mannours,
parks and chase, lying round together,
contain at least xix or xx miles in a pleasant country, the like both for strength,

state, and pleasure, not being within the
realme of England.' The Park of Kenilworth, the ancient seat of the Clintons, is
mentioned as early as the eleventh of
Henry II., when it was in the hands of
the sheriff; other notices respecting it will
be found in Dugdale's 'Warwickshire.'
It was finally destroyed during the Interregnum, ' when Oliver Cromwell gave the
whole manor to several officers of his
army, who demolished the castle, drained
the great pool, cut down the king's woods,
destroyed his parks and chase, and divided
the lands into farms among themselves.'[2]

Perhaps the remainder of the parks of
Warwickshire may be most conveniently
noticed as they occur in their respective
hundreds. In Knightlow Hundred, besides the parks attached to the castles of
Warwick and *Kenilworth*, there was a park
noticed in the thirty-third year of Henry
III. at *Cheylesmore*, near Coventry, which
then belonged to Roger de Montalt. There
were deer here in the eighth of Richard II.,
observes Dugdale, as appears by a lease
of the pasturage, which reserves sufficient
grass for them. In other leases of the
time of Henry VIII. the deer are not
mentioned, and were no doubt long removed before this park was granted to
the Mayor and Corporation of Coventry
by Queen Elizabeth in the tenth year of
her reign.[3] At *Astley Castle*, in this hundred, the seat of the Astleys, and afterwards of Thomas Grey Marquis of Dorset, were two parks, 'the little parke,' imparked by the marquis, and 'the great
parke,' enlarged by him with 90 acres of
land in the twelfth of Henry VII., taken out
of the precincts of Arley, ' which to this

[1] Dugdale, vol. ii. p. 742.
[2] Ib.. vol. i. p. 242, &c.

[3] Dugdale, vol. i. p. 140.

day,' writes Dugdale, 'bears the name of Arley Laund.' These parks are marked in the surveys of Saxton and Speed, but have been long disparked.

At *Flechamsted*, near Coventry, a park is also marked in Dugdale's map, but not in the more ancient surveys, although a park was enclosed in Nether Flechamsted, by Henry Smith, Esq., in the twelfth of Henry VII., and by Sir Thomas Leigh, at Over Flechamsted, now long disparked, in the reign of James I.

The same Sir Thomas Leigh is believed to have made the park at Stoneley, now called *Stoneley Old Park*, which contains at present 574 acres, with a herd of 450 fallow-deer. It is the property of Lord Leigh, and is remarkable for its rural beauty and the picturesque oak trees which are to be seen here.

Combe Abbey.—There were deer here in 1714, as appears from Kip's view of this place at that time : they have been of late years removed to Lord Craven's other seat at Hamstead-Marshall in Berkshire.

Newbold Revell.—Here was a park enclosed by Sir Fulwer Skipwith, Bart., early in the eighteenth century, which was disparked after the decease of Selina, Dowager Lady Skipwith, in 1832.

Newland, near Coventry.—Here the Prior of Coventry had license to impark 246 acres of waste and wood, in the sixth of Edward III.

Shuckburgh.—Here was a park in the year 1600, which is not noticed, however, in the ancient published maps of the county. It contains about 120 acres of a deep rich loam, in which elms and oaks

grow to a large size. There is a herd of 200 spotted fallow-deer.[1]

In Kineton Hundred there are, or were, the following parks :—*Charlecote, Compton Wyniate, Weston, Eatington, Compton Verney,* and *Honington.*

Charlecote.—Deer are represented in ' The prospect of Charlecote in Warwickshire, the seat of the Rev. William Lucy, Esq.,' in 1722. It is at present a park of 210 acres, with a herd of 400 fallow and red-deer.

Compton Wyniate.—' The parke,' says Dugdale, ' is very large, begun by Sir William Compton about the xi year of Henry VIII., for then he had license not only to impark certain grounds there enclosed at that time, but to include and lay to the same 2,000 acres more of land and wood, lying in Compton superior, and Compton inferior, for the use of himself and his heirs for ever.'[2] This park was probably disparked when Compton ceased to be the residence of the Earls of Northampton, about the year 1760.

Weston, the ancient seat of the Sheldons, 'imparked by William Sheldon, of Beoly in Worcestershire, Esq., their principal seat, who, liking well the situation hereof, in 37 Henry VIII. obtained license from the king to impark ccc acres of land, meadow, pasture, and wood, to be called by the name of Weston Park for ever.'[3] Disparked also about the middle of the eighteenth century.

Eatington.—There was a park here in 1653, as appears by a lease of that date, and it is laid down in a map made in 1738. It was restocked with deer by the Hon. George Shirley, in 1762. The

[1] Information of Sir Francis Shuckburgh, Bart.

[2] Dugdale, vol. i. p. 548.
[3] Ib. p. 584.

present park contains 436 acres, the deer, 200 in number, occupy but 200 acres; they are fallow-deer, both dark and light. Eatington Park is, for the midland counties, wild and romantic in its character, and celebrated for its ancient hawthorns. The doe venison is thought to be particularly good.

Compton Verney.—There is said to have been a park here in former times. In 1647, two deer were stolen from the park of Sir Grevil Verney.[1] It has been long disparked.

At *Honington,* the seat of the Townsend family, was a small park or paddock, as appears by Buck's print of the house in 1731. The old lodge, built in James II.'s time, still remains.

Barlichway Hundred contains the parks of *Fulbroke, Clopton, Ragley, Beauchamps Court, Coughton, Skilts,* and *Lapworth*; and also Beldesert, Grove Park, and Haseley, which have been already described.

Of *Fulbroke* Leland, in his 'Itinerary,' writes as follows,—'I roade from Warwick to Bereford (Barford) Bridge of 8 arches, a 2 miles of Warwicke. Here I sawe half a mile lower upon Avon on the right side, a fayre parke called Fulbroke. In this park was a praty castle made of stone and bricks, and as one tould mee, a Duke of Bedford laye in it. There is a litle lodge or piece of building in this parke called Bergeiney, made, as I conjecture, by some Lord or Lady Bergeiney (Bergavenny). This castle of Fulbroke

was an eyesore to the Earles that lay in Warwick Castle, and was cause of displeasure betweene each Lord. Sir William Compton, keeper of Fulbroke parke and castle, seeing it go to ruine helped it forward, takinge part of it (as some saye) for the buildinge of his house at Compton by Brailes in Warwickshire, and gave or permitted others to take pieces of it downe.'[2] Rous, in his 'History of the Kings of England,' also refers to this place as 'imparked by John Duke of Bedford,[3] brother of Henry V.,' and to the sumptuous gate below the pales of the park, built by Joan, Lady Bergavenny, and proceeds to lament the insecure state of the roads in consequence of the darkness of the way by the hedges and pales become 'a shelter for robbers.'[4] Fulbroke, in the reign of Elizabeth, was held *in capite* from the Crown by Sir Francis Englefield, and was purchased by Sir Thomas Lucy from his nephew in 1615. 'He renewed the park, and by the addition of Hampton Woods thereto, enlarged it much.'[5] It was during the time that Fulbroke belonged to, or rather had been forfeited by, Sir Francis Englefield, that it has been supposed by Mr. Bracebridge in his 'Shakespeare no Deerstealer,'[6] that the celebrated incident occurred which has connected the name of Lucy with that of the great dramatist, and to which I must refer the reader. The following graceful description of the site of the ancient Park of Fulbroke is by the same author :—'On the right of the road

---

[1] Halliwell's Historical Account of The New Place, Stratford-on-Avon. Fo. London, 1864, p. 117.

[2] Leland's Itin. vol. iv. p. 68, fol. 166 *b.*

[3] In anno 1432.

[4] Rous's Hist. Reg. Angliæ, ed. 1745, p. 123.

[5] Dugdale, vol. ii. p. 668.

[6] 8vo. London, 1862.

from Warwick to Stratford are the woodlands of Hampton-on-the-Hill, Grove
Park, Hatton, Snitterfield, Edston, and
Welcomb, forming part of the oak woods
of the forest of Arden,[1] of which this is
the south-western extremity. On the left
are the meadows of the Avon, and the
rich valley of Wasperton, Charlecote, Al-
veston, and the alluvial and clay lands
beyond, where the elm is indigenous and
abundant. Fulbroke Park pales extended
for more than a mile along the Warwick
and Stratford road, in the time of Richard
III. A lane still marks one boundary of
the park, Hampton parish another. The
north-west and south-east sides are formed
by the before-named road and the meadows along the Avon. The ground breaks
away from the red sandstone plateau in
endless combes, gentle slopes, and rounded
heights, to the meadows. In flood-time
the bright waters appear below; Hampton
Wood, with the little eminences near it,
closes in the view: in a line with this
wood the brick and lime fragments in a
ploughed field even now prove where the
castle stood. Further on by the river is
a substantial farm-house, with a moat, the
ancient park lodge; and near this is the
site of the church noted in Henry VIII.'s
first survey, but which had disappeared
before the last (survey) of his reign, commonly called the King's Book. A few
large trunks of ancient living trees remind
one of the self-grown oak forest still existing here in the year 1560, but most of
the ground is under the plough.'
  A small park of 80 acres, with a herd
of 130 fallow-deer, was enclosed at Clop-

ton, near Stratford-on-Avon, in the year
1850.
  In the neighbourhood of Alcester were
the parks of *Arrow, Beauchamps-Court,*
and *Coughton. Arrow* was imparked by
Sir Robert Burdet, Kt., by license in the
seventh of Edward III., and is well
known as the park where King Edward
IV. killed a white buck, which the owner,
Thomas Burdet, set much store by, 'who
passionately wishing the hornes in his
belly that moved the king so to do, being
arraigned and convicted of high treason
for those words, upon inference made that
his meaning was mischievous to the king
himself, he lost his life for the same.'[2]
The present park of Ragley, in the parish
of Arrow, is extensive; the deer, however,
about 230 in number, occupy only a small
portion of it, about 90 acres. It has long
been the principal seat of the Seymour-
Conways, Marquises of Hertford.
  At *Beauchamps-Court,* in the parish of
Alcester, was a park, which appears to
have been made by Foulk Grevile, who
married the heiress of Willoughby in the
reign of Henry VIII.[3]
  At *Coughton,* the ancient seat of the
Throckmorton family, was also a park,
enclosed in the second year of Henry VII.
by Sir Robert Throckmorton, Kt.[4] It
appears in the maps of Saxton and Speed,
but has been long disparked.
  Skelts, in the parish of Studley, 'im-
parkt for deer' by William Sheldon, Esq.,
in the reign of Elizabeth, but disparked
and turned into farms before the time of
Dugdale.
  Lapworth Park is marked both in the

[1] Rather the woodlands of Arden, as there
was never, strictly speaking, any forest.—
E. P. S.

[2] Dugdale, vol. ii. p. 848.
[3] Ib. vol. ii. p. 766.
[4] Ib. vol. ii. p. 756.

maps of Saxton and Speed, though it seems to have been disparked long before Dugdale's time. 'It was enclosed by William Catesby, Esq., a great favourite to king Richard III., who granted him in the second year of his reign under his signet at Kenilworth Castle, an Hundred Oaks, to be taken within the king's old park of Tanworth and Earlswood in Tanworth, within this county, and 500 trees for rails in Lodbroke's Park in Tanworth, for making his new park here at Lapworth.'[1]

In the hundred of Hemlingford we have to notice the parks of *Nuthurst, Aston, Nechells, Park-Hall, Kingshurst, Coleshill, Maxtoke, Berkswell, Packington, Arbury, Midleton, Merevale,* and *Pooley Park. Sutton* has been already mentioned.

Nuthurst.—In the fifth of Edward III. William Trussell had license to make a park of his woods in this place.[2]

Aston, juxta Birmingham.—A fair park was enclosed here by Sir Thomas Holt, Bart., in the reign of James I.[3] It was not disparked till the beginning of the present century, about the year 1818.

Nechells Parke is marked in the map of Hemlingford Hundred, in the first edition of Dugdale's 'Warwickshire' (1656). It then belonged to Sir Thomas Holt.

Park-Hall was imparked by the Arden family, 'this being for the last 300 years,' says Dugdale, 'their principal seat,' and in the second year of Henry VIII. it was considerably enlarged by John Arden, Esq. It was afterwards called 'Man-

sionne de la Logge, *alias* Park Hall.'[4] It appears to have been disparked before Dugdale's time, probably upon the attainder of Edward Arden, Esq., in the twenty-seventh of Elizabeth.

Kingshurst and *Coleshill,* ancient parks of the Montforts; the first imparked by Sir Edmund Montfort in the twenty-sixth of Henry VI. ;[5] afterwards both came to the Digby family on the attainder of Sir Simon Montfort in the eleventh of Henry VII. The park at Coleshill retained its deer and was not disparked till about the year 1812.

Maxtoke Castle had its park in the time of Edward Stafford, Duke of Buckingham, attainted in the thirteenth of Henry VIII.,[6] and, as there is reason to believe, for many ages before, when it belonged to the Clintons, 'the pale of the park of Maxtoke' being found mentioned in a grant of Sir William Clinton to the Church in the fifth of Edward III.

Packington, imparked by Sir Clement Fisher, in the reign of King James I. 'out of the outwood, and some other grounds here.'[7] It is at present a park of 500 acres, with a herd of 300 fallow-deer.

Berkswell was the site of a very ancient park, which belonged in the reign of Henry II. to Nigel de Mundeville, and which appears to have been kept up and used as a park as late as the reign of Elizabeth.

Arbury, recte Erdburie.—Here a park, which still continues, appears to have been enclosed by the Newdigate family in the eighteenth century.

---

[1] Dugdale, vol. ii. p. 789.
[2] Ib. vol. ii. p. 958.
[3] Ib. vol. ii. p. 872.
[4] Ib. vol. ii. p. 887.

[5] Dugdale, vol. ii. p. 1020.
[6] Ib. vol. ii. p. 995.
[7] Ib. vol. ii. p. 989.

Midleton.—'I passed by Middleton parke,' writes Leland in his 'Itinerary,'[1] 'wherof Sʳ John Willoughby, son and heir to Sʳ Henry Willoughby (an ould knight of yᵉ sepulchre), hath a fayre mannour-place.' This park, which is marked both by Dugdale and Speed, is now, I believe, disparked.

Merevale.—A park here is marked in Dugdale's map of 1656, and one is known to have belonged to this place after it had been granted to the Devereux family, being mentioned in the will of Robert second Earl of Essex. Of late years the park has been restored by the present owner, Mr. Dugdale, who brought the deer, now about 120 in number, from Bordesley in Worcestershire. The park occupies about 180 acres. The oaks here are remarkably fine.

Pooley Park, in the parish of Polesworth, near Tamworth. Here was an ancient park, enclosed by Sir Thomas Cokain, Kt., in the twenty-second of Henry VII., who lies buried at Ashbourn in Derbyshire, with the following inscription:—

'Here lyeth Sir Thomas Cockaine,
Made knight at Turney and Turwyne ;
Who builded here fayre houses twayne,
With many profittes that remayne ;
And three fayre parks impaled he,
For his successors here to be.'[2]

Dugdale[3] gives this inscription somewhat differently:—

'Three goodly houses he did build, to his great praise and fame,
With profits great and manifold belonging to the same.
Three parks he did impale, therein to chase the Deere,
The lofty lodge within this park he also builded here.'[4]

When Pooley Park was disparked I have not discovered, but it was probably early in the seventeenth century, as Dugdale mentions that in his time the Cockain family 'seldom dwelt at this place.'

List of existing Deer Parks in the County of Warwick.

1. WEDGENOCK . Earl of Warwick.
2. GROVE PARK . Lord Dormer.
3. STONELEY . . Lord Leigh.
4. SHUCKBURGH . Sir Francis Shuckburgh, Bart.
5. CHARLECOTE . Mr. Lucy.
6. EATINGTON . Mr. Shirley.
7. RAGLEY . . . Marquis of Hertford.
8. CLOPTON . . Late Mr. Warde.
9. MAXTOKE . . Mr. Dilke.
10. PACKINGTON . Earl of Aylesford.
11. ARBURY . . Mr. Newdigate.
12. MEREVALE . Mr. Dugdale.

[1] Vol. iv. p. 123, fol. 190 a.
[2] Ashbourn and the Valley of the Dove, 8vo. 1839, p. 64.

[3] Dugdale, vol. ii. p. 1141.
[4] This must be Ashbourn, where a park is marked in Saxton's Map of 1577.

M

WORCESTERSHIRE.

Two Domesday parks are to be noted in this county: one at Salewarpe (*Salwarp*), near Droitwich, which belonged to. Earl Roger, and which we do not hear of again ; and the other at Wadberge, the modern *Wadborough*, in the parish of Pershore, the property of the Church of St. Mary at that place. At the time of the Conquest it was held under it by one Robert, and afterwards came to the Beauchamps Earls of Warwick, and their heirs the Lords Latymer. In the time of Nash it belonged to Sir Charles Cocks, Baronet.[1] Wadborough was probably disparked long before the beginning .of the eighteenth century, but is marked as a park both in the Surveys of Saxton (1577) and Speed (1610).

Besides the parks, hays are also noticed in the Domesday Survey at Holt (Holt Castle), and at Chintune, Kinton or Kingston, 'in qua capiebant feræ.' They were held respectively by Urso d'Abetot, the sheriff, and Roger de Laci.

The town and Royal Park of *Bewdley*, a corruption of ' Beaulieu,' in Latin ' Belluslocus,' is in the parish of Ribbesford, and came to the Crown from the Mortimers Earls of March. It was also called Ticknell, and is thus noticed by Leland in his ' Itinerary:' ' The fayre mannour place by west of the Towne (of Bewdley), standing in a goodly park well wooded, on the very knappe of an hill that the town standeth

on, this place is called Tikenhill.'[2] A Court Roll held in the tenth year of James I. thus described it: ' The Prince' (Henry Prince of Wales) 'has a capital messuage within the sayd manor called Ticknell, and a stable called the King's Stable, together with a parke, called Bewdley Parke, and fair meadows adjoining, called Lady Meadows, which contayne above thirty-four acres, and are worth 4*l.* per ann. There be growing within the park 3,500 old trees, and 1,000 of them are valued at 1,000*l.*, another 1,000 at 1,000 marks, and 1,000 at 500*l.*, and 500 at 500 nobles, the park containeth about 400 acres, most of it is heath ground. Here are by estimation between 100 and 80 head of deere, beside the feeding of which deere, the herbage may be esteemed to be worth 20*l.* per annum.'[3] Bewdley appears to have been disparked at the period of the Rebellion, and was not afterwards restocked. In 1621 three bucks were ordered to be supplied by the keeper of Bewdley Park, for the use of his Majesty's household in the Castle of Ludlow,[4] and at the same period three bucks were charged to Malvern Chase, and to several other places in that neighbourhood.

The Bishops of Worcester possessed at least three parks in the county, at *Hartlebury*, *Alchurch*, and *Blockley.* ' At *Hartlebury*,' still the residence of the bishop, 'there is a parke and deere,'

---

[1] Nash's History of Worcestershire, vol. i. p. 249.
[2] Itin. vol. iv. p. 106, fol. 183.

[3] Nash's History of Worcestershire, vol. ii. p. 276.
[4] Dineley MS. *penes* the Duke of Beaufort, copied by Sir T. Winnington, Bart.

says Leland, 'a warren for conyes, and
fayre pooles, but the soyle about the
Castle is barren.'[1]   A Parliamentary survey of about the year 1648 notes, 'to this
Castle adjoins a fair park, containing 86
acres and 20 perches, yearly value 43*li*.'[2]
Hartlebury was disparked after the death
of Bishop Carr, in the year 1841.

Alchurch, recte Alvechurch, is also mentioned by Leland.   'The Bishop of Worcester,' he writes, 'hath a fayre mannour
place a little by north-east without the
towne, standinge on an hill, and it was
lately in decay, and Bishop Latymer re-
payred it.   There is a parke.'[1]   Long
before Nash's time the park had been
converted into farms.

Blockley.—Opposite the vicar's garden
is a hill called the park, supposed to have
been the Bishop of Worcester's park, who
had a palace here before the Reformation.[3]   Both the parks of Alchurch and
Blockley are marked in Saxton's Map of
1577.

Hallow or *Hollow Park*, in Grimley,
near Worcester, originally belonged to
the Priory of Worcester,[4] and afterwards
to the Dean and Chapter, and then to the
See of Worcester.   The park here is given
by Saxton ; and here Queen Elizabeth,
according to the following record, hunted
on Thursday, the 18th of August, 1575.
'Her Majesty rode to Hallow Parke, being Mr. Abyngton's, on her palfrey—where
she hunted, and with her bow kylled one
buck, and struck another buck, wth beyng

recovered, she called for Mr. Abyngton,
asking hym how many bucks be kylled ?
and he said two bucks.   And then said
she, "Let one of the bucks be brought
to the one Bayliff's house, and the other
buck to the other Bayliff's house, with a
better good turn," which bucks were
brought to the Bayliffs' houses accordingly.'[5]

At *Baltenhall*, or Battenhall, near Worcester, was another park which anciently
belonged to the Prior.   Here Queen Elizabeth intended to hunt the next day, and
rode there accordingly.   'But that she
found the game very scarce, she returned
again without hunting at all.'[5]

The mitred Abbots of Evesham possessed several parks in Worcestershire.

Schrewenhulle, or *Shrevell Park*, in
Bengeworth, enclosed by Abbot William
de Chiriton, between the years 1317 and
1344, as appears from the 'Chronicle of
Evesham,'[6] 'ubi seminare fecit quercus et
fraxinos et alias arbores.'   After the Dissolution it was granted to Sir Philip
Hoby, Knight, in the thirtieth of Henry
VIII.   In 1376 (fiftieth of Edward III.)
Abbot John de Ombresley obtained a
patent from the king to impark his wood
of 'Lynholte,' containing 300 acres of land
and wood within the Manor of Ombresley,
now *Ombersley*, which remained with the
Abbey till the Dissolution.[7]   At *Offenham*
also there appears to have been a park
appertaining to this great Abbey,[7] for John
Norton, elected Abbot in 1483 (1 R. III.),

[1] Leland Itin. vol. iv. p. 113, fol. 186a.
[2] Nash's Worcestershire, vol. i. p. 568.
[3] Ib. vol. i. p. 98.
[4] In the 3rd of Edw. II. the Prior of Worcester had license to impark his Wood of
Monkwood, in the Manor of Grimley. Cal. of
Inq., p. 71.

[5] Progresses of Queen Elizabeth, vol. i.
p. 541, extracted from the Chamber Order
Book of the City of Worcester.
[6] Printed in 1863, 8vo. London, ed. W. D.
Macray.
[7] Ib. pp. 301, 339.

provided 'that on the day of his anni-
versary, the brothers should have one doe
from the deer park of Offenham, with wine
from the cellar of the Abbot.'

The Abbots of Pershore had also their
park at *Goldicote*, in the parish of Aldermarston, in that detached part of Worcestershire which extends from near Stratford-on-Avon to Shipston-on-Stour. The
ancient park of *Goldicote* is marked in all
the old maps, and its site is well known,
though no park is believed to have existed
here since the Reformation.

Within the limits of Malvern Chase
were formerly two parks, *Hanley* and
Blackmore. Of the former Leland observes :—

'Hanley is from Upton a mile in dextra
ripa Sabrinæ, a mile above Upton, and a
flite shotte from Severne. It is an up-
landisch Towne, the Castelle standith in
a park at the weste parte of the Towne.
Syr John Savage and his Father, and
Grandfather lay much aboute Hanley and
Theokesbyri, as kepers of Hanley. The
Erles of Glocester were owners of this
Castel, and lay much there. Mr. Come-
ton clene defacid it yn his tyme beyng
keper of it after Savage.'[1] Hanley Park
does not appear in the ancient maps,
having probably been disparked by Mr.
Compton, afterwards Sir William, and the
ancestor of the Earls and Marquisses of
Northampton, and the same who destroyed the Castle of Fulbroke in Warwickshire.

Blackmore Park is mentioned in all
the surveys, though no deer appear to
have been kept here within the memory
of man. At *Severn-End* in the parish of

Hanley, the venerable seat of the Lech-
meres, it may be observed, there was a
small park or paddock of deer in the last
century. It was disparked about the year
1790, and the deer sent to Ludford in
Herefordshire.

At *Croome*, the seat of the Earl of Coventry, in this southern part of the county,
is a large park, which with the pleasure-
grounds are estimated by Nash at near
1,200 acres. It was probably enclosed at
the commencement of the eighteenth century, and contains a herd of 400 fallow-
deer.

At *Strensham*, the ancient seat of the
Russells, near Croome, was a park, marked
in the Surveys of Saxton and Speed, but
which has been long disparked.

At *Bushley*, near Tewkesbury, was a
large park which belonged to the Le De-
spencers Earls of Gloucester, afterwards
to the Crown and to the Bishops of London. It is not marked in the ancient
maps.

Ridmerley Park, in this neighbourhood,
on the borders of Gloucestershire, was
one of the numerous parks belonging to
the Beauchamps, and came afterwards by
attainder to the Crown, by whom it was
granted, like Bushley, to the See of London, before the reign of Queen Elizabeth.[2]

Adjoining to Ridmerley is Staunton,
where in the seventeenth of Edward III.
free warren was granted to Robert de
Staunton, and license for his park of
Haukesshurne in Hawgrove.[3]

The ruins of *Elmley Castle*, in former
ages a principal seat of the Beauchamps,
near Bredon Hill, stands in a deer park,
containing 105 acres and a herd of from

[1] Leland's Itn. vol. vi. p. 76, fol. 80.
[2] Nash, vol. ii. p. 304.

[3] Cal. of Patent Rolls, p. 230.

60 to 70 fallow-deer. Whether this is an ancient park I have not been able to ascertain.

Northwich Park is in the parish of Blockley, and contains 290 acres with a large herd of fallow-deer. It was a park 'well stocked with deer' in Nash's time (1781), and was probably imparked in the early part of the eighteenth century.

Near the Forest of Feckenham, on the eastern verge of the county, were several parks. *Feckenham Park* itself, in the parish of Hanbury, was a very ancient Royal park, granted by the Crown in the reign of Queen Elizabeth, and eventually sold to Lord Keeper Coventry.

Hanbury Park, enclosed late in the seventeenth century, contains 63 acres, with a herd of 184 fallow-deer. The handsome seat of the Vernon family, in the midst of it, was erected in 1710.

The Calendar of Patent Rolls contains the notice of a park granted to Simon de Wauton at *Bradell*, in the thirty-seventh of Henry III., within the Forest of Feckenham ; and in the twentieth of Edward I. William de Valence had license to impark a certain preserve (vivarium) and 80 acres of land on either side to increase his park of Inkberg (*Inkberrow*) within the bounds of the same forest.[1]

In this neighbourhood is *Beoley* and *Bordesley*. The first is noticed in the ancient maps, and was a park of the Sheldon family, disparked probably at the period of the Great Rebellion when the house was destroyed.

Bordesley Park, from whence the deer were removed by the present Mr. Dug-

dale to his seat at Merevale in Warwickshire, is said not to be ancient. I find it, however, mentioned, together with 'the pleasant park' of *Hewell Grange*, in Nash's 'History of Worcestershire,' printed in 1781.

Grafton Park, an ancient seat of the Earls of Shrewsbury, is thus noticed by Leland (the park has been long disparked): 'I came by a parke about a mile ere I came to Bromsgrove, on the left hand. It is called Grafton. It longid, before Bosworth Field, to the Staffordes, noble knightes, since by attainder it came to the Kinge, and was given by King Henry VII. to Sᵣ. Gilbert Talbot, and in that name it yet remayneth. In this Parke is a fayre Mannour place, and one Talbot at this present dwellith in it.'[2]

The Park of *Westwood*, near Droitwich, does not occur in the ancient surveys, but is said to have been long established. It contains a range for fallow-deer of 200 acres, with a hundred head of deer.

At *Hagley*, Lord Lyttelton's, there appears to have been a park as early as the reign of Edward III., when it belonged to Sir John Botetourt, but it was for ages disparked, and restored by Sir Charles Lyttelton about the year 1694.[3] It contains 220 acres, and about 70 fallow-deer.

The park at *Great Witley*, now Lord Dudley's, was certainly imparked before it belonged to the Foley family in the eighteenth century, as it is marked in Saxton's Map of 1577. It contains 400 acres and 700 head of fallow-deer.

Near Witley is *Abberley*, the site of

[1] Cal. of Pat. Rolls, pp. 26, 56. At p. 108 reference is made to a license granted in the 3rd Edw. III. to Wm. Corbett, to impark his

wood of Prodesor in this county.
[2] Leland's Itin. vol. iv. p. 113, fol. 186 a.
[3] Nash, vol. i. p. 490.

an ancient park, which also is noted by Saxton. It has been long disparked.

At *Stanford*, the seat of the Winningtons, was a park formed in the early part of the last century, and disparked about the year 1790. There were also parks at *Ham Castle* and *Eastham*, in this neighbourhood. The first, which formerly belonged to the family of Jeffreys, was disparked at the close of the eighteenth century. At the latter a farm called Park Farm still exists. It once belonged to the Cornewalls.[1]

Kyre Park was enclosed by John Kyare in the third year of Edward III., originally said to have contained 500 acres. In Nash's time but 180. Mr. Habington mentions 'the tall and mighty oaks as scarce any ground in England, within that quantity of acres, can show so many.'[2] It was disparked by the present proprietor, Mr. Child, within the last ten years.

Sutton Park, in Tenbury near Kyre, was the seat of the Actons in the reign of Henry IV., and afterwards passed to the Lucys of Charlecote in Warwickshire. It occurs in Saxton's Map.

Spetchley Park, near Worcester, contains about 130 acres, and 170 fallow and a few red-deer. It was enclosed in the reign of Charles I.

List of Existing Deer Parks in the County of Worcester.

1. CROOME	.	. Earl of Coventry.
2. ELMLEY CASTLE	.	Lady Pakington.
3. NORTHWICK	.	Lord Northwick.
4. HANBURY	.	. Mr. Vernon.
5. WESTWOOD	.	. Sir John Pakington, Bart.
6. HAGLEY	.	. Lord Lyttelton.
7. WITLEY	.	. Earl of Dudley.
8. SPETCHLEY	.	. Mr. Berkeley.

[1] Information of Sir Thomas Winnington, Bart.

[2] Nash, vol. ii. p. 70.

CHAPTER VIII.

NOTES ON DEER PARKS IN THE COUNTIES

OF

DERBYSHIRE,   NOTTINGHAMSHIRE, AND

STAFFORDSHIRE,   LINCOLNSHIRE.

Chartley Park, Staffordshire.

CHAPTER VIII.

DERBYSHIRE.

YSONS, in his 'History of Derbyshire,'[1] observes that 'there were anciently seven parks belonging to the Earls of Lancaster, and afterwards to the Duchy of Lancaster, within this county, besides that there were in the early part of the fourteenth century, not less than fifty-four deer-parks in Derbyshire, belonging to monastic bodies and individuals.' He proceeds to give a list of these parks in their different parishes, but it will be more convenient for our present purpose to notice them in detail, beginning first with those which belonged to the Duchy of Lancaster. These were mostly in and around Duffield, one of the castles of the great House of Ferrers, and which came to the Crown on the fall of the Earl of Derby, and was granted by Henry III. to his son Edward Earl of Lancaster. In the year 1330, in answer to a *quo warranto*, Henry Earl of Lancaster claimed seven parks in the frith or forest of Duffield ; these (which have been all long disparked) were, *Shottull, Mauncell,*

[1] P. clxix.

Postern, *Belper*, *Morley*, *Ravensdale*, and *Schymynd-cliffe*. They were all in the neighbourhood of Belper and Duffield, in the centre part of the southern division of Derbyshire.

The Park of Shottull is marked in Saxton's Map of 1577 as Shotley Park, but was then probably disparked, as it is represented without pales: it appears to have been the most considerable of the Duffield Parks, and is thus noticed in an original wardmote[1] of 'Duffield Fryth,' held at 'Rowhouse,' die Lunæ px̃ post fm̃ Aĩschĩ ep̃i anno Reg. Henrici Septimi xiii. 'P̃cus de Shottull. On the Sunday next after Saynt Barnaby Day, a doo was kylled in the blak broke, and cared out of the pale and stollen, by whom it can not as yet be ꝑved. On the Tuysday next aftr Saynt Barnaby Day a doo was kylled and drawen aftr to Thoms̃ Pk̃er hous. Roger Vernon had a buk by the keꝑ. My Lord of Shrewsbury kylled a buk, ii sowres, and a sowrell, and gaff theym to Sr Harry Willoughby, Knyght, and other squyers and gentilmen that were there. Antony Babyngton a sowre by the keꝑ. Mastr Thoms̃ Talbot a sowre and a doo by his own auctorite. Nicholas Shirley a sowre. The Bailiffe of Derby and other of the same town had a buk on the Monday next aftr Saynt Gyly's Day, a chaunce buk and a sowre that the keꝑ had to his own use the same tyme. Godfrey Foliambe a buk by a warrant. Thoms̃ Leyke a buk by a warrant. Mastre Elton had a buk by the keꝑ. Harry Sacheverell a sowre by the keꝑ; William Sacheverell a buk by the wodmastr̃. Edward Savege a buk by the keꝑ. Mastre Stokes a buk by the keꝑ. The keꝑ had a buk the same tyme. Thomas Molyneux a buk by the keꝑ. William Gresley a buk by the keꝑ. The Abbot of Sale a buk by the keꝑ. John Alsop and other of his friends had a buk by the keꝑ. Itm̃ the keꝑ had ii bukks when he removed to Wyndloy hill.' The reversion of Shottle, or Shothill Park, together with that of Postern, was granted by Queen Elizabeth to the Earl of Shrewsbury for forty-one years, in the thirteenth year of her reign. The herbage of these parks was at that time valued at 86*l.*[2]

Mauncell, or Mansell Park, is also noticed in the wardmote above referred to. It is at present, with the Park of *Revensdale*, comprehended within the parish of Mugginton.

Postern Park occurs also in the same wardmote. It adjoined Shottle, and is marked in Saxton's Survey as Postern Wood.

Morley Park is a little to the east of the preceding parks, in the great parish of Duffield. According to Lysons,[3] this park was granted by Queen Elizabeth, about the year 1573, to John Stanhope, Esq. The wardmote before alluded to observes :—'Nicholas Kneveton and Roger Vernon cam into Morley ꝑke and hunted by there own autorite and kylled no thyng. Itm̃ the said Nicholas Kneveton brak the pale another tyme as he went to Butterley.'

Belper, now a considerable place, is about three miles north of Duffield, of which it was originally a chapelry. The name—*Beau-repaire*—was given to it, as it is supposed, by Edward Crouchback, Earl of Lancaster, who died in 1296, from its beautiful situation, afterwards corrupted to

[1] *Penes* the Earl Ferrers.
[2] Cotton MS. Titus, B. iv. fo. 297.
[3] P. 141.

Belper.[1] The park here was called ' *The Lady Park.*'[2] The herbage and pasturage, worth 13s. 4d. per annum, was granted in reversion for thirty years to Robert Holmes in the seventeenth of Queen Elizabeth,[3] and finally passed from the Crown in the reign of Charles I.[4]

The Park of *Schymynd-cliffe* I find only noticed by Lysons as one of the Duffield Parks, unless indeed it is identical with *Holland Park* and Holland Wood, a manor in the parish of Wirksworth, which was given by Thomas Earl of Lancaster to Sir Robert Holland, and forfeited by the attainder of Henry Holland Duke of Exeter in 1411. The park is marked by Saxton.

To the east of this group of Duchy Parks (the ancient hunting preserves of the House of Lancaster), there were in the Elizabethan period, as we find by Saxton's Survey, several parks, of which the largest was *Codnor*, in Heanor parish, the ancient seat of the Greys, and afterwards of the Zouches. Here Robert Lord Grey in 1330 claimed four parks, and Robert Strelley, Esq., two parks, in the manor of Shipley, in the same parish : but one was allowed, the other, *Estinker*, was stocked with deer, but being only a new enclosure was not allowed as a park.[5] There were also parks, now, with the others above-mentioned, long disused, at two other places in this parish, at *Aldercar* and at *Loscoe.* Two more must be noted in this part of the county, *Denby Park* and *Kiddesley Park*: the former belonged to the Rosels, in the reign of Henry III.,

and the latter to the Abbot of Chester in 1235.[6] At both *Pentrich* and *South Winfield*, a little to the south of Morley Park, were two parks : those of Pentrich belonged to the Abbot and Convent of Darley, ' and the site of one of them,' adds Lysons, ' tho' long since disparked, retains the name.'[7] Of the Winfield Parks, the larger, extending into the parish of Pentrich, contained nearly 1,000 acres.[7]

In the adjoining parishes of *Alfreton* and *Shirland* there were ancient parks, the former belonging to the Chaworth and the latter to the Grey family. Both were claimed as parks in 1330,[8] and both appear in Saxton's Survey of 1577. Alfreton was an existing park in 1817. Shirland was then long disparked.

In 1380, also, Roger Deincourt claimed a park at *Morton*, a manor in the immediate neighbourhood.[8]

Further north, in the parish of Chesterfield, there was a park at *Wingeworth*, the seat of the Hunloke family in 1817, and at *Walton*, the ancient seat of the Foljambes, existing in 1577.

At *Sutton-in-the-Dale*, belonging to the Leakes and to Lord Ormond in 1817, and at *Bolsover*, enclosed in the year 1200 (and long ago converted into tillage).[9] Lysons quotes the pipe roll of the second of John to prove that 30l. was expended at that period for its enclosure by the King.

East of Bolsover, on the borders of Nottinghamshire, is Langwith, where the Bassett family had two parks in 1330,[10] and more to the south *Hardwick*, the fine

---

[1] Lysons, p. 140.
[2] Wardmote of Duffield Frith, *penes* Earl Ferrers.
[3] Cotton MSS. Titus, B. iv. fo. 297.
[4] Lysons, p. 136.

[5] Ib. p. 181, quoting the *quo warranto* roll of the fourth Edward III.
[6] Lysons, pp. 188–214.
[7] Ib. pp. 230–292.   [8] Ib. pp. 4, 214, 254.
[9] Ib. p. 54.   [10] Ib. p. 198.

old seat of the Duke of Devonshire. Here is an existing deer park, which, although ancient, is not found marked in the Surveys of Saxton or Speed. It is noticed, however, by Leland in his 'Itinerary.'[1]

In the adjoining parish of *Pleasley* was a park in the fifteenth century,[2] and at *Scarcliffe* the Prior of Newsted had a park in 1330, which was granted to the Pierrepont family in 1344.[3]

To the north of Chesterfield Saxton marks parks at *Stavely* and *Woodthorpe*, in the same parish.

Stavely was the chief house of the noble family of Frecheville. The park is alluded to in a letter from the Earl of Shrewsbury to his Countess, among 'the Talbot Papers,' in which he recounts a frolic of his stepson, Charles Cavendish, 'enticed to go a stealing into Stavely Park in the night.' This took place in the reign of Queen Elizabeth.[4]

Woodthorpe was the ancient seat of the Rodes family, before they removed to the adjoining parish of *Barlborough*, where also there was said to have been three parks, containing about 400 acres of land, according to a survey of the year 1630.[5]

At *Holmsfield*, in the parish of Dronfield, and at *Norton*, on the borders of Yorkshire, the Chaworth family had parks in 1330, as appears by the *quo warranto* roll of that year;[6] and at the same period another was owned by Ralph de Rye at *Whitwell*, on the Nottinghamshire border, claimed from time immemorial. A park also existed at *Norton*, in 1817, belonging to Mr. Shore.

In the parish of Bakewell, about the centre of the northern division of Derbyshire, were two ancient parks, at *Haddon* and *Harthill*, the former the well-known and venerable seat of the Vernons, 'The Kings of the Park,' and the latter of the Cokaynes. Both these parks, existing in the Elizabethan period, have been long disused and disparked. Two existing parks have, however, taken their places, *Chatsworth* and *Stanton-in-the-Peak*, the former the magnificent palace of the Duke of Devonshire in the parish of Edensor. There was a park here when it belonged to the Leche family, previous to the year 1550, and it appears in Saxton's Map in 1577, 'the Stand' being particularly mentioned. The present park is said to be nine miles in circumference.

Stanton is in the parish of Youlgrave. The park here, a wild and rocky enclosure of 130 acres, dates from the year 1800. The deer, entirely black or dark, came from the ancient park of Chartley in Staffordshire.

Returning towards the south, about the centre of the county, there is an existing park at *Alderwasley*, in the parish of Wicksworth, enclosed about the year 1715. It contains 187 acres, and about 130 fallow-deer.

In the neighbourhood of *Ashbourn* were several parks; one founded by Sir Thomas Cokaine, who died in the reign of Henry VIII., was in that parish, and another at *Tissington*,[7] the seat of the Fitzherbert family. At Bradley also, three miles east of Ashbourn, was a park according to Saxton, and another called 'Hugh Park,' closely adjoining to it.

[1] Leland's Itin. vol. v. p. 108, fol. 94.
[2] Lysons, p. 232.
[3] Ib. p. 252.
[4] Hunter's nev Illustrations of the Life of
Shakespeare, p. 55.
[5] Lysons, p. 44.
[6] Ib. pp. 220, 134–285.
[7] Ib. p. clxix.

Birchwood Park, a few miles south of Ashbourn, is in the parish of Norbury, and is marked in Saxton's Map.

At *Shirley*, a little to the east, and four miles south of Ashbourn, were two parks, belonging to the ancient family who derive their name from this place. They are thus described in Sir Thomas Shirley's MS. account of his own family, now in the British Museum,[1] but have been long disparked : the site, now woodland, is still called Shirley Park. 'On the one side, Shirley is encompassed by two ancient stately parks of a large extension and most pleasant to behold, in respect of the fair woods and their chrystal brook, &c.' 'The hayes adjoining to the parks are called "Shirley Hayes," which for the large compass of ground and great plenty of high hedges and stately oaks in them, and the ancient woods belonging to the same manor, may be more aptly called a forest.'

The family of *Longford* had a park in the adjoining parish of that name in 1330. The license for its enclosure was granted by King Henry III. in 1251.[2] Saxton also marks a park called *Myddleton*, near Longford, and another at *Barton*, closely adjoining.

Cubley was the chief seat of the Montgomery family, who had a park there, which is noticed in Saxton's Survey.

At Doveridge, on the borders of Staffordshire, the monks of Tutbury are said to have had a park called *Holt*.

Sudbury Park, not far from Doveridge, was enclosed in the year 1614, as appears by a MS. poem by John Harstaff, in Lord Vernon's possession. It contains about 600 acres and a herd of 300 fallow-deer.

There had, however, been a more ancient park here in 1330.[2]

Another existing park, famous for the magnificence of its oak timber, is at *Keddleston*, four miles north-west of Derby. It is an area of between 500 and 600 acres, with about 450 fallow-deer. It is said to have been enclosed about the year 1760, but there appears to have been an ancient park here before, according to Saxton's Survey. The park at *Langley* adjoining, now disparked, was at that time larger and more important. It suffered terribly in 1545, during a great tempest in the month of June of that year, which according to the ideas of the time was ascribed to the devil. A letter giving an account of the devastation is printed by Lysons,[3] and records :—' Syr Wyllam Bassett's place rente and pully'd downe, and the wood that growethe aboute his place, and in his parke he (the devil as we do suppose) pulled down his pale, and dryve out his deere, &c.'

To the east of Derby, in the parish of *Kirk-Hallam*, were two parks, one belonging to the family of Willoughby at *Maperley*, and one to the Abbot of Dale, in the reign of Edward III.[4]

In Horsley parish, to the north of the county town, was the Castle of *Horeston*, at one time a Royal possession. A park appears to have been attached to it, and here King James I. is recorded to have hunted during a progress in Derbyshire. The park has long ago been converted into tillage.[5]

There was also another park in this parish, at *Denby*, as early as the reign of Henry III.[6]

---

[1] Harl. MSS. 4928.
[2] Lysons, pp. 199, 269.
[3] Ib. p. 160, note.

[4] Lysons, p. 73.
[5] Ib. p. 187.
[6] Ib. p. 188.

At *Ilkeston* also, a parish in the neighbourhood, on the borders of Nottinghamshire, the family of Cantilupe are said to have had two parks in 1330.[1]

More to the south, but still to the east of Derby, is the parish of Spandon. Here was an ancient park called *Stanley*, wherein Dale Abbey was founded;[2] here also is an existing park, called *Locko*, originally Lockhay. It is said to be an ancient park, of 260 acres and about 200 fallow-deer. The Bardolfs had an ancient park at *Ockbrook*, and the Abbot of Dale another, which had been made by the Grendons, in the early part of the thirteenth century.

Three parks are marked by Saxton in the immediate neighbourhood of Ockbrook—at *Hopwell, Risley,* and *Sandiacre.* The second appears to have been called *Woodhall Park*, and belonged to the Babington and afterwards to the Sheffield family. It has been long converted into tillage.[3]

At *Little-Eaton*, three miles north of Derby, Philip de Wilughby enclosed a park in the reign of Richard I.[4]

In that part of Derbyshire south of the county town were the parks of *Melbourne, Repton, Smisby, Croxall,* and *Drakelow,* and the existing parks of *Calke* and *Bretby.*

Melbourne was the palace and park of the Bishops of Carlisle. It passed to the Coke family by agreement and an Act of Parliament in 1704. The park has been long cultivated and destroyed.[5]

Repton Park was the inheritance of the Findernes and afterwards of the Harpurs. The park paling existed in 1817.[6]

At *Smisby*, John Shepey, in answer to a *quo warranto*, in 1330, stated that his ancestors had from time immemorial had a park within their manor there.[7]

Croxall Park is marked in Saxton's Survey. It was a seat of the Curzon family.

Drakelow, the ancient seat of the Gresleys, appears among Lysons' list of parks, existing in the year 1817. It is marked by Saxton.

Sir John Harpur Crewe's park at *Calke Abbey* does not appear in the ancient maps, but is by no means a modern park. It is a fine and richly wooded area of 500 acres, with a herd of between 600 and 700 head of fallow and red-deer.

The date of Lord Chesterfield's beautiful park at *Bretby* is also uncertain, though undoubtedly ancient. Mr. Wolley in his MS. account of Derbyshire (1712) speaks of it as 'a very large park, well wooded and stored with several kinds of deer and exotic beasts.' There is a curious view of it in Kip's 'Noveaux Theatre de la Grande Bretagne.' Bretby contains at present 450 acres, and a large herd of menil, Manilla, or spotted deer, only.

Existing Deer Parks in Derbyshire.

1. HARDWICK .	} The Duke of Devonshire.	
2. CHATSWORTH		
3. KEDDLESTON	. Lord Scarsdale.	
4. SUDBURY .	. Lord Vernon.	
5. BRETBY .	. Earl of Chesterfield	
6. CALKE .	. Sir John Harpur Crewe, Bart.	
7. ALDERWASLEY	. Mr. Hurt.	
8. LOCKO .	. Mr. Lowe.	
9. STANTON .	. Mr. Thornhill.	

---

[1]. Lysons, p. 193. [2] Ib. p.261.
[3] Ib. p. 225. [4] Ib. p. 123.
[5] Ib. p. 211. The keepers of this park of Melbourne are said to have had their offerings free on Candlemas Day : 'and their parson and curate found them a taper of wax for their

offering that day free, without paying anything for the same.' The head of the Melbourne family is said also to have by custom an annual buck from Hardwick Hall. See the Reliquary, vol. i. p. 240.
[6] Ib. p. 237. [7] Ib. p. 245. [8] Ib. p. 240.

STAFFORDSHIRE.

THE Castle and Honor of Tutbury, the principal seat of the great House of Ferrers, and after the fall of that House, of the Earls and Dukes of Lancaster, is built on the banks of the Dove, on the borders of Derbyshire, flanked on the west by what was once the Forest of Needwood and an attendant group of eight ancient parks,[1] 'besides the little park that the castle stands in.'[2] These parks were called *Castle-hay, Stockley, Rolleston, Hanbury, Agardesley, Barton, Heylyns,* recte Highlands, and *Sherrold*; besides *Rowley* and *Newpark,* according to Sir Simon Degge's list in Harwood's edition of Erdeswick's 'Staffordshire.' All of them are described as belonging to the Crown before the Great Rebellion, though some had been granted out, both for terms of years and in fee, before that period. The following description of these parks is from the Harleian MS. No. 71 and No. 568, written in the reign of Queen Elizabeth and in that of James I.

' The *Castle Park* is in circuit one mile, in good meadow XL acres, the rest all very good and *bateful* pasture. It will bear well seven score deer, and sufficient herbage to make the king's rent. There are in it at the present XXX deer. There is no covert in all the park, but the clyff, whereupon the castle standeth. The keeper therof is appointed by the King's Majesty's Letters Patent, under the Duchy seal. His fee is

yearly 4*l.*, one horse grass for himself, one other for his deputy ; six beasts' grass for himself, and two for his deputy ; and such other fees and rewards as belong to a keeper.'

' The park called *Castle-hay,* distant from the castle a little mile, contains three miles and a half about, and the deere viewed to CCCCLXXX, and old dottred oakes MMMMMC, and in timber trees young and old CCCCXX, noe underwood, but in meadow ground severed XI acres and half and more.' This park is said to have been divided from Needwood by a hay or hedge by the first Robert Earl Ferrers, who died in 1139, and hence its name of Castle-Hay.[3]

' *Stockley Park* contains in compass XXI furlongs and an half.' This, together with several of the other parks, was taken out of the forest of Needwood during the lives of the two last Earls of Derby, before the year 1262.[3] It was sold by the Crown in the sixth of Charles I.[4]

Rolleston, ' half a mile distant from the castle on the east side, contains in compass one mile and quarter : the deer viewed to CXX : in old dottred oaks M and XL.' Rolleston was also alienated by King Charles I. in the fourth year of his reign.[4]

' *Hanbury Park* adjoyns on the south side of the said Castle-Hay, within one

[1] Leland restricts the number to four, viz., Castle-Hay, Hanbury, Barton, and the New Park.
[2] Harl. MS. No. 568, quoted in the Topo-grapher, vol. ii. p. 174.
[3] Mosley's History of Tutbury, p. 15.
[4] Mosley's Tutbury, p. 216.

quarter of a mile, containing in compasse two miles and an halfe : the deere viewed CLXX : in old trees dottred and stubbs of oakes M and timber trees XXX.'

'The park of *Agardesley* contains in compass XXI furlongs.'

'The park of *Barton* contains in compass XVI furlongs and dim. and X poles.'

The park of *Heylyn's*, in compass one part XVIII furlongs and XIII poles, and every part XV furlongs.' It appears from a note in the State Paper Office that this park was purchased from the usurping powers during the Commonwealth, by Gregory Walklett, who 'destroyed the deer, felled the timber and ploughed up the soil,' &c.[1] According to Mr. Wilkes' 'List of Staffordshire Parks,' however, Heylins, belonging to John Turton, Esq., 'was stored with deer' in 1735.[2]

'The park of *Sherrold* contains in compass X furlongs and dim. and X poles.'

'The number of all the timber-trees within the parks of Needwood are MMMCCCCVI.'

'The number of dottrell trees within the said parks XXIᵐDCCCXLI after XIIᵈ a tree, for the dottrells come to DCXIIl. and XXIᵈ.'

Of these parks the four last are said to have been stocked with deer about the time of the Civil Wars, according to Sir Simon Degge,'[3] who also includes the parks of *Rowley* and *New-Park* as belonging to the king, and stocked with deer. The former had been granted to Sir Thomas Leigh.

Other parks independent of the Castle of Tutbury, but originally, no doubt,

granted by its lords, and taken out of the forest on the western side of it, were those at *Hamstall-Ridware, Bagots Park, Bromley, Horecross*, and *Wichnor*.

Of the great antiquity of *Bagots Park*, so celebrated for its magnificent oaks, there can be no doubt, although the precise date of its enclosure is unknown. It contains at present about 1,000 acres, and about 400 fallow-deer, chiefly black and dun, the ancient Needwood Forest colour ; also from 50 to 60 red-deer. In this park is also a herd of wild goats, which have been there from time immemorial, and according to Strutt, in his 'Sylva Brittanica,' were originally presented to one of Lord Bagot's ancestors by Richard II.[4]

Bromley was disparked before the period of the Civil Wars, but is marked, as Bagots Park, Horecross, and Wichnor, are, in Saxton's Survey of 1577.

Horecross is an existing park. It is mentioned as such in Erdeswick's Survey of this county ; began about 1593.

Wichnor was a seat of the Somerviles, and afterwards of the Offleys. Horace Walpole was here in 1760, and describes 'the pretty park, the situation a brow of a hill commanding sweet meadows, through which the Trent serpentines in numberless windings and branches. The spires of the Cathedral of Lichfield are in front at a distance, with a variety of other steeples, seats, and farms, and the horizon bounded by rich hills covered with blue woods. If you love a prospect, or bacon,[5] you will certainly come hither.' Wichnor now belongs to the family of Levett.

---

[1] S. P. O. Domestic. Charles II. Aug. 26, 1666, p. 69.

[2] Shaw's Saffordshire, vol. i. p. xxiv.

[3] Harwood's Erdeswick's Staffordshire, p. xix.

[4] Strutt's Sylva Brittanica, p. 3.

[5] Alluding to the Wichnor flitch.

The father of the present owner disparked it, but there is a probability that it will shortly be restored.

At *Dunstall*, the seat of Mr. Hardy, a small park or paddock of deer has lately been enclosed.

At *Sinai Park*, near Burton, the Pagets had a deer park in 1660 and in 1735, and there were deer at *Loxley*, the seat of the Kinnersley family, between Needwood and Chartley, at the same period,[1] and according to Neale, in his 'Views of Seats,' in 1821.

Of the early history of the wild and historical park of *Chartley*, which lies still farther to the west of the Forest of Needwood, we know but little. Originally enclosed by the great House of Ferrers, it is said that the breed of wild cattle still preserved here were driven into the park from the forest in the reign of Henry III.[2] The wild cattle of Chartley are, like those of Craven, Chillingham, and Lyme Park in Cheshire, of a white, or rather cream colour, but they differ from them in some minute particulars; for instance, the Craven cattle are destitute of horns, while those at Chartley have sharp horns, the points of which, together with their ears, are tipped with black; those of Chillingham and Lyme have similar horns, but their ears are red. The size of all these varieties is rather below that of the common breed of cows. It is the opinion of Professor Owen that they are descended from domestic cattle introduced by the Romans, which subsequently became half wild from breeding together for many years in an unreclaimed state; and, in a similar way, the numerous herds of wild cattle in South America owe their origin to the tame ones originally imported into that country by Europeans.[3] Leland, in his 'Itinerary,' notices 'the mighty large park' of Chartley, and Erdeswick, in his survey of this county, observes of it :— 'The park is very large, and hath therein red-deer, fallow-deer, wild beasts, and swine.' Wild beasts, it may be necessary to remark, is still the local name for the wild cattle, about twenty in number. The wild swine have long disappeared, but in an account-book of the steward of the manor as late as 1683–4, I find the following item :—' P^d the cooper for a paile for ye wild swine 2^s.' The extent of Chartley Park is about 900 acres of heathy land in a wild and uncultivated state. Here is a herd of about 300 red and fallow-deer, but little fine timber. The ancient oaks are represented as dead, in the map in Plot's 'History of Staffordshire,' printed in 1686.

A little to the north of Chartley, Saxton marks a park at *Birchwood*: this originally belonged to the Aston family, and in Sir Symon Degge's time to Mr. Goring. There were deer in it at the period of the Civil Wars, but it has been long disparked.

Above Birchwood was *Paynsley Park*, on the banks of the Blyth, the ancient seat of the Draycotes: disparked before the time of Sir S. Degge.

Passing to the north-eastern quarter of the county, on the borders of Derbyshire, parks are marked by Saxton both at *Croxden* and at *Alton*; the one an abbey

---

[1] List of Parks by R. Wilkes, quoted in Shaw's Staffordshire, vol. i. p. xxiv.
[2] Mosley's Hist. of Tutbury, p. 12.
[3] Mosley and Brown's Natural History of Tutbury, p. 16.

founded by the Verdons, the other the castle of the same family and of their descendants the Furnivalls and the Talbots.

A park 'stored with deer' is said to be at Wotton, belonging to Mr. Wheler in 1735.[1]

An ancient existing park is to be remarked at *Okeover*, the beautiful seat of the venerable family of that name on the banks of the Dove. Its origin is unknown, but it is supposed to be of great antiquity, and has the appearance of genuine forest land. The park, which contains 200 acres and a herd of 150 fallow-deer, is remarkable for its fine oak and fir timber. Erdeswick notices 'the fair old house, park, and goodly demesne' of this enchanting spot.

He also records 'the goodly ancient house and park' of *Blore*, nearly adjoining, once the seat of the Bassets of Staffordshire, and in Degge's time of their descendant William Cavendish Marquis and Duke of Newcastle. It was then a park with deer, and remained so till after the Restoration, and is marked as a park by Plot in his map of the county in 1686, but both house and park have been long destroyed.

At *Throwley*, a little to the east, was the house and park of the Cromwells Earls of Ardglass in Ireland, and formerly of the Meverells. It was an existing park in Plot's time, but has been long disparked.

In the more northern parts of Staffordshire no ancient parks occur in the Surveys of Saxton and Speed, though an existing park at *Swythamley*, in the town-

ship of Heaton, on the borders of Cheshire, may possibly lay claim to antiquity. Swythamley was a grange to Dieulacres Abbey, and 'the parke-land,' near Swythamley Grange, occurs in a lease granted in the twenty-ninth of Henry VIII.[2] It is said that deer have been always kept here. There is at present a herd of 150 deer of the menil breed. The park contains 200 acres of soil of a peaty nature.

The park of *Knypersley*, formerly the seat of the Bowyers, is given in Sir Simon Degge's list, as containing deer. It was disparked in 1795, and re-stocked with deer in 1859. The park at present contains 120 acres, and about 80 fallow-deer.

Returning towards the south we come to *Bradwell*, the ancient house of the Sneyds, where there were deer at the period of the Civil Wars.[3] The family afterwards removing to their present seat of *Keel*, it appears that the deer alsowere removed thither, as they are particularly mentioned in a book of ' Poems on several occasions,' published in 1733 ;[4] but Keel has been long disparked.

Near Keel is *Madeley*, 'a goodly manor,' the seat of the family of Crew ; and here there was a park in the time of Degge and Plot.

Healey Castle, at one time the principal residence of the House of Audley, adjoins Madeley. Here there was a park, for in 1223 King Henry III. gave to Henry de Audley twelve hinds to be taken out of the forest of Canoc, to store his park at Hethley.[5] No other record of it appears to exist.

To the east is *Trentham*, the beautiful

[1] Shaw's Staffordshire, vol. i. p. xxiv.
[2] Sleigh's History of Leek, p. 55.
[3] Sir S. Degge's list.
[4] Printed for the author at Manchester.
[5] Dugdale's Baronage, vol. i. p. 746.

seat and park of the Duke of Sutherland. It is a park of 540 acres, and a herd of 320 fallow-deer. This park appears to have been enclosed by Lord Gower about the year 1735. The Gower family had also a park at *Stone* at the same period, which in Degge's time had belonged to Mr. Crompton. He notices also parks at *Stoke* and. *Sandon* 'stocked with deer.'

On the borders of Shropshire was the Park of *Willowbridge*, in the parish of Meare, noted in all the old maps, and about the time of the Civil Wars belonging to the Earl of Shrewsbury, but without deer. *Gerards-Bromley*, and *Broughton* are a little to the south ; both are marked as parks in Plot's Survey : the former belonged to Lord Gerard, the latter to Mr. Broughton.

The Bishops of Lichfield had also a large park at *Blore*, in the neighbourhood of their residence at Eccleshall Castle. It has been long disparked. And another at *Brewood*, noticed below. Leland mentions 'the wonderful fair wood' in Blore Park.

Near Eccleshall is *Ellenhall*, the site of an ancient park, noticed by Saxton ; and south of it *Knightley* and *Norbury Parks*, which occur in the same survey. There were deer in the latter belonging to the Skrymshire family, in the middle of the seventeenth century, and at *Horsley*, belonging to the Peshalls, at the same period ; and also at *Aqualate*, south of Norbury, a park, still existing, and which belonged also to the Skrymshires in former times.

In the neighbourhood of Stafford were the parks of *Ingestrie* and *Tixall*, besides

that which was attached to the castle of *Stafford*. The first is an existing park, belonging to the Earl of Shrewsbury and Talbot, and formerly to his ancestors of the Chetwind family. The latter has been disparked since the year 1735.

South of Stafford is the forest, or more properly, chase of Cannock, generally called Cannock (pronounced Cank) Wood. Leland describes it as 'a great thing, merely longging to the Bishoprick of Lichfield. . There is *Bewdesert* his place and parke, and Shucborough his place (where is a park now of red dere) is yn the side of Cankwoode.' This, observes Harwood, in his edition of ' Erdeswick's Staffordshire,' 'is probably *Heywood* Park, which belongs to the Marquis of Anglesey, and is remarkable for the beautiful woody dingles that wind into the sides of the forest.' Near this is *Oakedge Park*, belonging to Lord Lichfield.

Adjoining Cannock Chase were the Parks of *Colton, Hawksyard, Pillerton, Teddesley*, and *Wolseley*, the last an existing park with the right of deer-leap from the chase. The park was originally enclosed by license granted to Ralph Wolseley, one of the Barons of the Exchequer in the reign of Edward IV. This right of saltory or deer-leap was once not uncommon throughout the realm, but the present instance of a chartered deer-leap still exercising its privileges is believed to be unique.[1]

The origin of the park which once belonged to the Bishops of Lichfield and Coventry at *Brewood*, on the borders of Shropshire, is preserved in Mr. Eyton's admirable history of that county. ' King John,' he says, ' on April 10th, 1200, after

[1] See page 14 for a note on deer-leaps, and hereafter, p. 191, for a view of this at Wolseley.

a visit to Brewood, having reached Worcester, addressed a precept to Geoffrey Fitz-piers and Hugh de Nevill (The Chief Justice of England and the Justice of the Forest) prohibiting them from hindering the Bishop of Coventry in enclosing a park in his wood of Brewood, for which park to be two leagues in circumference the Bishop had the King's license. A further precept of King John, dated 20th July, 1213, allows the Archbishop of Dublin to take thirty stags in Brewood Park, the See of Coventry being vacant.[1]

At *Weston-under-Lizard*, near this ancient Episcopal park, the late Earl of Bradford established a deer park.

The following parks were existing in this part of the county during the seventeenth and eighteenth centuries :—

At *Chillington*, the seat of the Giffords; *Hilton*, that of a younger branch of the Vernons; *Wrottesley*, belonging to the very ancient family of that name, now Barons Wrottesley, and founded by Hugh Wrottesley, son and heir of Sir William, who had license to make a park here in the twenty-first of Edward III.[2] At *Pepperhill*, which belonged to the Talbots Earls of Shrewsbury, and at *Patteshull*, once the seats of the Astleys of Staffordshire, and now of Lord Dartmouth.

In the south-western corner of the county Saxton marks parks at *Envill* and *Compton* ; the former a seat of the Greys, the latter of the Whorwoods. ' The fair park' at Compton is noticed by Erdeswick, but appears to have been

without deer at the period of the Civil Wars.

A more modern park was at *Himley*, Lord Ward's, in 1735, and an ancient one at *Sedgeley*, belonging to his ancestor Lord Dudley, and which Erdeswick calls ' a large goodly park.' Another park was at *Dudley Castle*, belonging to the same nobleman.

At *Sandwell*, the now deserted seat of the Legges Earls of Dartmouth, there appears to have been deer in 1735 ; and at *Bentley*, once the seat of the family of Lane, in the parish of Wolverhampton, were two parks, as we find on the authority of Sir Simon Degge. One of them was existing and ' stored with deer' in 1735.

Shenston Park, on the borders of Warwickshire, can lay claim to great antiquity. It was first enclosed in the twentieth of Henry III. by one of the Grendons, and, was three miles in circumference, and in the time of Henry VIII. stocked with deer and game. It was disparked in the reign of Charles II.[3] Erdeswick characterises it as ' a goodly manor and park,' and Leland observes, ' Shenston, a park of the Kinges, and 3 miles about, well deered.'[4]

At *Drayton-Basset*, near Tamworth, there was probably a park from a very early period. It is recognised by Saxton and all the ancient surveys. It was disparked at the latter end of the last century.

Fisherwick, the seat of the Skeffingtons, and afterwards of the Chichesters Earls and Marquesses of Donegal, was a park

[1] Eyton's Shropshire, vol. ii. p. 186 ; quoting the Close Rolls.
[2] Harwood's Erdeswick, 2nd ed. p. 360.
[3] Harwood's Erdeswick, p. 421.
[4] Itin. vol. iv. p. 116, fol. 186 b.

with deer in 1735. It was disparked and divided into farms in the early part of the present century.

The last, though not the most recent, of the parks of Staffordshire which requires to be noticed, is that enclosed by the present Mr. Newton Lane at *Kings-Bromley*, in the neighbourhood of Rugeley.

Existing Deer Parks in Staffordshire.

1. CHARTLEY . . Earl Ferrers.
2. BAGOTS PARK . Lord Bagot.
3. HORECROSS . . Mr. Meynell Ingram.
4. OKEOVER . . . Mr. Okeover.

5. WOLSELEY . . Sir Charles Wolseley, Bart.
6. WROTTESLEY . Lord Wrottesley.
7. BEAUDESERT . Marq. of Anglesey.
8. INGESTRIE . . Earl of Shrewsbury and Talbot.
9. AQUELATE . . Sir Thos. Boughey, Bart.
10. TRENTHAM . Duke of Sutherland
11. OAKEDGE . . . Earl of Lichfield.
12. HIMLEY . . . Earl of Dudley.
13. SWITHAMLEY . Mr. Brocklehurst.
14. WESTON . . . Earl of Bradford.
15. KINGS-BROMLEY, Mr. Newton Lane.
16. KNYPERSLEY. . Mr. Bateman.
17. DUNSTALL . . Mr. Hardy.

NOTTINGHAMSHIRE.

THE far-famed Forest of Sherwood on the western borders of this county, contained within its extensive limits several Royal and Episcopal parks, of which the largest was *Beskwood*, described by Leland as ' a mighty great park,' a few miles north of Nottingham, and computed, according to a survey taken in 1609, to contain 3,672 acres. The first grant concerning it is in the time of Henry I. In an inquisition of the thirty-fifth of Henry III. it is called ' An Hay or Park of Our Lord the King wherein no man commons.' Among the Patent Rolls of the twenty-fifth of Edward III. is an order for its enclosure and impalement, and in the regard of the thirty-first of the same reign, the king's Hay of Beskwood is said to be closed in

with a pale. Thoroton in his 'History of Nottinghamshire,' printed in 1677, thus describes it : 'It hath a very fair Lodge in it, and in respect of the pleasant situation of the place, and conveniency of hunting and pleasure, this Park and Lodge hath for these many years been the desire and atchievement of great men, &c. Three Earls of Rutland had it. Before the Troubles it was well stored with red-deer,[1] but now it is parcelled into little closes on one side, and much of it hath been plowed, so that there is scarce either wood or venison, which is also too likely to be the fate of the whole Forest of Shire-wood.'[2] Whereas in Leland's time had been ' great game of deere.' Thoroton, it may be scarcely necessary to add, was

---

[1] In 1604, there were 140 red-deer and 700 fallow-deer in Beskwood Park. Lambeth MSS.

No. 709.
[2] Thoroton's Notts, p. 258.

right in these anticipations. According to the Reports of the Commissioners of the Land Revenue of the Crown, there were in 1616, 1263 head of red-deer in Sherwood Forest ; in the year 1722 they had greatly diminished, and the last of the race were destroyed about the year 1773, except as regards Thorney Wood, claimed by Lord Chesterfield, in consequence of a grant to his ancestor, John Stanhope, in the forty-second year of Queen Elizabeth (100 head of deer being kept for the use of the queen). There were in 1789 about 500 head of deer in that part of the forest ; which long since that time have entirely disappeared, the Royal rights in Sherwood Forest having been sold in the year 1827. To the above notice of Beskwood Park, and in illustration of the rights of the Crown in Royal parks, it may be added that Lord Willoughby (de Eresby), having a grant in the year 1664 of the Custody Herbage and Pannage of Beskwood Park, Sir Jeffrey Palmer, then Attorney-General, gave his opinion thereon as follows :—'I conceive that by this grant the Lord Willoughby hath an interest in the office of keepership, with all the usual fees belonging to it, and hath an interest in the surplusage of the herbage, over and above the sustenance and feeding of the game, so long as the park continues a park ; but the king may increase the deer, and if there be no surplusage, he that hath the herbage cannot put in any beasts ; and if the king do dispark the park (as he may), both the office of custody, and the interest in the herbage, will thereby determine ; yet in such cases it hath been held reason-

able to give compensation for the custody and herbage.'[1]

North of Beskwood was the Royal park of *Clypston* or *Clipston*, estimated in 1609 to contain 1,583 acres, and in 1604 no red and 60 fallow-deer.[2] In the first of Edward III., as we are told by Thoroton,[3] 'The Hunters or Huntsmen of the Town of King's Clipston might have Common of Pasture, and *Fugeria* and *Folia* (Fern or Gorste-grass, and leaves) in the said park, paying 13s. 4d. p' annum : Robert de Clipston in the second of Edward III. had the care of the park, and was bound to keep the manor in repair at the king's cost, and the park pale at his own, receiving for the reparation of the said pale, timber of the dry wood there, and taking every day for himself the palers and makers of the said pale 7d.'

Clipston Park, as I have had occasion to notice before,[4] was totally destroyed during the Usurpation ; it was at that time held by William Cavendish Duke of Newcastle, and is described as being seven miles in compass, and before the Civil Wars well stocked with deer and game. The timber, valued at 20,000l., was cut down at this period, 'there being not one timber tree left in it.'[5]

Nearer Nottingham was the Royal park of *Bulwell*, besides that which was attached to the Castle of *Nottingham*. The former contained in 1609 326 acres, the latter 129. Bulwell, according to Thoroton, was granted in the thirty-second of Henry VIII., together with Newstead Priory, to Sir John Byron. The park belonging to Nottingham Castle was restocked and

[1] Ninth Report on Woods and Forests, 8vo. p. 549.
[2] Lambeth MSS., No. 709.
[3] Notts, p. 435.
[4] See p. 49.
[5] Collins's Noble Families, p. 42.

paled after the Restoration of Charles II.
by William Cavendish Duke of Newcastle.[1] It has been long disparked.

In 1709 his son, the second Duke of
Newcastle, as Lord Warden of the Forest
of Sherwood, obtained by Letters Patent,
license to make a park within the forest,
to contain at least 3,000 acres of his own
land, and in consideration of thus extin-
guishing the rent of such a quantity of his
own lands, and of finding hay and pasture ground, not only for the deer to be
kept in the said park, but for those in the
forest also, and of paying all the keepers
both in the park and forest, a yearly fee
or salary of 1,000*l.* was granted to him,
payable out of the Exchequer. It was
paid till the death of Queen Anne in
1714.[2]

Of *Newstead* Thoroton observes that it
'was once ornamented with 2.700 head of
deer.' It is believed to have been disparked about the middle of the last century by William Lord Byron.[3]

Near Newstead is the existing park of
Annesley, the seat of Mr. Chaworth Musters. It contains about 780 acres, of
which only 450 are open to the deer—a
herd of 300 of the small black forest fallow
breed, which have never been crossed in
the memory of man. This park was enclosed by Patrick Viscount Chaworth, by
license granted under the Privy Seal, the
17th of July 1673, in the thirteenth year
of Charles II. A wood with ridings had
previously existed here, of which a plan
may be seen in Thoroton's 'Nottinghamshire.' In the common centre of the various ridings was one of the stands for com-

manding the game common at that period.
Two of them still retain their names; 'The
Yew Tree Stand,' now a row of six very
large old yew trees on the brow of the hill
inside the park, and 'The Buck's Head
Stand,' the name of a wood adjoining.

Lord Middleton has an ancient and still
existing park at his beautiful seat at *Wollaton* near Nottingham.

To the south of Nottingham, and not
far from the borders of Leicestershire, is
Bunny. Here Sir Thomas Parkyns, the
third baronet, who succeeded to his
father in 1684, built a park wall of brick,
three miles in compass, all on arches, being the first that was built, according to
Kimber in his 'Baronetage,'[4] in England
after that method.

Parks which are now disused existed once
at *Colewick* near Nottingham, disparked
about twenty years ago, when the deer
were removed to Annesley Park, and at
Wiverton near Bingham, said to have
been enclosed by Sir Thomas Chaworth
in the twenty-fourth of Henry VI, and
probably disparked between the years
1640 and 1650.[3]

In the midland parts of Nottinghamshire is the town of *Southwell*. In this
neighbourhood the Archbishop of York
had three parks; two were in the immediate vicinity of the town, the one called
the *New* or *Little Park*, the site of the
palace, and the other *Norwood Park*. By
far the largest was *Hexgrave*; this was
supposed by Thoroton to have been enclosed by Walter Archbishop of York in
the time of Henry III. It is noticed by
Leland in his 'Itinerary,' who says, 'I

[1] Collins's Noble Families, p. 42.
[2] Fourteenth Report of Commissioners on Woods and Forests, p. 1103.
[3] Information of Mrs. Chaworth Musters, 1865.
[4] Vol. ii. p. 453.

came hard by Hexgrave Park on the right hand, and a little beyond on the left hand, I saw nere at hand, Mr. Newman's a knighte's parke, and prati manor. It is in Keklington (Kirklington) paroche.'[1] This appears to be the park marked in Saxton's Survey at *Bellow*.

A little more to the north two more parks are noticed by Saxton at *Knesall* and *Rufford*. The latter was, I presume, originally a monastic park ; it is an existing one, belonging to Henry Savile, Esq;, and is said to contain 400 head of deer.

We now approach the well-known 'Dukeries,' the contiguous domains of Worksop, Welbeck, Clumber, and Thoresby, to which may be added *Houghton*, at one time the seat of the Holles's Earls of Clare and Dukes of Newcastle. It is marked as a park in Saxton's Map, together with *Worksop* and *Welbeck*, but has been long disparked and the mansion demolished.

'*Worksop*,' writes Leland, 'is a parke of a vi. or vii. miles in compass, longging to the Erle of Shreusbiry. The stones of the castil were fetched, as sum say, to make the fair lodge in Wyrksoppe Parke not yet finished. This Erle of Shrewsbyri's Father was aboute to have finished hit, as apperith by much hewyd stone lying there.'[2] 'Wirsop' is noticed as a park, when it belonged to Thomas de Furnivall, in the twenty-ninth of Edward III.[3]

Worksop Manor, purchased in 1838 by the Duke of Newcastle from Bernard twelfth Duke of Norfolk, was at that time disparked, and the greater part of the mansion taken down. A mile from Worksop, Leland notices the Park of *Newhagge*, 'longging to the king.' This appears to be the park laid down in Saxton's Map as north of Worksop Manor.

Welbeck is an existing and very extensive park belonging to the Duke of Portland. The park of Thomas de Furnivall here is noticed 'by the King's Highway' as early as the twenty-ninth of Edward I.[4] In 1654 Welbeck belonged to William Cavendish Duke of Newcastle, and was visited by Evelyn, who calls it 'a noble yet melancholy seate.' It was the only one of eight parks belonging to the Duke which escaped destruction from the rebels in the Civil Wars.

Clumber never appears to have had a deer park, and the adjoining park of *Thoresby* is not found in the ancient maps. It is a very extensive park, said to be thirteen miles in circumference, with 1,000 head of deer.

To the north of Worksop is *Hodsock*, 'a park where Master Clifton hath a fair House,' writes Leland. Thoroton calls it 'a fair park,' but it has been long since disparked. Two other ancient parks were, in Henry VIII.'s time, in this vicinity thus noticed by Leland : ' Riding a very little beyond Scroby Manor Place, I passid by a forde over the Ryver : and so betwixt the pales of two parkes longging to *Scroby*, I came to Bautre.'[5] Scroby was a palace of the Archbishops of York, and here Archbishop Savage, one of the keenest sportsmen of the age, often re-

---

[1] Leland's Itin. vol. v. p. 104, fol. 93.
[2] Itin. vol. v. p. 103, fol. 92.
[3] Abbr. Rot. Orig. 239.

[4] Thoroton, p. 451.
[5] Leland's Itin. vol, i. p. 36, fol. 37.

sided to be near Hatfield Chase, in Yorkshire.[1]

North of Scroby, Saxton marks a park
at *Finningley*, and another at *Gringley*
near East Retford. The last was a park
belonging to the Duchy of Lancaster, in
the twenty-seventh year of Queen Elizabeth let to Thomas Markham, Esq , for
thirty-one years at the rent of 7*l.* 6*s.* 8*d.*
The park was divided into the East and

West Parks;[2] it has been long disused
and disparked.

*Existing Deer Parks in Nottingham-
shire.*

1. WOLLATON . Lord Middleton.
2. RUFFORD . Mr. Savile.
3. ANNESLEY . Mr. Chaworth Musters.
4. THORESBY . Earl Manvers.
5. WELBECK . The Duke of Portland.

LINCOLNSHIRE.

INDICATIONS of fourteen parks appear in
Saxton's Survey of this extensive county,
engraved in 1576. They were generally
on its north-western bounds, and towards
the south on the marches of Leicestershire, Rutlandshire, and Northamptonshire. In this latter locality two parks,
called 'The Red-dere pk,' and 'The
Fallow-dere pk,' are marked at *Grimsthorpe*, the ancestral seat of Lord Willoughby de Eresby. One of these parks,
characterised by Leland as 'a fayre parke
betwixt Vauldey and Grimsthorpe,' is
noticed in the 'Itinerary' of that most
accurate and agreeable topographer. In
Kip's 'Views of Seats,' engraved in 1714,
there are two birdseye views of this grand
old place, exhibiting the various avenues
and rides in the woods. At present the
whole extent of Grimsthorpe Park is 1,992
acres. The deer, which still comprehend
both red and fallow, are confined to 1,190
acres. There were formerly about 1,800
of the latter, but the number is now re-

duced, and the deer greatly increased in
size and weight. There are about 60 red-
deer at Grimsthorpe. The following are
the dimensions of two stag-heads killed
here in September 1864 :—No. 1. Length
of horns, 35½ inches ; width between the
horns, 34 in. ; size round the horn at
the root, 8 in. ; number of points, 12.—
No. 2. Length 40½ in. ; width, 35¾ in. ;
size round, 8½ in. ; number of points, 11.
The timber in this park is very fine, oaks,
horse-chestnuts, and thorns growing to a
great size, and many of them of very great
age. When Grimsthorpe was first imparked appears to be uncertain, but it is
undoubtedly a park of great antiquity,
and if we may believe the tradition of the
place, the keepership of the park remained
in the same family, of the name of Scole,
from the first beginning of the park till
the reign of George IV.[3]

A little north of Grimsthorpe two other
parks are marked in Saxton's map, at *Irnham*, and near *Aslackby*. The former is a

[1] See Godwin, p. 71, and Stowe, p. 309.
[2] Cotton MS., Titus B., iv. p. 297.

[3] Partly derived from the information of the
late Lady Willoughby de Eresby.

small existing park, once the inheritance of the Conquest, Arundell and Clifford families. A little to the west of Irnham is *Easton*. Here is a small park enclosed within the last twenty-five years by Sir Montagu Cholmeley, Bart., containing about 100 fallow-deer.

A modern and still existing park is at *Havei holm* Priory, on the borders of the Fen Country, near Sleaford. It contains about 220 acres, and was enclosed between the years 1780 and 1790. There is a herd of 200 fallow-deer.

Nearly adjoining is *North Kyme*, ' a goodly House and Park,' noticed by Leland, and also given in Saxton's Survey.

Near Grantham are two parks, nearly adjoining, *Belton* and *Syston*. The former is an extensive park, said to have been enlarged in 1656, and again in 1824, and which at present contains a herd of 800 fallow-deer.

Syston Park contains 546 acres. The deer (120 fallow and 20 red-deer) are confined to 270 acres. Neither of these parks appears in the ancient surveys. The same remark applies to *Doddington*, in 1714 the seat of Sir Thomas Hussey, Bart., and where there was a deer park at that period.[1] It lies to the north-east of Syston. More to the north, on the edge of Nottinghamshire, is *Norton Disney*, where, according to Saxton, there was a park in the Elizabethan period. The same survey notices a group of parks still on the borders of Nottinghamshire, and still more towards the north, at or near *Stow, Knathe*, and *Gainsborough*. These parks are also marked in the modern maps. The park at Gains-

borough, 'longging to the Lord Borow,' is mentioned by Leland in the ' Itinerary.'[2] *Knathe*, or *Knaythe*, was imparked by John Darcy, with the Royal license, in the fourth year of Edward III.[3]

In the Isle of Axholm, which occupies the north-western angle of Lincolnshire, were two ancient parks, *Melwood* and *West Butterwick*. The last appears to have been disparked before 1610, as it is not noticed in Speed's survey of that date. It was the seat of the ancient family of Sheffield.

Between Flixborough and Burton is the modern park of *Normanby*, belonging to Sir Robert Sheffield, and enclosed about the year 1804. It is a park of 300 acres, with a herd of 200 fallow-deer. This park appears to be nearly identical with one which is laid down in the ancient surveys at ' *Canesbye*.' In them also, to the east of Glanford-bridge, a park is also noticed at *Kettleby*.

But two other old Lincolnshire parks are given in Saxton's Survey, one in the part of Lindesay near *Snarford*, unnoticed by Speed, and the other at *Kirkby* near Bolingbroke Castle, on the borders of the eastern fen country.

To this scanty list of ancient parks, two should be added which are mentioned in Leland's ' Itinerary.' ' Lude alias *Louth* Park,' and the following notice of one near Spilsby : ' The Lord Wylloughby had a House at Heresby (Eresby), and a parke of blak Dere a 2 miles from Spilesby, wher, as I heere say, he entendithe to build sumptuously.'[4] The former was doubtless attached to the Abbey of Louth, and appears to have been imparked in the

---

[1] Kip's Views of Seats.
[2] Vol. i. p. 35, fol. 36.

[3] Cal. Pat. Rolls, p. 109.
[4] Itin. vol. vii. p. 40, fol. 50.

eleventh of Edward III., when the Abbot 'de Parco Ludi,' obtained license to im- park 140 acres of pasture in the waste of Foulstowe, and 30 acres of marsh in that of Foulsthorp in this county.[1]

Existing Deer Parks in Lincolnshire.

1. GRIMSTHORPE, Lord Willoughby de Eresby.

2. IRNHAM . . . Mr. Woodhouse.

3. HAVERHOLM . Countess Dowager of Winchilsea.

4. BELTON . . . Earl of Brownlow.

5. SYSTON . . . Sir John Thorold, Bart.

6. NORMANBY. . Sir Richard Sheffield, Bart.

7. EASTON . . . Sir Montagu Cholme- ley, Bart.

[1] Cal. Pat. Rolls, p. 128.

CHAPTER IX.

NOTES ON DEER PARKS IN THE COUNTIES

OF

GLOUCESTERSHIRE,   MONMOUTHSHIRE,

HEREFORDSHIRE,   SHROPSHIRE, AND

CHESHIRE.

The Deer-Leap at Wolseley Park, in Staffordshire, on the borders of Cannock Chase.

CHAPTER IX.

GLOUCESTERSHIRE.

THE county of Gloucester, remarkable for the number of its deer parks, and generally also for their small extent, can boast, however, of but one park which is known to have existed at the period of the Norman Conquest, and which is noticed in the Domesday Survey, that at *Sopeberie*, the modern Sodbury, and which belonged to the king. In Leland's time a park still existed here, which is thus mentioned in his ' Itinerary' : ' There is a Parke of the Kyng's by this towne (Cheping Sodbiry) sumtyme the Warwicks,' and also at *Little Sodbury* adjoining. 'Walshe is Lord of Little Sodbyri, and hathe a fayr place there in the syde of Sodbyri high hill, and a parke.'¹ Three other ancient parks, two of them still existing, are noticed also by Leland in this neighbourhood : those of *Acton, Dyrham,* and *Badminton* ; the latter since the destruction of Ragland Castle in the great Civil Wars, the well-known and principal seat of the Dukes of Beaufort. Of *Acton* (Iron Acton) Leland observes, ' There is a goodly House and 2 parks by the House, one of Redde Dere, an other of Fallow,' and of *Dyrham,* ' from Cotherington to Derham, a mile and a halfe of, where master Dionise dwellithe, havinge a fair Howse of achelei stones, and a parke.'² The ' meane,' that is moderate, ' manor place and park of Badminton,'³ in Leland's time belonged to the Boteler family. A curious view of this magnificent place is given in Kip's ' Views of Seats,' engraved in 1714. The whole country was at that time laid out in straight avenues of trees, intersecting each other, most of them meeting in a single tree or ' standing ' near the house. No less than five parks were at that time kept up at Badminton, distinguished as ' The Virginia Deere Parke, The East India Deere Parke, The Fallow Deere Parke, The Red Deere Parke, The Great Parke.'

At present the park contains 971 acres, with a herd of 300 red, and 1,200 fallow-deer.

The forest or chase of Kingswood occupied the southern extremity of the county near the city of Bristol. In Saxton's ' Survey of Gloucestershire ' (1577), a park is marked adjoining it at *Stoke.*

Here, we are told in Smyth's ' Lives of the Berkeleys,'⁴ ' that the people, warlikely arrayed, made an attack upon Sʳ. Maurice Berkeley's park, recently enclosed from the Common.' This was in the reign of Edward III.

A few miles to the north is *Thornbury Castle,* once the seat of the great House of Stafford Dukes of Buckingham. Here was a park of which Leland observes, ' Edward Duke of Bukkyngham made a fayre parke hard by the Castle, and tooke much faire ground in it very frutefull of corne, now fayr launds for coursynge. The Inhabitaunts cursyd the Duke for ther lands so inclosyd. There was a parke by the Manor of Thornbyry afore, and yet is caullyd Morlewodde. There was also afore Duke Edward's tyme a parke at Estewood a myle or more of : But Duke Edward at 2 tymes enlarged it to the compass of 6 myles not without many curses of the poore Tenaunts.'⁵ This park must have been destroyed before the Elizabethan period, as it is not given in Saxton's Survey. It was enclosed by Gilbert de Clare Earl of Gloucester and Hereford in the ninth year of Edward I.⁶

There is an existing park at *Knowle,* south of Thornbury, belonging to Colonel Master, and one also at *Tortworth,* a little to the east, the seat of the Earl of Ducie.

To the north is *Berkeley,* the baronial castle of the great Norman house of that name, and which once arrogated to itself two chases, Micklewood and Redwood, and no less than twelve attendant parks. These, according to Rudder in his ' History of Gloucestershire,' were the *Castle*

¹ Leland's Itin. vol. vii. p. 97, fol. 72 *a.*
² Itin. vol. vii. p. 97, fol. 72 *a,* and 101, fol. 74 *b.*
³ Ibid. vol. vi. p. 73, fol. 76.

⁴ P. 121.
⁵ Leland's Itin. vol. vii. p. 102, fol. 73 *a.*
⁶ Cal. Pat. Rolls, p. 49.

Park, Whitley and *New Park, Okeley, Shipnash, Ham Park, Beverstone, Hill Park, Ozleworth, Almondesbury, Cromhall,* and *Uley Parks.* Leland, however, only notices four parks, 'Okeley Parke hard by, Whitwike, New Parke, Hawlle Parke.'

We find, from Fosbroke's amusing and valuable extracts from Smyth's 'Lives of the Berkeleys,' 'The Chase of the Barons of Berkeley was always and is still called Michaelwood. It was partly disparked 10th James I., and wholly converted into farms 3d Charles I. It had been reduced in the 13th century, Maurice the second Lord having granted various small estates out of it, and again in the year 1301 a farm, afterwards called " Bassets Court," was further taken out of this Chase.' In the year 1568 Henry Lord Berkeley issued his warrant to Henry Ligon to build a new lodge at the Park Hill in Michaelwood Chase.[1]

Of the parks which belonged to the Castle of Berkeley, that which was called ' The Worthy' appears to have been enclosed by Thomas the fourth Lord Berkeley, in the reign of Henry IV. It was also called the 'Castle Park.' After Berkeley Castle fell by attainder into the power of the Crown, this park was enlarged by ' King Henry VIII., who in the year 1514, granted to Maurice the 6th Lord Berkeley, the keeping of the Castle Park called " The Worthy," and of the Portership thereof, and the keeping of the red and fallow-deer in Chisalhanger and Redwood.'[2] Henry Lord Berkeley is said

'passionately to have disparked that ground' (The Worthy) in consequence of the slaughter of twenty-seven stags by Queen Elizabeth and her Court in one day, in the year 1574.[3]

The ancient park of *Whitley* or *Whitecliffe,* is the present park belonging to Berkeley Castle. It was first imparked, according to Smyth's ' Lives of the Berkeleys,' by Maurice second Lord Berkeley in the reign of Henry III. Thomas the third Lord is said to have first paled it, ' instead of the hedge of Whitcliffe Park, which each three years was, with the excrescence of thorns there growing, new made, and the old sold.' Here he is said to have put certain white deer which he had of William de Montacute Earl of Salisbury. Henry Lord Berkeley in the sixteenth century, enlarged this park by throwing into it a farm called Cowley, and in the lodge here his widow is said sometimes to have resided.[4]

New Park was enclosed by Thomas third Lord Berkeley in 1327-8. At the same time with the enclosure, Lord Thomas 'built a square pile of stoneworke for a lodge for this park.' It was enlarged between the years 1368 and 1417.[4]

Lord Berkeley had a park at Shobenash in the time of Richard I. In the thirteenth century Thomas the first Lord made Horley and Shobenash, now called *Oakley* and *Shepnasse,* into two parks ; they were disparked by Sir Edward Seymour in the reign of Edward VI.,[5] and the same fate probably overtook most of the Berkeley parks ; but *Cromhall* was again imparked in the

---

[1] Fosbroke's Lives of the Berkeleys, pp. 35, 197.
[2] Ib, p. 23.
[3] See p. 38.

[4] Fosbroke's Lives of the Berkeleys, pp. 36, 131.
[5] Lives of the Berkeleys, p. 35.

O

reign of Charles II., Sir William Ducy having obtained a license for enclosing it in the year 1661.[1]

Uley Park, mentioned above, appears to have been identical with Weoly Park, of which Smyth relates that, being in the king's hands in right of Roger de Somery his ward, Maurice the second Lord Berkeley killed two bucks here, and was consequently fined 5*l.*[2]

At *Newark,* near Wooton-under-Edge, there was a deer park which has been only lately disused.

Between Tetbury and Cirencester is *Cherington.* Here is a small park of about 78 acres, with a herd of 65 fallow-deer. It has been imparked 'beyond the memory of the oldest inhabitant,' but is not noticed in the surveys of Saxton or Speed.

Near Cirencester is *Oakley Park,* belonging to Lord Bathurst, containing about 300 acres and 550 fallow-deer of all the varieties. A plan of this fine park is given in Rudder's history of this county, printed in 1779, when it was 'well stocked with deer.'

There are existing parks also at *Ampney, Williamstrip, Barnsley,* and *Fairford,* places to the east of Cirencester ; and at *Miserden* and *Rendcomb,* ancient parks to the north of that town. The former is described, in 1779, as being about seven miles in circuit, and full of fine beech-wood.

East of Northleach is *Sherborne.* 'There are two parks belonging to this seat,' according to Rudder ; 'one adjoining to the house ; the other lies at a little distance from it, with a beautiful lodge house, and a paddock-course near it.'

The park at Sherborne at present consists of 350 acres, with 280 fallow-deer.

Not far from Sherborne, on the edge of Oxfordshire, is *Barrington.* Here was a deer park in 1717, as we find by a view of the place in Kip's 'Views of Seats.' Sherborne is also represented as a deer park in the same work.

In the north-eastern district of Gloucestershire, adjoining an outlying part of Worcestershire, is *Batsford.* Here is a small but beautiful and well-ordered park of about 95 acres, with a herd of 200 fallow-deer. It has been enclosed about 150 years.

Still further north, on the borders of Warwickshire, is *Alscot,* in the parish of Preston-upon-Stour. Here is a park containing 220 acres and 120 fallow-deer. It has existed upwards of a century, and is thus mentioned in Rudder's 'History':[3] 'At this place I saw a natural curiosity ; it was the skulls of two stags [he means probably bucks] with their horns so entangled by the animals' fighting in the Park when alive, that they could never disengage themselves, and so perished with hunger. They now remain not to be separated by human force, without cutting or breaking some part of them.' These horns are no longer preserved at Alscot.

Near Winchcomb is *Sudeley Castle,* where, in the Elizabethan period, was a very extensive park, which has been long since disused and thrown open. It is thus noticed in Leland's 'Itinerary' : 'There runneth a praty lake out of Sudeey parke Towne by the Castle, and runneth into Esseburne brooke, at the south syde of Winchcombe.'[4]

---

[1] Rudder, p. 397.
[2] Lives of the Berkeleys, p. 84.

[3] P. 608.
[4] Itin. vol. iv. p. 76, fol. 169.

A deer park is marked at *Southam* near Cheltenham in Saxton's Survey, engraved in 1577. It has been long disparked. More modern and existing parks are at *Dowdeswell* and *Colesbourn*, in the same neighbourhood.

Nearer Gloucester were the ancient parks of *Prinkash, Painswick*, and *Brimsfield.* The first belonged to the Abbot of St. Peters at Gloucester, and is characterised by Leland as 'a *fayr parke* 3 miles from Gloucester by East.' *Whitcomb Park*, where there were deer in 1717, nearly adjoins it. To the north of Gloucester two ancient parks, disused before the time of Saxton, are mentioned in Leland's 'Itinerary;' one at *Boddington*, '4 miles north from Glocester, a fair Manor place and a park, it cam to one Rede, Servante to the Lord Beauchamp, that married his Lordes Daughter, the eldest of 3, and the Redes have it still.'[1] Of the other near *Tewksbury*,he observes: 'There is a parke bytwixt the old plot of Holm castelle & it (Deerhurst), but it longgid to Holme the Erles of Glocester's House, and not to it. There is a fair Manor place of tymbre and stone yn this Theokesbyri Parke, where the Lord Edward Spencer lay, and late my Lady Mary.'[2]

Highnam, once a seat of the Guises, and now of Mr. Gambier Parry, is on the western bank of the Severn near Gloucester. Here there was a very extensive park, now disused. A more ancient park was, in the time of Elizabeth, at *Pantley* or Pauntley, directly north of Highnam on the bounds of the county of Worcester.

In recent times one has been established at *Stancombe* near Gloucester, and another is in course of completion at *Fretherne* on the eastern banks of the Severn.

It remains to notice the district which intervenes between the Severn and the Wye, well known as the Forest of Dean, and which appears from the earliest time to have contained more than one ancient park. Saxton's Map, indeed, marks one without name about the centre of the forest. '*Whitemead Park*,' and 'Park End' still attest the site.[3] Another, also given by him, still exists at *Lydney*, a seat of the Bathurst family, on the western banks of the Severn. There were deer also at *Clearwell*, the ancient seat of the Wyndhams in 1717, on the opposite side of the forest, and they still remain there. A more modern park exists at *Flaxley*, in the north-eastern frontiers of it. At different periods there have been, no doubt, many other parks within this extensive county. The foregoing notes will be sufficient to show that Gloucestershire has at all times been noted for their number and variety.

Existing Deer Parks in Gloucestershire.

1. WHITECLIFF PARK, Lord Fitzharding.
2. BADMINTON . . Duke of Beaufort.
3. DYRHAM . . . Mr. Blathwayte.
4. KNOWLE . . . Colonel Master.
5. TORTWORTH . . Earl of Ducie.
6. CHERINGTON . Rev. Mr. George.
7. OAKLEY PARK . Earl Bathurst.
8. AMPNEY . . . Mr. Blackwell.

---

[1] Itin. vol. vi. p. 74, fol. 78.
[2] Ib. p. 75, fol. 79.
[3] Whitemead Park contained 227 acres, 1 r. 9 p. and timber worth 11,736*l*. This was in 1809, when Lord Berkeley applied unsuccessfully for a new lease. See Appendix to 4th Report of Surveyor-General of Land Revenue, p. 210.

9. WILLIAMSTRIP . Sir M. H. Beach, Bart.
10. BARNSLEY . . Sir T. Musgrave, Bart.
11. FAIRFORD . . Mr. Barker.
12. MISERDEN . . Mr. Rald.
13. RENDCOMB . . Sir F. Goldsmidt.
14. SHERBORNE . . Lord Sherborne.
15. BATSFORD . . Lord Redesdale.
16. ALSCOT . . . Mr. West.

17. DOWDESWELL . Mr. Lawrence.
18. COLESBOURN . Mr. Elwes.
19. CLEARWELL, The Dowager Countess of Dunraven.
20. LYDNEY . . . Rev. Mr. Bathurst.
21. FLAXLEY . . . Sir T. C. Bowey, Bart.
22. STANCOMBE . . Mr. Purnell.
23. FRETHERNE . . Rev. Sir L. Darell, Bart.

HEREFORDSHIRE.

ANYONE who ascends the steep crest of the Malvern Hills in Worcestershire, and looks down from the summit of the ridge on the western side of the hills, upon the richly wooded and beautifully undulating surface which lies stretched beneath, as far as the mountains of South Wales, would at once be struck with the 'bosky' nature of the scenery and its perfect adaptation, according to our modern notions, for the formation of deer parks and sylvan residences. Herefordshire, indeed, from the earliest historical times appears to have been remarkable for the number of its forests, chases, and parks, though the merits of its surpassing beauty of scenery could scarcely have been understood before the middle of the last century.

Duncumb, in his 'Herefordshire Collections,' observes that there were four forests and the same number of chases within this county, viz., the forests of Aconbury, Deerfold, Ewyas, and Haywood, and the chases of Bringwood, Mocktree, Ledbury, and Penyard. Parks, he adds, have been much more abundant;

and he proceeds to give a list of thirty-two, the major part of which were, at that time (1804), disused, and adapted to the common purposes of agriculture ; but before we notice some of them in detail, it will be well to begin with those two venerable parks which appear in the Herefordshire Domesday, one of which belonged to the King, and the other to Roger de Lacy. The Royal park alluded to was at Haloede, and the Survey adds, ' Ibi ē parcus ferarū sed missus est exī m̄ cū tota silva.' This place is at present unknown, but it was in Naisse Hundred, in or near Worcestershire.[1]

Roger de Lacy's park was at Wibelei, the modern *Weobley*, and was probably identical with that at *Lenshall* or *Leonshall* adjoining, noticed by Leland, and which belonged to the Devereux family. The Domesday Survey also informs us that there were several 'hayes' in various parts of Herefordshire, the nature of which has been already described.

Saxton, in his survey of this county, which was engraved in 1577, notices but

[1] Duncumb, vol. i. p. 62.

eight parks within its limits. They were at Netherwood, in the north-eastern part of the county, on the borders of Worcestershire, at Richards-Castle, Wigmore-Castle, and Brampton-Bryan-Castle, in the north-western angle; a park at Erdesley in the west; and two at Newcourt and Morehampton, in the south of the county; and one at Holm-Lacy, six miles south-east of Hereford, the well-known seat of the Scudamore family.

The park of *Netherwood*, or Northwood, belonged to the House of Devereux. It contained about 300 acres, which has long been enclosed and converted into tillage.[1]

Near Netherwood a park is marked in the modern maps at *Wolverlow*, on the edge of the county of Worcester, and there was one at *Sapey* adjoining.

Close to Ludlow is *Ludford*, an ancient seat of the extinct family of Charlton. Here was a small deer park, disparked in the early part of the present century. The parks at *Richards-Castle* and *Wigmore-Castle* have been long disparked, that at *Brampton-Bryan*, the old Harley seat, still exists. It is a park of 500 acres, and a herd of 300 fallow-deer, and is a good specimen of a thorough English park, with well-broken ground, and fine oak timber.

In this neighbourhood were the more modern parks of *Shobden, Staunton, Pembridge, Croft Castle, Titley, Eyewood,* and *Newport.*

Staunton Park contains 110 acres, though the deer have access to but a third of the park, which was enclosed about the year 1770–5. The number of the herd of fallow-deer here is about 90.

Erdesley has been long disparked, but

modern parks exist at *Garnstone* and *Moccas* in this part of the county. The former has been enclosed upwards of sixty years, and contains about 200 acres, and the same number of black and dun-coloured fallow-deer.

A large park exists at *Hampton Court*, once the fine seat of the Coningsby family, six miles south of Leominster; it appears originally to have been enclosed in the thirteenth of Henry VI. by Sir Rowland Lentall, Knt., who obtained license to impark 1,000 acres of land here, and to crenelate, or embattle his mansion at the same time.[2] In former times this park is said to have been nearly eight miles in circumference, containing a separate enclosure for red deer. At present it contains but 150 acres, with 160 fallow-deer.

The ancient parks of *Newcourt* and *Morehampton*, noticed in Saxton's Survey, no longer contain deer, and the same may be said of several other parks which figure in Duncumbe's List.

Meend Park is now disparked, but *Kentchurch*, on the borders of the county of Monmouth, an ancient seat of the Scudamore family, is an existing park. It contains between 300 and 400 acres, and a herd of about 130 fallow-deer. This park appears to have been enclosed before the reign of Henry VIII. Near Hereford is *Rotherwas*, once a deer park, but now disused, and on the western side of the city, *Sugwas*, on the banks of the Wye, disparked in Leland's time.[3]

The ancient park of *Holm-Lacy* still exists, and is celebrated for the beauty of its scenery and the magnificence of the timber. It is a park of 280 acres, with a herd of 130 fallow-deer.

---

[1] Duncumb's Herefordshire, vol. ii. p. 225.
[2] Cal. Pat. Rolls, p. 278.
[3] Leland's Itin. vol. viii. p. 57, fol. 87 a.

Near it is *Fownhope*, where the Chandos family had a park as early as the year 1354. No vestiges of it now remain, beyond the name of the park, retained by a part of the woodlands.[1] Duncumb informs us there were parks at *Pengethley* and *Harewood*, in the southern parts of the county, both of which are now disparked.

At *Stoke-Edith* is an existing park, containing 214 acres and 220 fallow-deer. Adjoining it are two more ancient parks, called, The *Middle Park* and *Devereux Park*, but both are at present without deer.

Near Ledbury is *Easnor Castle*. Here is a wild and beautiful park of 515 acres, half of which is open grove covered with fern and gorse. It was enclosed about the year 1820.

Following the base of the Malvern Hills we come to *Collwall.* Here was a park belonging to the Bishops of Hereford. It is noticed in Leland's ' Itinerary,' but was disparked before Saxton's time.

A few miles to the west is *Asperton*, or Ashpurton. Here there appears to have

been a park held under the Duchy of Lancaster. The herbage and pannage of this park was let to John Norton for thirty-one years, in the nineteenth of Elizabeth, and it was again granted in reversion to John de Cardinas, for thirty-one years, in the twenty-eighth of the same reign.[2]

Existing Deer Parks in Herefordshire.

1. BRAMPTON-BRYAN . Lady Langdale.
2. SHOBDEN . . . . . Lord Bateman.
3. STAUNTON . . . . Mr. King.
4. TITLEY . . . . . Sir Thomas Hastings.
5. GARNSTONE . . . Mr. Peploe.
6. MOCCAS . . . . Sir V. Cornwall, Bart.
7. HAMPTON-COURT . Mr. Arkwright.
8. KENTCHURCH . . Col. Scudamore.
9. HOLM-LACY . . . Sir E. S. Stanhope, Bart.
10. STOKE-EDITH . . Lady Emily Foley.
11. EASNOR . . . . Earl Somers.

MONMOUTHSHIRE.

BY an Act of Parliament passed in 1536 (twenty-seventh of Henry VIII.), Monmouthshire became an English county. Before that period but little information can be gleaned as to the parks within the district, eight of which are given in Saxton's map of Monmouthshire, engraved in 1577. The first is that at ' *Grace Dieu*,' near Monmouth. This park belonged to the small Cistertian Abbey of

Grace Dieu, founded, according to Dugdale, in 1229 by John of Monmouth, and suppressed at the Dissolution, when it was probably disparked. Its memory still lingers in the name of a farm called Parkersdue, a corruption of Parc gracedieu.

Llantilio Crasseny.—This park most probably belonged to an ancient moated mansion in this parish, destroyed time out

[1] Duncumb's Herefordshire, vol. ii. p. 347.

[2] Cotton MS. Titus B. iv. fol. 297.

of mind, said to have belonged to Sir David Gam, Knt. It was also near White-Castle, which with the Castles of Grasmont and Skenfrith belonged from an early time to the Duchy of Lancaster. *Raglan Castle.*—There were two parks belonging to the Castle, noticed in Leland's ' Itinerary,' with a series of lakes or fish-ponds. These appear to have been disparked and destroyed when the castle was dismantled after the famous siege during the Civil Wars.

' *Llanyrhangle Tonneygroyse.*' — This must have been the park of the abbey of that name ; after the Dissolution in the reign of Elizabeth, the abbey, which was then probably dismantled, came into possession of a branch of the Morgan family, and a mansion was erected on the site of the abbey. The enclosure of the park by a wall still in some degree exists ; but there have been no deer within the memory of man.

St. Julians.—This was an ancient mansion of the Herbert family, and belonged to Lord Herbert of Cherbury, and in his time doubtless the park existed. It has, however, been disparked for very many generations.

Tredegar.—This, the chief seat of the elder line of the Morgan family, is a very ancient park. Of the time of its enclosure there is no record ; it may probably have taken place after the dissolution of the Lordship Marcher of Wentllwch or Newport, in the time of Henry VIII., but this is only conjecture, for the family was certainly established there as far back as the early part of the fourteenth century. The park is surrounded by an ancient wall, and contains about 400 acres and about 600 fallow-deer. It occupies the mouth

of the valley of the river Ebbw, which flows through it, embracing a portion of the hills on either side. This is called ' the Old Park,' in maps ; there were two other parks, one called ' the New Park,' now the Home Farm, and the other *Cleppa Park*, which once belonged to another mansion of a branch of the family of Morgan. Lord Tredegar is in possession of a grant of Free-warren, given by James I. to Sir William Morgan, Knt., in 1617, authorising the enclosure of parks in certain parishes. ' The New Park,' above alluded to, was probably then enclosed. The following curious account of this place is from 'The Life of Marmaduke Rawdon of York,[1] written in the year 1664 :—' Tredegar, a seate belonging to Squier Morgan, which we were told was the chiefe Morgan in Wales. He hath there a stately parke through which runs the river Ebwith, soe that in his parke he hath salmon, trouts, and what fish that river doth afford. He hath likewise severall fish ponds, with what fish will live in ponds ; He hath a warren near his parke, and in his parke a thousand head of deere, besides wild goates and other cattle about his grounds, soe that I thinke he is pretty well provided towards house-keepinge.'

In a document of 1498, mention is made of certain lands having been excepted from the rental of the Manor of Develes, near the village of Castleton, in the Lordship Marcher of Wentllwch or Newport, for the purpose of forming a park by the lord's order. This is the park mentioned by Leland by the name of Parkvehan, or the Little Park, which he says ' hath neither deer or pale, now it is the king's,' the king having come into

---

[1] Printed by the Camden Society, 1863, p. 185.

possession of the lordship by the attainder of Edward Duke of Buckingham in 1521. The custom of the manor was, that the tenants should fence out the lord, so that the lord took the lands and made a park chiefly at the expense of the tenants, who were in their own defence obliged to fence out the lord's deer.

Manghen or *Machen Park.*—Here was an ancient mansion of a junior branch of the Morgan family. All traces of the park are gone, except indeed that a large wood bears the name of Caedy-Parc, or the Park-Wood, which was probably the site of it.

Chepstow Park.—This was never impaled, and seems to have been a large unenclosed chase attached to the Castle and Lordship of Chepstow.

The following Parks are not noticed in Saxton's Survey.

St. Pierre Park, near Chepstow.—This is a very ancient seat of the Lewis family

(a branch of that of Tredegar in the fourteenth century). There is no record of the first enclosure of the park, which contains about 140 acres and a herd of about 300 fallow-deer.

Llangibby, near Usk.—The seat of the ancient family of Williams, who formerly possessed the old castle here, and defended it during the civil wars. The park was ancient, and may have belonged to the castle. It did not contain many deer, and was disparked and the deer killed a few years ago.

Pontypool Park.—This is not an ancient park, and was enclosed when the mansion was built during the last century. It is a park of 91 acres, and contains 180 fallow-deer.

Existing Monmouthshire Deer Parks.

1. TREDEGAR   .   Lord Tredegar.
2. ST. PIERRE .   Mr. Lewis.
3. PONTYPOOL .   Mrs. Hanbury Leigh.

SHROPSHIRE.

MR. EYTON, in his invaluable 'Antiquities of Shropshire,' has identified ' *Marsetelie*' the only park particularly mentioned in the Domesday Survey in this county. ' It is recorded,' he writes, ' among the ancient customs of Shrewsbury, that when the king visited the town, " The Sheriff used to send thirty-six footmen as his body-guard (*ad stabilitionem*), for so long as he

remained there. But for the Park of Marsetlie (the Sheriff) used customarily to find thirty-six men for eight days." That is, I presume, the Sheriff provided the king's body-guard when he went to hunt at *Marstley*, and in the adjacent Royal Forest of the Stiperstones.'[1] Marsetelie, Mr. Eyton considers, to be the modern Marstley, a place in Habberley, a member of the

[1] Eyton's Antiquities of Shropshire, vol. vii. p. 46.

manor and chapelry of Minsterley in Ruesset Hundred, adjoining what is called in Saxton's Survey, Hockestow Forest. But besides the Park of Marsetelie, there are several 'Hayes' recorded in Domesday as existing in this county.

At Lege, the present Longnor, were three *firm Hayes*, by which we may understand three Hayes or Enclosures, in good repair. There was a divided Hay, that is a Hay divided between two proprietors, at Rorrington, near Chirbury. Another at Burford. Three at Stanage, on the borders of Radnorshire ; and here, as appears by an Inquest taken in February, 1295, on the death of Brian de Brompton, there was a park called *Ammareslit*. The writ ordering an Inquest taken in December, 1308, had directed the jurors to value the late Brian de Brompton's manor of Ambreslyth, but the jurors explained, that *Ambreslyth* was no manor but only a park pertaining to the manor of Stanegge, separately worth 20*s*. per annum.[1]

One Haye was at Cascob, at present an insulated part of Herefordshire, within the county of Radnor, and of which Domesday observes, ' in these waste lands the woods have grown up. Therein Osbern exercises the chase, and therein he has what he can catch ; nothing else.'

Lingham, the modern Lingen, is also in Herefordshire, though in the Domesday Shropshire. Here were at that period three Hayes 'capreolis capiendis,' for taking young deer or kids.

Hayes are also mentioned at the following places: at Wenlock, Corfton, Stretton (Church Stretton), Wentnor, Westune (Whitchurch), Munek (Myndtown), Chenton, Hopesay, Cheenpitune (Kempton), Baitune (Batton), and in many other places in this county.

Arranging the ancient and modern parks of Shropshire around the nucleus of Shrewsbury, we find in the north-western districts a few miles south of Ellesmere, the large and important park of *Kenwick*, very conspicuously marked in Saxton's Maps of 1577. This appears to have belonged to Haghmond Abbey, but I have found no mention of the park till the year 1604, when William Penrhyn, writing on the 27th of January to Hugh Nannay, observes, 'S[r]. Jevan Lloid spent at Kenwik parke fortye markes in takynge of six young Rascalls.'[2] This place has been long disparked.

A little north of Kenwick is *Otley*, an ancient and existing park, said to have been imparked at the beginning of the fourteenth century; it is recognised by Saxton, and at present contains about 150 acres and 160 fallow-deer.

Another ancient park was at *Ruyton* juxta Baschurch, near Knockin, the seat of the great Le Strange family, and which appears to have been imparked by John Le Strange about the year 1195, when he came to the following agreement with Hugh, Abbot of Shrewsbury. The Abbot conceded to Le Strange a corner of his wood of Birch, extending from the place

---

[1] Eyton, vol. xi. p. 341.
[2] Hengwrt MS., No. 529, at Peniarth. By the term 'Rascal Deer,' commonly used in the seventeenth century, is to be understood the 'lean animals fit neither to hunt or kill' (Halliwell's Dictionary, *sub voce*). The *rake* of the deer is used in the same sense : thus Sir

Reginald Forster petitioned Charles II., April 15, 1663, to give him the '*rake of the king's deer*' from Hambledon Chase, belonging to the Bishop of Winchester, &c. (S.P.O. Domestic). So late as the year 1733, I find the Steward of Woodsome Park in Yorkshire advising the destruction of all the young and *rascally* deer.

where Le Strange's Park fence came down to the water of Peveree (Perry,) to the end of Le Strange's meadow on the side of Plettebrug Mill. This was to enlarge Le Strange's Park, and he was to pay a rent of one doe yearly in acknowledgment.[1] Very close to Ruyton is *Boreatton*, where there exists a park said to be ancient, though it is not marked in Saxton's Survey ; it contains about 150 acres, and about 40 fallow-deer.

Further south and nearer to Shrewsbury is *Shrawardine*; here was an ancient castle, which at one time belonged to the Fitz-Alans Earls of Arundel ; here a park appears to be indicated in Saxton's Survey.

In the most northern part of this county on the borders of Cheshire, four ancient parks nearly contiguous are given by Saxton : at *Blakemere, Ightfield, Shenton* (Shavington), and *Atherley* (Adderley). The first, which originally belonged to the Le Stranges, is thus noticed by Leland in his ' Itinerary' :—From Whitchurch a mile and a half, I cam by the pale of the large parke of Blackmer longying to the Erle of Shrewsbiri, wherin is a very fair place or loge. The Park hath both redde dere and falow. In the park (as I herd say) be iii faire poles, of the wich I saw by the pale the largest, caullid Blakein, whereof the park is named.'[2] Of *Ightfield* he writes:—' Syr Richard Manoring, chefe of that name, dwelleth a iii miles be est from Price (Prees) village, at a village caullid Hightfelde, having a Parke and greate plenty of wood about hym.'[3]

The park at *Adderley* was enclosed by Walter de Dunstanvill by agreement with the Abbot of Shrewsbury, between the years 1175 and 1190.[4]

The great House of Le Strange had also a park at *Cheswardine* on the borders of Staffordshire, and here Sir John Mainwaryng, Knt., was keeper of the park and of that of Blakemere, in the thirteenth Edward IV.[5]

Saxton marks a park at *Hodnet*, midway between Cheswardine and Wem: this was an ancient park, recognised as early as the year 1257,[6] when it was held by a family who assumed their name from hence. Near Hodnet is *Hawkstone*, the seat of Viscount Hill. Here is a very extensive park (1,200 acres), celebrated for its romantic scenery. It is said to have been disparked about the year 1770, and restored in the year 1830. It does not appear, however, to have been an ancient park. At present it is stocked with a herd of 500 black fallow-deer, and 30 Barbary deer.

Saxton recognises a park, now long disused, at *Stanton* upon Hine-heath, a few miles south of Hodnet, and another at *Shawbury*, near adjoining: here Giles de Erdington had license from Henry III. in the thirty-seventh year of his reign to make a saltory or deer-leap in his park.[7] The site is still called Shawbury park.'

At *Haughmond* Abbey, nearer to Shrewsbury, a large park is noticed by Saxton: its origin may apparently be traced to the Patent granted by Edward I. in the twenty-fourth year of his reign to enclose 20 acres, and by Edward II. in 1313 to enclose 60 acres, of their bosc or wood, which lay within the Royal Forest of Haghmon.[8]

[1] Eyton, vol. x. p. 113.
[2] Leland's Itin. vol. v. p. 90, fol. 81.
[3] Ib. vol. vii. p. 24, fol. 35.
[4] Eyton, vol. x. p. 2.

[5] Duke's Antiquities of Salop, p. 143.
[6] Eyton, vol. ix. p. 330.
[7] Pat. 37, Hen. III. m. 10.
[8] Eyton, vol. vii. p. 296.

At *High Ercel* also, a little more to the east, there was a park according to the same authority; it is also mentioned by Leland.

A modern park which dates soon after the year 1803 is at *Chetwynd*, on the confines of Staffordshire. It contains 212 acres, and from 150 to 160 fallow-deer. But this is not the original park here; there had been one before, as appears by an Inquest on the death of John de Chetwynd in 1281.[1]

South of Chetwynd is *Lilleshall*: the park belonging to the Abbot of this place was in the adjoining parish of Preston on the Wealdmoors, still called *Lubstree* Park. It is now a farm belonging to the Duke of Sutherland.[2]

Farther south, and still on the Staffordshire borders, were ancient parks at *Shiffnal, Tongcastle*, and *Albrighton*: the latter is thus noticed by Leland in his 'Itinerary:' ' Syr John Talbot that maried Troutbeks Heire dwellith in a goodly logge in the hy toppe of Albrighton parke, it is in the very egge of Shropshire, 3 miles from Tunge.'[3] In another place[4] he tells us the park is called ' *Pepper-Hill*,' as it is marked in Saxton's Survey.

Madeley, which lies to the south of Shiffnal, but on the northern bank of the Severn, was a park belonging to the Prior and Convent of Wenlock licensed by King Edward I. in the year 1283.[5]

South of the Severn, near Wenlock, Leland notices a park at *Willey*: it was on the bounds of the Royal Hay or Forest of Shirlot ; and south of this wood or forest, Saxton marks a park at *Upton Cressett*.

A comparatively modern park should be noticed at Apley near Bridgenorth, containing 245 acres and about 200 fallow-deer. It is celebrated for the great beauty of its sylvan scenery.

In the central part of Shropshire, south of Shrewsbury and the Severn, according to Saxton also, there were parks at *Langley* and *Plash*. The Castle of Acton-Burnell is a little north of these places, and here also was an ancient park, enclosed by the celebrated Bishop of Bath, Robert Burnell, as early as the fiftieth of Henry III.[6] This is an existing park belonging to Sir F. C. Smyth, Bart.: contiguous to it is *Longnor*, the ancient seat of the Corbetts. Here a park is noticed by Leland,[7] which at present contains 40 acres and a herd of 60 fallow-deer.

A modern and existing park is at *Attingham* or Atcham, on the banks of the Severn near Shrewsbury, belonging to Lord Berwick.

About eight miles west of Shrewsbury and south of the Severn, is *Rowton*. Here was an ancient castle, and a park, which is given in Saxton's Survey; adjoining is *Loton*, the seat of Sir Baldwyn Leighton, where there is an existing park of 260 acres, with about 100 head of fallow-deer. The date of this park is unknown, but it is not in the ancient surveys. It may be noted here that Sir Richard Leighton, Bart., an ancestor of this venerable family, reserved to himself in a certain deed of feoffment power to make a park in his Manor of Leghton in the year 1300. This manor is near Buildwas Abbey on the Severn.[8]

[1] Eyton, vol. viii. p. 86.
[2] Ib. p. 258.
[3] Itin. vol. v. p. 29, fol. 30.
[4] Ib. vol. vii. p. 24, fol. 35.
[5] Eyton, vol. iii. p. 320.
[6] Cal. Pat. Rolls, p. 38.
[7] Itin. vol. v. p. 30, fol. 31.
[8] Eyton, vol. vii. p. 337.

Immediately south of Shrewsbury was the Lye Forest, now Lythwood. Here in the nineteenth of Edward III., and again in the first of Richard II., license was granted to the Abbot of Shrewsbury to impark 459 acres.[1]

In the southern parts of this county several other parks remain to be noticed. In 1813 there was one at *Walcot*, near Bishops-Castle, ' very extensive, finely laid out and abundantly stocked with deer.'[2] Another and a more ancient one, as it is laid down by Saxton, was at *Stoke* St. Milburgh in this neighbourhood, and also at *Oakley* near Ludlow, and at *Dean Park* near Burford, near the verge of the county of Worcester.

Saxton also marks a large park at *Cleobury*, within that part of the once large and Royal forest of Wyre, which was within the bounds of this county. This was originally a Royal chase or park, but in very early times came to the Mortimers, and again merged in the Crown.

Earnwood, now a manor in the parish of Kinlet, in this district, was originally a forest residence (with a park attached) of the Mortimers. On February 13, 1225, King Henry III. ' commands Hugh de Neville (he was justice of the forest) to let Hugh de Mortimer have ten fallow-deer, (*damas*) from the Royal Forest of Feckenham, which the king has given him towards stocking his park of Ernewood.[3]

A park at Mr. Child's at *Kinlet* has been only recently disparked.

Existing Deer Parks in Shropshire.

1. OTLEY	. . . .	Mr. Mainwaring.
2. BOREATTON	. .	Mr. Hunt.
3. HAWKSTONE	. .	Viscount Hill.
4. CHETWYND	. . .	Mr. Borough.
5. APLEY	. . . . .	Mr. Whitmore.
6. ACTON-BURNELL	.	Sir F.C. Smyth, Bt.
7. LONGNOR	. . .	Mr. Corbett.
8. ATTINGHAM	. .	Lord Berwick.
9. LOTON	. . . .	Sir Baldwyn Leighton, Bart.

CHESHIRE.

'SMITH, writing in the reign of Elizabeth,' observes Ormerod in his admirable ' History of Cheshire,' 'mentions "the great store of parks, for every gentleman almost hath his own park." The same might yet be said of park-like enclosures, but the number of those imparked by license, in which the vert venison and enclosure have been uninterruptedly maintained, is extremely limited.'[4]

Before we notice in detail the Cheshire parks, it will not be out of place to remark that although there is no mention in the Domesday Survey of any *park* within the county, there are frequent notices of Haiæ or Hayes in various parts of it, and that these Hayes differed but little from parks we have already observed;[5] they were rather intended for the capture of deer from the forests, than for their permanent

---

[1] Cal. Pat. Rolls, pp. 152, 199.
[2] Beauties of England and Wales, Shropshire, p. 256.

[3] Eyton, vol. iv. p. 278.
[4] Ormerod's Cheshire (1819), vol. i. p. l.
[5] See p. 12.

preservation, and appear also to have been very unequal in size, as well as in number, in the various lordships where we find them established. In one place in this county (Edulwintune, Adlington, in the Hundred of Macclesfield) no less than seven hayes and four eyries of hawks are mentioned.

The Earls of Chester being in fact the local sovereigns of the county, held, after the manner of their royal superiors, the forests or chases in their own hands. Of these there were three—De la Mere, Wirral, and Macclesfield — situated, respectively, the former in the more central part of the county, south of the Mersey, the second between the Mersey and the Dee, and the latter on the eastern borders of Cheshire, on the confines of Derbyshire and Staffordshire. In the forest or chase of De la Mere are two elevated points on the side which overlooks the Mersey and the vale of Chester, ' The new pale,' enclosed in the seventeenth century, 'The old pale,' enclosed by virtue of a precept now remaining in the Exchequer of Chester, directed to John Done in the eleventh year of Edward III., commanding him to make a ' *chamber in the forest* ' for the preservation of vert and venison. In this pale is the site of a lodge which bears that name, and where the foresters occasionally resided. In 1617, it appears by the account given of the progress of James I. through this county, that the chase or forest of De la Mere contained ' no small store of deer both red and fallow ;'[1] both are now extinct, though the woody character of the forest remains. In the twenty-seventh of Edward I., Walter de Langton, Bishop of Coventry

and Lichfield, obtained a license to impark his wood of *Tervyn*, contiguous to this forest.[2] The place is now called Tarvin on the western angle of Delamere Forest. Immediately south of it is *Oulton*, the existing park of Sir Philip Egerton. It is an area of about 350 acres, with a herd of 300 fallow-deer, and was enclosed with a brick wall about the year 1743.

West of the Forest of Delamere on the outlying tongue of land between the Mersey and the Dee, is the hundred of Wirral, the whole of which was formed into a forest by Randle Meschines, third Earl of Chester. Five ancient parks are marked within this district in Saxton's Survey of the county, engraved in 1577, three on the banks of the Dee at *Shotwick*, *Puddington*, and *Neston* ; and two towards the north at *Bydston*, and *Hooton*.

The Royal Castle and Park of *Shotwick* is noticed as early as the fifteenth of Henry VI., when the king granted to William Troutbek, and John his son, the office of park-keeper of Shotwyk, for their joint lives and that of the survivor. Shotwick was sold by the Crown in the seventeenth of Charles II., to Sir Thomas Wilbraham. It has been long disparked.[3]

King, in his 'Vale Royal,' speaks of the 'goodly ancient House and fair park of Hooton,' the seat of the Stanleys, and the park belonging to the 'fair ancient seat' of *Pool* adjoining. The last is not given in Saxton's Survey.

North of Delamere Forest, on the banks of the Mersey, were the large parks of *Halton Castle* and *Rocksavage*. The former was held under the Duchy of Lancaster, and in the fifteenth year of the

[1] Ormerod's Cheshire, vol. ii. p. 50.
[2] Cal. Pat. Rolls, p. 60.

[3] Ormerod, vol. ii. p. 314.

reign of Elizabeth let to Sir John Savage, Knt., the owner of the adjoining seat of Rocksavage, for thirty-one years at the annual rent of 6*l.* 7*s.* 8*d.* It was granted in reversion to Mr. Davison for fifty years in the twenty-sixth year of the same sovereign.[1] Both these parks have been long disparked, as is the case also with two ancient parks of small dimensions on the northern side of the river Wever, at *Aston* and *Dutton*, which appear in Saxton's Survey.

The same authority notices but two parks between Northwich and Altringham, those of *Warburton* and *Dunham-Massey.* The latter is an existing park, belonging to the Earl of Stamford and Warrington, being the seat of his ancestors of the family of *Boothe.* Leland writes, ' I cam by a park on the lifte Honde, wher Mr. Leyrcestre dwellith [*Tabley?*], and a iiii. miles farther I cam by a parke on the lifte Hond wher Master Bouth dwellith.'[2] Ormerod observes of Dunham-Massey, ' There are two parks, one of which is enclosed by a wall and supports four or five hundred head of deer. Both of the parks and the adjacent domain are full of fine timber, which in several instances has attained an extraordinary growth.'[3] ' Le of Bouth, half a mile from Knuttesford, hath a park,'[4] writes Leland. This no longer exists, but immediately north of Knutsford is the very extensive and well-wooded park of *Tatton*, from ten to eleven miles in circumference, and containing about 2,500 acres, and herds of 800 fallow and 40 red deer. This park is noticed in Speed's map of the county engraved in the reign of James I. It was greatly en-

larged by Samuel Egerton, Esq., about the year 1760. It is at present by far the largest park in the county, if not throughout the whole of England.

East of Knutsford is the hundred of Macclesfield, where there have been ever several parks. In connection with this hundred Ormerod writes, ' From the tenures specified in the inquisitions given under Wilmslow, Cheadle, &c., it will be found that the lords of these districts (which appear to have been formed out of the wastes attached to the earl's demesne of Macclesfield and Adlington) were bound yearly to repair the fences of the " combes " in Macclesfield Forest, and the former of them to send a guard for the protection of the earl when hunting in the forest. The combes were probably earthworks, or a kind of forest pale, constructed for a retiring place in case of danger, and were probably situated near the chamber of the forest.'[5]

Of *Adlington* Ormerod observes, ' King Edward IV., in the second year of his reign, by letters patent dated at Westminster, gave leave to Robert Legh of Adlington and his heirs to enclose certain lands in Adlington and Whitley, in the Forest of Macclesfield.'[6] If a park, however, existed here it had been probably disused before Saxton's time. He marks but five in the hundred of Macclesfield—at *Lyme, Poynton, Bromhall, Wynslow,* and *Gawsworth.*

The Park of *Lyme*, which is very extensive, is celebrated for the fine flavour of its venison, and contains a herd of wild cattle, the remains of a breed which has been kept there from time imme-

---

[1] Cotton MSS. Titus B. iv. f. 297.
[2] Leland's Itin. vol. v. p. 93, fol. 82.
[3] Ormerod's Cheshire, vol. i. p. 406.

[4] Leland's Itin. vol. vii. pp. 32-3, fol. 42.
[5] Ormerod's Cheshire, vol. iii. p. 281 note.
[6] Ib. vol. iii. p. 334.

morial, and is supposed indigenous. In the last century a custom was observed here of driving the Red Deer round the park, about Midsummer or rather earlier, collecting them in a body before the house, and then swimming them through a pool of water, with which the exhibition terminated. There is a large print of it by Vivares, after a painting by T. Smith, representing Lyme Park during the performance of the annual ceremony, with the great vale of Cheshire and Lancashire as far as the Rivington Hills in the distance, and in the foreground the great body of the deer passing through the pool, the last just entering it, and the old stags emerging on the opposite bank, two of which are contending with their forefeet, the horns at that season being too tender to combat with; this 'art of driving the deer,' like a herd of ordinary cattle, is stated on a monument at Disley to have been first perfected by Joseph Watson, who died in 1753, at the age of 104, 'having been park-keeper at Lyme more than sixty-four years.' The custom, however, appears not to have been peculiar to Lyme, as Dr. Whitaker observes in his account of Townley (the seat of a collateral line of Legh, in the county of Lancaster).[1] It is said of this Joseph Watson that he once undertook at the bidding of his master to drive twelve brace of stags to Windsor Forest, for a wager of 500 guineas, which he performed accordingly. This was in the reign of Queen Anne.[2]

' At Poynton is a parke,' writes Leland ; and again, ' The auncienter House longging to Warines, was Poynton yn the

mydle way, betwixt Stopford (Stockfort) and Mexwell Towne' (Macclesfield).[3] There appear to have been deer at one time at *Alderley*, the seat of Lord Stanley, of that place, as 'The Park House' is mentioned, but there are no deer at present.[4] In Northwich Hundred were the parks of *Kinderton* and *Brereton.* The former belonged to the Venables family, called Barons of Kinderton, and the latter to the ancient family who took their name from hence. The ancient park at Brereton, which has been long disparked, was situated north of the Hall.

One ancient park alone is marked in Speed's map of this county, and none in Saxton's, within the hundred of Nantwich, at *Wrenbury*, on the river Wever, not far from Combermere. It is thus noticed by Leland : ' Starkey, the auncients of that stokke, dwellith at Wenbyri, a mile and a half from Cumbermare ; there is a parke ful of marvelus faire wood, but no Dere.'[5] ' In imitation of their local sovereigns,' Ormerod remarks, ' the Barons of Nantwich formed a forest within the district of Nantwich, on the banks of the Weever, which is noticed by the name of the forest of Couhul, in the Charters of Hugh and William Melbank to their Abbey of Combermere, with reference to this forest, from which the township of Coole appears to derive its name ; they reserve "*cervum cervam et aprum*," in their grants to the monks of the adjacent abbey.'[6] Five miles south-east of Nantwich is *Doddington*, an extensive park, containing both red and fallow-deer.

More to the east, in the parish of Malpas, in Broxton Hundred, is *Cholmondeley*

[1] Ormerod's Cheshire, vol. ii. p. 339.
[2] See the Reliquary, vol. ii. p. 246.
[3] Itin. vol. vii. p. 30, fol. 40.

[4] Ormerod, vol. iii. p. 301.
[5] Itin. vol. vii. p. 34, fol. 43.
[6] Ormerod, vol. iii. p. 150, note.

Park, the ancient seat of the Marquis of Cholmondeley. It contains 137 acres, and about 200 fallow-deer. A park a little to the north in the borders of Eddisbury Hundred is marked in Speed's map at *Ridley* ; it is near *Peckforton,* the modern castle of Mr. Tollemache, where there are a few tame fallow-deer.

In the hundred of Broxton is *Carden,* the seat of the ancient family of Leche, where there is an existing deer park. More to the north is *Saighton,* once the Grange of the Abbots of St. Werburgh in Chester, to one of whom in the sixth of Henry VIII. license was granted to make a park of 1,000 acres, in Huntington, Cheveley, and Saighton. The project, adds Ormerod, was most probably put an end to by the Reformation.[1] Closely adjoining is *Eaton,* the seat of the Marquis

of Westminster. Here is a park of 388 acres, with a herd of 300 fallow-deer. It has been stocked with deer since the year 1714, as appears by Kips 'Views of Seats' at that period. The park has, however, within the last sixty years been considerably increased.

Existing Deer Parks in Cheshire.

1. LYME . . . Mr. Legh.
2. DUNHAM-}
   MASSEY } . Earl of Stamford.
3. TATTON . . Lord Egerton of Tatton.
4. OULTON . . Sir Philip Egerton, Bart.
5. EATON . . Marquis of Westminster
6. CHOLMONDE-} Marquis of Cholmon-
   LEY . . } deley.
7. DODDINGTON, Sir Henry Broughton, Bart.
8. CARDEN . . Mr. Leche.

[1] Ormerod's Cheshire, vol. ii. p. 420.

CHAPTER X.

NOTES ON DEER PARKS IN THE COUNTIES

OF

LANCASHIRE,   DURHAM,
YORKSHIRE,   CUMBERLAND, AND
WESTMORELAND,   NORTHUMBERLAND.

The View from Wharncliffe Chase.

CHAPTER X.

LANCASHIRE.

HE County Palatine of Lancaster, distinguished in former times for the number of its ancient families, could also boast of a considerable number of ancient deer parks. More than thirty are marked in Saxton's map of 1577. They were generally in the southern parts of the county, though there were several, disparked before the Elizabethan period, in the northern district of Furness. Thus in the twelfth year of Edward III., in the year 1338, the Abbot of the great Cistertian Abbey of Furness was permitted by Royal license to impark his woods of *Ramshead*, now corruptly spelt *Rampside*, *Sowerby*,

Rouhead, Greenscogh, Hagg, and *Millwood* in Low Furness, and of *Claife,* and some other parts of the Fells. In a Rental of the Lands of the Abbey I find ' The new parke vocatum Dereparke,' estimated at 6*l.* 13*s.* 4*d.*[1] A park at *Broughton,* in this district, is marked in Saxton's Survey. At *Holker* Hall near Cartmell, is an existing park belonging to the Duke of Devonshire, containing 200 acres, and 180 fallow-deer.

In the neighbourhood of Lancaster were the parks of *Leghton, Hornby Castle,* where there were two parks, *Leck, Gresgarth,* and *Ashton.* The latter appears to have been identical with that imparked by John de Ashton called ' Lymparke' in Ashton, in the eleventh year of Edward III.[2]

An existing park at *Ashton,* which formerly belonged to the Dukes of Hamilton, and now to Mr. Starkie, contains 130 acres, and a herd of 30 menil or spotted deer.

South of the Forests of Wyerdale and Bowland, was the great Park or Chase of *Mirescough*: it is mentioned by Leland in his ' Itinerary' as follows: ' or I cam to Garstone by a mile and a half, I left Marscow, a great parke partely enclosid with Hegge, partely al on the moore side with pale, on the right. It is replenishid with Redde Deere. The Erle of Derby hath hit in farme of the King.'[3] In the ninth year of Elizabeth, the Herbage and Pannage of this park was let to Edward Tildisley for fifty years, at an annual rent of 25*l.*[4]

Among the Domestic State Papers of the year 1633-4 (Feb. 15), is a Petition from Carew Raleigh, farmer of this park, to the King, for an order from the Chancellor of the Duchy of Lancaster to compound with the Petitioner. It appears that the rent of the park was to be increased to 35*l.* per annum, and the Crown to be discharged of the annual fee of 4*l.*, granted to the keeper for life.

A letter is also preserved in the State Paper Office, dated the 3rd of September, 1662, from the King to Edward Tyldesley, chief ranger of this park, to the effect that whereas several fallow-deer having been driven out of the park by the injury of the late times, and bred and increased in the adjacent grounds, he is ordered to hunt and drive in any not belonging to a chartered park.[5]

Another and smaller park is marked in the ancient maps at *Grenno* or *Grenagh* Castle, a little north of Garstang.

Whitaker in his ' History of Whalley' has preserved much information with regard to the forests, chases, and parks within the Honor of Clitheroe.[6] Of the Royal park of *Ightenhill* he observes, that it was separated from the Forest of Pendle by the Calder, and was one of the demesnes of Clitheroe Castle. The ancient orthography, he says, is *Hightenhull*; within the pale was a very ancient manor-house of the Lacies, in existence as early as the twenty-second of Henry III. (1238). In 1311, it is mentioned in an Inquisition as being one league and a half (leuca) in circuit.

A note of ' sundry parks within the Duchy of Lancaster,' preserved among the Cotton MSS.,[7] tells us that sometime

---

[1] Beck's Annales Furnesienses, 4to. 1844, p. 71.
[2] Cal. Pat. Rolls, p. 128.
[3] Itin. vol. v. p. 98, fol. 84.

[4] Cotton MS. Titus B. iv. f. 297.
[5] S. P. O. Domestic.
[6] 4to. London, 1818, p. 218, &c.
[7] Titus B. iv. fol. 297.

the Duke of Lancaster kept house here, but that it was disparked and granted by lease to Sir John Townley, Knt., for seventy years in the tenth of the reign of Henry VIII., at an annual rent of 30*l.* Whitaker adds, that Sir Richard Shuttleworth appears as the lessee about the fifteenth of Elizabeth, ' which they have since converted into fee-simple.'

The Forest of Blackburnshire, observes Whitaker, appears to have been divided into four subordinate divisions, viz. : *Ightenhill* Park, *Trawden* Chase, *Rossendale* Chase with the Park of *Musbury*, and the Chase of *Accrington.* Custody of the Herbage of Musbury was granted to James de Radcliffe by John of Gaunt in the eighteenth of Richard II.,and a lease was also granted of this park to Richard Radcliffe of Radcliffe for twenty years at the rent of 8*l.* 6*s.* 8*d.* in the ninth of Edward IV.[1]

In Bowland Forest, of which the family of Parker of Browsholme were hereditary bow-bearers, and where the deer were finally destroyed in the year 1805,[2] there were too ' Launds ' or enclosures for the deer—*Radholme* Park or Lawn, in Yorkshire, and the park of *Lathgram* or *Leagram*, in Lancashire.

An ancient park existed also at *Stonyhurst* on the borders of Yorkshire, ' but when it was enclosed,' says Whitaker, ' I have not been able to learn.' ' The Dean or Abbot,' he tells us, ' had a park at *Whalley*,and here,according to tradition, bubali or wild cattle were transplanted from Blakely, and after the Dissolution removed to Gisburne Park, where their

descendants still remain.'[3] By Inquisition in the ninth of Henry VIII., it was found that the Abbot's Park of Whalley was enclosed in the twenty-second of Henry VII., but it is probable that this refers only to a *licientia imparcandi*, of later date than the time at which it was actually enclosed.'[4]

Whitaker describes the warm and fertile country on the left bank of the river Ribble from Walton to Salisbury, ten miles in length, as one of the finest portions of Ribblesdale : it was once possessed, he says, by five knightly families, all resident on their own estates. In this tract were four parks, as many manor-houses of the first rank, furnished with domestic chapels, all now gone, the parks divided, and the woods destroyed. The parks appear to have been *Osbaldeston,Salesbury, Samlesbury,* and *Dinkley.*[5]

At *Rishton* in this neighbourhood was once an ancient park, as appears by the petition of Richard Walmesley to King Charles II. in May 1664, asking for a confirmation of the Charter of Edward II., granting free warren and liberty of hunting in the demesne lands of Rishton, and for permission to impark and employ for breeding deer his other lands adjoining, lying in the parish of Whalley.[6]

At *Hopton* was also an ancient park first mentioned in the second year of Edward III. It then belonged to the Arches family. Prior to the year 1181, Robert de Lacy,who died in 1193, granted to William de Arches a confirmation of all the privileges which his ancestors had conferred upon the ancestors of the latter,

[1] Whitaker's Whalley, p. 222.
[2] See Mr. Lister Parker's Description of Browsholme Hall, p. 12.
[3] Whitaker's Whalley, p. 205. Tradition says they were drawn to Gisburne by the

power of music. — *Bewick's Quadrupeds,* p. 39 *n.*
[4] Ib. p. 251.
[5] Ib. p. 433.
[6] Calendar of State Papers Domestic.

particularly the venison caught (venatio-nem captam), in Hopton; a proof that the range of deer was not then confined to the forests. Besides the ancient park of Hopton, there were others of later date imparked by Sir John Townley, the first comparatively of small extent, consisting of old enclosed lands, for which the license bears date twelfth Henry VII., but the second, which was almost a complete enclosure of the open fields and wastes of the township, did not take place till the year 1514 or 1515, as appears by the license. This consisted of no less than 1,100 Lancashire acres, and after Knowes-ley appears to have been the largest park in the county. The deer of this park had been destroyed before the year 1615, though it was not divided into tenements before the beginning of the present cen-tury.[1]

Within the contiguous demesne of *Habergham*, is an hollow in the ground, which, adds Whitaker, tradition points out as a pit-fall, dug for impounding the stray deer when the two families of Town-ley and Habergham lived upon terms of bad neighbourhood together. Near the summit of the park, and where it declines to the south, are the remains of a large pool, through which tradition reports that the deer were driven by their keepers in the manner still practised in the park at Lyme. 'It is impossible,' is the remark of Dr. Whitaker, 'not to be struck with the mixture of ancient simplicity and splendour in this once favoured residence of the family, where from the windows of their castellated mansion, high and bleak, with no eyes for landscape, and little feel-

ing of cold, they could survey with undi-minished pleasure, vast herds of deer, sheep, and cattle, grazing in a park of ten miles in circumference, where like the " old courtier who never hunted but in his own grounds," they could enjoy the pleasures of the chase without interruption or intrusion, and whence they derived inexhaustible supplies of that plain hos-pitality which never consumed a great estate.'[2]

The license for enclosing the old park of Townley, which lay west from the house, bears date, as per Inquisition, in the sixth of Henry VII.[3]

Near Bolton and Bury is *Radcliffe*, the original seat of the great family of that name; it is described by Whitaker as 'a fertile domain of the finest grazing ground, once a park, upon the south-west bank of Irwell;'[4] adjoining it was the Park of *Pilkington*, which, with those of *Myd-dleton*, *Barton*, *Holme* and *Trafford*, is laid down in the Surveys of Saxton and Speed. The park at Middleton, belonging to Sir Ralph Ashton, is noticed by Leigh in his ' Natural History of Lan-cashire' (p.3) as containing at that period (1700) wild cattle, supposed to have been brought from the Highlands of Scotland. Trafford is an existing park of about 500 acres, with a herd of 300 fallow-deer.

Near Wigan were the following ancient parks: *Hulton* not impaled, *Atherton*, *Bryn*, *Ashton*, *Newton*, *Bradley*, and *Bewsey*. To the north-west is *Lathom*, where there were two parks, one called ' New Park.' This park is stated in 1818 to be nearly four miles in circumference, finely wooded, and well stocked with deer.[5]

---

[1] Whitaker's Whalley, p. 271.
[2] Ib. p. 277.
[3] Ib. p. 342.
[4] Whitaker's Whalley, p. 412.
[5] Neale's Views of Seats, 1818, vol. i.

At present it contains about 200 acres including woods, and from 100 to 130 fallow-deer. To the south is *Knowesley,* the magnificent seat of the Earl of Derby, and the largest park in the county; it was described in 1776 as 'having a fine variety of ground, and good covert for the deer.'[1] Leland merely says, ' Knollesley a park having a pretty House of the Erles of Derby within a mile of Prestcod.' Knowesley Park is an area of 2,000 acres including some young plantations, containing 300 fallow and as many red deer. It was enclosed by Sir Thomas de Lathom by license granted by Edward III. in the year 1348. Two other parks given by Saxton remain to be mentioned—*Croxteth* and *Tocksteth*; the first near Knowesley,

the last near Liverpool. Leland observes of the former, that it was 'a parke of the Kinges hard by Molineux's House,'[2] and I find it noticed in the thirty-third of Edward III. as ' parcus de Croxtath super le mosse de Leverpole.'[3] Toxteth belonged to the Duchy of Lancaster.

Existing Deer Parks in Lancashire.

1. KNOWESLEY . The Earl of Derby.
2. LATHOM .   . . Lord Skelmersdale.
3. ASHTON .   . . Mr. Starkie.
4. TRAFFORD . . Sir Humphrey Trafford, Bart.
5. HOLKER . . . The Duke of Devonshire.

YORKSHIRE. WEST RIDING.

HUNTER, in his valuable Histories of Hallamshire and South Yorkshire, has given many interesting notices of some of the numerous deer parks of the West Riding. We will begin with his account of the great park of *Sheffield*, at the southern extremity of the great county. ' This park, according to Harrison's survey made in 1637, contained 2,461 acres, 3 roods, and 11 perches, all within a ring fence of eight miles. This was the park of the Lords of the Manor of Sheffield. It was a park by prescription, at least no royal charter can now be produced for

converting this fine tract of land to the purposes of a park. Dodsworth[4] has preserved the memory of a singular and indeed a savage custom of which this park was formerly the scene. In the topographical notes which he made at Sheffield in 1620, he writes that "the late Gilbert Earl of Shrewsbury was wont on every year on a certain day to have many bucks lodged in a meadow near the townside, about a mile in compass, to which place repaired almost all the men of the parish, and had liberty to kill and carry away as many as they could with their

[1] Beauties of England, vol. ii. p. 205.
[2] Leland's Itin. vol. vii. p. 48, fol. 36.
[3] Cal. Pat. Rolls, p. 170.
[4] Dodsworth's MSS. in Bibl. Bodl. vol. clx. f. 132 b.

hands, and did kill sometimes twenty, and had money given them for wine by the Earl." In Harrison's time there were still a thousand fallow-deer in the park, and of deer of antler two hundred.' This park was divided into farms about the commencement of the eighteenth century.[1] Leland makes mention of 'the goodly Lodge or Manor place on a hill top in Shefield Park.'[2]

In the immediate neighbourhood of Rotherham, Saxton, in his Survey of Yorkshire, marks several ancient parks,—at *Greasborough, Thriburgh, Conisbrough,* and two parks near the site of *Keveton Park* on the borders of Derbyshire. Coningborough, once the castle of the great House of Warren, was in the hands of the Crown in the reign of Henry VII., who, by a warrant dated November 11th, the seventh of Henry VII., the original of which, says Hunter, was in the possession of F. F. Fuljambe, Esq. (in 1828), directed to Sir Thomas Fitzwilliam, Knight, keeper of our park of Cunesburgh Hawe, commanded him to deliver 'twelve quick does to be taken within our parc of Cunesburgh Hawe, to our trusty and well beloved squire for our body Bryan Sandeford, towards the storing of his park at *Thorp.*' This was at Thorpe Salvin in the parish of Laughton, on the borders of Yorkshire, Nottinghamshire, and Derbyshire. There were 440 fallow-deer in Conisborough Park in 1604.[3]

Near Greasborough is the extensive and magnificent but comparatively modern park of *Wentworth-Woodhouse,* and the ancient park of *Tankersley.* Of the

latter it was said, in 1731, that the finest red deer in England were here fed.[4]

A little to the west is *Wortley* and *Wharncliffe,* 'partly,' says Hunter, 'a Forest, and partly a Deer Park.' Here is the famous inscription of Sir Thomas Wortley, inscribed in 1510, to the effect that he had built the lodge here ' that he might hear the hart bel in the midst of Wharncliffe.'[5] Two hundred head of deer are still kept in Wharncliffe Chase.[6]

North of Wortley is the modern park of *Wentworth Castle,* and the smaller one of *Cannon Hall,* containing 157 acres, and about 170 fallow-deer. It was enclosed about the year 1730. To the east of Barnsley a park is marked by Saxton at *Brearly*; a subsequent park was, in the early part of the eighteenth century, at *Woodsome,* near Huddersfield, belonging at that period to the Kaye family : it appears to have been disparked about the year 1733, after the death of Lord Lewisham, who had married the heiress of the Kayes. An existing park is at *Wolley,* between Barnsley and Wakefield.

On the eastern confines of this southern part of Yorkshire, on the borders of Lincolnshire, was the celebrated *Hatfield Chase,* of which Hunter, in his 'South Yorkshire,' has given the following account :[7] 'Hither the Earls of Warren were accustomed to resort for the enjoyment of these sports [hunting, fowling, and fishing], and near the centre of the chase, at which is now the town of Hatfield, they had a house at which they might remain when, fatigued with their day's exertion, they were unwilling to

[1] Hunter's Hallamshire Fo. 1819, pp. 7, 189.
[2] Itin. vol. v. p. 107, fol. 94.
[3] Lambeth MSS. No. 709.
[4] Mag. Britt. 1731, vol. vi. p. 506.
[5] See *antè,* p. 22.
[6] Hunter's S. Yorkshire, p. 332.
[7] Vol. i. p. 155, &c.

return to Coningsborough. Near this house was a park of five hundred acres, the memory of which is still retained in the local nomenclature of the district. This park was at all times well stocked with deer, who were also to be seen roaming at large through the whole limits of the chase.'

'When Edward Balliol, the Ex-king of Scotland, was residing at Wheatley, he amused himself with sporting on these lands. There is a curious instrument in the Fœdera, dated October 18, 1356, in which a pardon is granted to him for the slaughter he had committed. In the chase he had killed 16 red deer, 6 hinds, 8 stags, 3 calves, and 6 kids, in the park; 8 fallow-deer, one sour, and one sorell; in the ponds, 2 pike of 3½ feet in length, 3 of 3 feet long, 20 of 2⅓ feet, 20 of 2 feet, 50 pickerels of 1½ feet, 6 of 1 foot, 109 perch, roach, tench, skelys, and 6 breames and bremettes.'[1]

'When Henry VIII. made his northern progress after the suppression of the Pilgrimage of Grace, it was a part of his plan to enjoy the diversion which Hatfield could afford. The Earl of Southampton wrote to the Earl of Shrewsbury, who was Surveyor-General of the Chase, enclosing warrants for taking twenty bucks, from some other park I presume of the king's, and conveying them to Hatfield a day or two before the king's coming. The Earl replied that he would provide for the king's pleasure, but would spare to use the warrants, and make up the number of bucks out of his own grounds at Sheffield, desiring at the same time that the king might be moved to see his

poor House at Winfield by the way. The Earl, however, issued fourteen warrants to the Regarders of Hatfield, to prepare so many bucks, and repaired himself to Bawtry to meet the king. This was in August 1541.'

About this period the antiquary Leland visited Hatfield, of which his account is as follows : 'From Doncaster to Heathfeld by champagn sandy ground is 5 miles. There is a faire Paroch Chirch in the village ; and a parke therby. The Logge or Manor-place is but meanely builded of Tymber. The quarters about Heathfeld be forest ground, and though wood be scars there, yet there is great plentie of red Deere that haunt the fennes, and the great mores thereabout.'[2]

The level of Hatfield Chase, containing about 70,000 acres, was surveyed in 1607. It is said that the red deer at that time amounted to about 1,000;[3] but that the herd was much impaired by the depredations of the borderers. In 1609, Henry Prince of Wales is said to have been at Hatfield. An account of his sport in the Chase has been preserved.[4] This was the last time that there was any royal hunting here, the Chase having been disparked and passed out of the Crown in 1629.

At *Cusworth*, very near Doncaster, is an existing park belonging to Mr. Wrightson.

At *Pontefract* was an ancient park noticed by Leland, containing 434 fallow-deer in 1604,[5] and near it a park called *Kridling*, in the surveys of Saxton and Speed.

Between Pontefract and Wakefield is

[1] Hunter's S. Yorkshire, vol. i. p. 135.
[2] Lel. Itin. vol. i. p. 38, fol 40.
[3] 700, according to the Lambeth MSS. anno 1604.
[4] Hunter's South Yorkshire, vol. i. p. 156.
[5] Lambeth MSS. No. 709.

Nostal. Here Sir Richard Gargrave, in the reign of James I., had a grant of a free park. At *Kinsley,* adjoining, was also a house and park. It had been an ancient estate of the Burtons, but was purchased by Sir Thomas Gargrave in the time of Queen Elizabeth.[1] Wakefield was surrounded by several parks. The largest, called ' *The New Park,*' contained 200 fallow-deer, and the smallest, or *Old Park,* 80, in the year 1604.[2] I find the latter mentioned in the Patent Rolls as early as the thirteenth of Edward III.

Still more to the north numerous ancient parks were scattered over the broad expanse of the West Riding. To the west, the large wild park of *Denholme,* which belonged to the Tempests, and was reserved for red deer ; others at *Bowling Hall, Calverley, Farnley Hall,* &c. Near Leeds was the well-known *Rothwell Haigh,* the park belonging to the manor-place of the Lacies of Rothwell ;[3] and here also still exists the ancient park of *Temple Newsam,* imparked by John Darcy, with the royal license in the eighteenth year of Edward III.[4] Ninety fallow-deer are stated to have been here in July 1604.

To the east, near Selby, six parks are marked by Saxton, including *Rust* and *Scaline Parks.* Near Wetherby and Tadcaster is the extensive park of *Bramham.*

In the more central district is *Kipax.* Here was a small park held under the Duchy of Lancaster, and containing 45 fallow-deer in 1604.[3]

South of Knaresborough were the great

parks of *Spoford* and *Healagh,* belonging to the Earls of Northumberland. Both were visited by Leland. Of the latter he writes : ' From Helegh Priory, scant a mile to Helegh village, there I saw great Ruines of an auncient Manor-place of stone that longgid with the fair woddid park thereby to the Erle of Northumberland.'[5] It appears from the 'Northumberland Household Book' that Spoford Park contained 180 fallow-deer, and the wood of Spoford 43, in the year 1512. At the same period Healagh Park had a herd of 319 red and fallow-deer. In 1604 Spoford is said to have contained 175 fallow-deer.[2] Healagh is not mentioned in Lambeth MSS.

Between Spoford (or Spofforth) and Knaresborough is *Plumpton,* where there was a park noticed by Leland, and which was enclosed in the thirteenth of Edward IV.[6] At *Knaresborough* there were three parks, ' metely welle woddid,' which, according to that accurate topographer, belonged to that place. The largest was called ' the Park of the Hay,' or ' Hay Park,' and its herbage and pannage were let to Francis Slingsby, Esq., for twenty-one years, in the thirtieth year of Queen Elizabeth (1587–8) at an annual rent of 6*l.* 18*s.* 8*d.*[7]

Of the parks about *Skipton,* belonging to the great House of Clifford Earls of Cumberland, we have an interesting account in Whitaker's ' History and Antiquities of Craven.'[8] There appear to have been several besides that adjoining to the castle, valued in the fourth year of Edward II., with the feeding of the

[1] Hunter's S. Yorkshire, vol. ii. p. 211.
[2] Lambeth MSS. No. 709.
[3] Whitaker's Whalley, p. 205 *n.*
[4] Cal. Pat. Rolls, p. 148.
[5] Leland's Itin. vol. i. p. 46, fol. 48.
[6] Cal. Pat. Rolls, p. 318.
[7] Cotton MSS. Titus B. iv. f. 297.
[8] 2nd ed. pp. 228, 230.

deer, at 60*s.*; in the year 1612, ' besyde the same feeding,' rated at 10*l.* This park, which lay immediately contiguous to the Castle, had one deep and beautiful dell, immediately beneath the walls.

Near Skipton is *Newbiggin*, in the parish of Carlton, where there was a park probably enclosed by the first earl. The Parks *De la Caudre* and *Heye* are first mentioned in a charter of William de Fortibus Earl of Albemarle, in the year 1257. *Calder* or *Cawder Park* stretched along the skirts of Romille Moor, and near the confines of Bradley, where a farm belonging to the Earl of Thanet still (observes Whitaker in 1812) retains the name; yet the Licentia imparcandi was not granted before the fortieth of Edward III. to Roger de Clifford. It is now a grazing farm.

The *Hawe Park*, or *Haye Park*, retaining some vestiges of the ancient ridings, was at the same period a bushy pasture.

Another park was called *George*, of which the particular site and dimensions are not remembered. There were besides, lodges and parks adjoining *Holden*, and the Forest of *Barden* with various ' lodges' within it, the lower part of which appears to have been wholly occupied in parks and chases. In the fourth of Edward II. there were here six lodges for the accommodation of the keepers, and the protection of the deer, viz., Dreblay, Barden, Laund, Gamleswath, Holgill, and Ungayne.

The Forest of Skipton, which, excepting Holden, comprehended all these parks and demesnes, consisted of that rocky and central part of Craven which extends

east and west from the Wharf to the Are, and is bounded on the north and south by the two great openings which connect those valleys. The whole may be estimated at an area of six miles by four, or 15,360 acres.[1]

Whitaker has preserved also many curious particulars on the subject of hunting the deer in these wild and extensive preserves. He tells us how the old Lady Clifford ' hounded' her greyhounds within the grounds of *Rilston*, and chased the deer both red and fallow ; and how Master Norton hath walled his grounds of Rilston, where the foresters were wont to walk, ' and to draw my Lord of Cumberland's deer into his ground he hath made a wall on an high rigge (or ridge) beside a quagmire, and at the end of the wall he hath rayled the ground, so that it is destruction to my Lord's deer so many as come.'[2]

The following extracts from the Household Books of the Clifford Family are curious in themselves, and will serve to throw light upon the domestic economy of our ancestors at the beginning of the seventeenth century:—

' Fees to Foresters and Park-keepers within Craven.

' 1609. To Lister Symonson, in part for kepyng his Lordship's deer at Birks (now Birk-House) near Buckden, xxv*s.*

' Robert Smith of Gressington, in part for his kepershippe there x*s.*

' Kepershippe at Old Park x*s.*

' Kepershippe at the Hawe, in part xv*s.*

' Kepershippe at Threshfield, xxx*s.*

' Kepershippe at Bradshawe, and the liberties thereof, l*s.*

' Walking of Craco Fell, and part of

---

[1] Whitaker's History and Antiquities of Craven, 2nd ed. p. 232.

[2] Whitaker's History and Antiquities of Craven, 2nd ed. p. 234.

Wm. Atkinson's office, due this Pentecost, xvi˟.

' S͛ Richd. Musgrave, Knt., his half year's annuities, xxv˭˭. [query as Master Forester?]

' Keeping Carlton Park iiii˭˭.

' Keepershippe at Barden, xxx˟.

' Keeping his Lp̄s deer in Longshotte, xl˟.

' Keepershippe of the great new Pk̄e here at Skipton at Pk̄e George, viii˭˭.

' Looking to my lo: deere on Thorpe Fell, xx˟.

' John Taylor of Littendale, for his keepershippe there, xl˟.'

[Thirteen keepers prove how large a portion of Craven was then ranged by deer.]

' For going to the Birks with a letter for bringing six red-deer hither picked out of Lister Simmons herd, xii˟.

' For going to Londesbro' with the great Buck of Threshfield, ix˟.

'Gave to Mr. Michael Lister's man and maide who brought 2 hyndes calves, and a cowe from their master, (the cowe he gave unto my Ld.), xii˟. John Wardman for the charge of himself and two men carrying xiii. kyne and 25 hynd calves to my lady Suffolk at Saffron Walden on whom my lord did bestow them, vii˭˭.'

[These items are curious. The Earl had engaged to supply the Countess of Suffolk with red-deer (which seem to have been rare in the south), in order to stock the park at Audley-End, and for that purpose appears to have had several hynd calves taught to suck cows, by which means the difficulty of conveyance was obviated, as the young creatures would spontaneously follow their foster dams.]

' Given to the keepers of *Wighil* Park, Mr. Henry Stapleton's men, my Lord having killed two buckes in his parke, xx˟.

' To the keepers of *Allerton Maulevery* parke where my Lord killed a buck, xiii˟. iv͟d.'[1]

Wighill is near Wetherby in the Ainsty Liberty; Allerton Maulevery was one of the Knaresborough parks.

In 1650, in consequence of the loyalty of the owner, Lord Clifford, the Park of Skipton was placed under sequestration by the usurping powers, 'who declared that they would let all the deer out of the park when the first of June is passed.'

' In 1654, however, the heiress of the elder and younger line of the Cliffords having succeeded to their respective portions of the family estates, the deer which had hitherto ranged at large over both, were now to be appropriated and enclosed. From this transaction, therefore, observes Whitaker, ' we are able to fix the era at which the ancient forests of Craven were finally depopulated of their old and stately inhabitants, and as the park of *Bolton* was the retreat provided for one moiety of them, we have here a positive proof that the stags which yet adorn its summits are lineal descendants of that wild race which anciently spread from Skipton to Longstruther; at once the pride of the chase, and the luxury of Romille and Albemarle, of Percy and Clifford.' The contract by which the above arrangement was carried out was dated the 20th of May 1654, and was between the Countess Dowager of Pembroke and Elizabeth Countess of Cork. ' Touching the Deer that are or shall be driven into Barden parke,—That as soon as a certain number shall be taken as well of those already come in, as of such deer as shall hereafter be driven into the said parke of *Barden*, which was lately

[1] Whitaker's Craven, 2nd ed. p. 319.

walled in by the said Countess of Pembroke, the said number so taken shall be and remain in the said parke of Barden, and be employed to the use and behoof of the said Countess of Pembroke, until such time as there shall be a parke walled in, and made staunch at *Bolton* or Stedhouse by the Countesse of Corke, and then the one half of the said number of deer shall be redelivered by the said Countess of Pembroke, or her appointment to the Countess of Corke or her appointment.'[1]

Nine or ten miles north of Shipton is *Threshfield.* 'Here the Nortons had a park noticed by Harrison in his Description of Britain,[2] where they kept their fallow-deer, of which in 1603 the number was 120. The park measured 80 acres, and must have been filled with valuable wood, as it was estimated at no less than 400*l.* while in the Crown; Sir Stephen Tempest was Ranger. After it came into possession of the Tempests it was still preserved. In 1639, 2*l.* 10*s.* were paid by the Earl of Cumberland's agents at Skipton for toils to catch the deer at Threshfield, and then it was, in all probability, that they were finally destroyed.'[3]

More modern parks were at *Broughton* in the immediate neighbourhood of Skipton, and at *Gisburne,* some miles to the west towards the Lancashire border. The latter appears to have been enclosed by the Prior of Gisburne by license in the thirty-ninth of Edward III.[4]

In the parish of Kettlewell on the confines of the North Riding was *Skale Park,* laid down in all the old surveys, and licensed in the sixth and seventh, and again in the eleventh year of Henry IV.,

by a grant to Ralph Earl of Westmoreland, 'to enclose 300 acres of land for a park, and to build and kernel a lodge within it.' The name of Skale is derived from a long and steep ascent within the park from Craven to Coverdale; it is now divided into two large enclosures.[5]

The Archbishops of York possessed from an early period a park at *Ripon,* of which John De Carleton was deputed keeper in the forty-fifth of Edward III.[6] Leland rates it as six miles in compass. The existing park of *Studley Royal* is in the immediate neighbourhood, and appears in Saxton's Survey of 1577.

Existing Deer Parks in the West Riding of Yorkshire.

1. WHARNCLIFFE . Lord Wharncliffe.
2. WENTWORTH-WOODHOUSE } Earl Fitzwilliam.
3. WENTWORTH CASTLE } Mr. Vernon Wentworth.
4. CANNON HALL . Mr. Spencer Stanhope.
5. WOLLEY . . . Mr. Wentworth.
6. NOSTAL PRIORY Mr. Winn.
7. CUSWORTH . . Mr. Wrightson.
8. KIRKLEES . . . Sir George Armytage, Bart.
9. METHLEY . . . Earl of Mexborough.
10. TEMPLE NEW-SHAM } Mr. Meynell Ingram.
11. BRAMHAM . . . Mr. Lane Fox.
12. BOLTON ABBEY . Duke of Devonshire.
13. GISBURNE . . . Lord Ribblesdale.
14. STUDLEY ROYAL Earl de Grey and Ripon.

[1] Whitaker's History of Craven, p. 239.
[2] P. 70. '**Tresfelde Parke.**'
[3] Whitaker's History of Craven, p. 472.
[4] Cal. Pat. Rolls, p. 180.
[5] Whitaker's History of Craven, p. 480.
[6] Cal. Pat. Rolls, p. 187.

YORKSHIRE. NORTH RIDING.

ALTHOUGH the North Riding of York-shire is much less in extent than the West Riding, yet about an equal number of parks in both, appear to be marked in Saxton's Survey of the county, engraved in 1577. The greater number of these parks were grouped near the towns of Middleham, Masham, and Thirsk ; south of Richmond and North Allerton. Those near the first mentioned place are thus noticed in Leland's 'Itinerary:' 'There be 4 or 5 parks about *Middleham*, and longing to it, whereof som be reasonaly wooddyd.'[1] Saxton preserves the names of three of them, '*Woodhall* Park,' '*Wan-las* Park,' and *Capilbank* Park.' Another in the same neighbourhood is also noticed by Leland: ' There is a parke waullyd with stone at *Bolton*.'[1] An ancient park is also recorded by Saxton at *Constable-Burton*, a little to the north of Middleham, which appears to have been enclosed by license granted to Walter le Scroop in the twelfth of Edward III.[2] There were deer here in 1714,[3] when it belonged to Sir Marmaduke Wyvill, 'Bárt. North of Bedal is *Hornby Castle*, where there has been long an ancient park, given in the older surveys; and to the south of that town five parks, of which the principal were *Snape*, and *Tanfield*, are also found in a group near the town of Masham. Leland describes ' Snape a goodly Castel in a Valley longing to the Lorde Latimer,

and ii or iii parkes welle woddid abowt hit. It is his chefe Howse and standith a ii mile from Great Tanfeld.' Of the latter he says: ' Tanfield village, a castell of the Lord Parrs, and a great woody parke.'[4]

South of Masham is the comparatively modern park of *Swinton*, enclosed about the middle of the seventeenth century, and containing 80 acres, and a herd of 200 spotted deer.

Nearer Ripon were the parks of *Norton-Conyers*, and *Newby*: the latter appears to have been imparked by a license granted to Sir William Robinson in 1634-5, which permitted the enclosure of 150 acres of his demesne lands of his Manor of Newby, with liberty of free warren.[5]

The group of parks about Thirsk com-prehended those of *Topclyf* and *Catton*, which belonged to the Earls of Northum-berland. It appears by the Household Book of that noble family, that there were in the year 1512, 558 fallow-deer in the great park of Topclyf, and 291 in the little park at the same place; while at Catton there were but 79 fallow-deer ; Leland, mentioning the two parks at Topclyf, tells us that ' the bigger is a 6 or 7 miles in cumpace and is well woddid.' ' At Tresk' (*Thirsk*), he adds, 'was a great castil of the Lord Mowbreys, and there is a Park with prety wood about it.'[6]

On the western confines of the forest of

---

[1] Itin. vol. viii. pp. 18, 19, fol. 66.
[2] Cal. Pat. Rolls, p. 133.
[3] Kip's Views.

[4] Itin. vol. v. p. 117, fol. 114, pp. 120-1, fol. 115.
[5] Cal. S. Papers Domestic. p. 523.
[6] Lel. Itin. vol. i. p. 69, fol. 75.

Gautres was the old park of *Raskill*: here were 120 fallow-deer in the year 1604.[1]

At *Newborough* in the same neighbourhood, the park was enclosed in the sixth year of Richard II. by a license granted to the Prior of that place. The park of *Crake*, a little to the south, belonged to the Bishops of Durham; it was noticed by Leland, but was disparked before Saxton's time.

An ancient park had long existed also at *Gilling Castle* not far from Newborough, to be traced to a license for imparking a thousand acres of land and wood, granted to Thomas Eaton in the forty-eighth year of Edward III.[2] Two other old parks remain to be mentioned in this district—those of *Sheriff-Hutton*, and *Hilderskill* Castles. The former appears to have been enclosed by Ralph de Nevill in the ninth year of Edward III., when the right of making a deer-leap (saltatorium) was also included in the license. This park is noticed in Leland's 'Itinerary,' and contained in the year 1604, 400 fallow-deer.[3] 'The park of Hinderskel,' writes Leland, 'by my estimation is a 4 miles yn cumpace, and hath much fair youg wod yn it.'[4] Here is the present house and park of *Castle Howard*, the seat of the Earl of Carlisle, a large demesne, including woods and water, 1,500 acres, with a herd of 500 fallow-deer. A little more to the north is *Helmsley*: here was an ancient park which is given in Saxton's Survey, a part of it is comprehended in the comparatively modern park of *Duncombe*, the greater part of which was enclosed about 150 years

ago; it is an area of 500 acres, with a herd of 600 fallow-deer of every variety of colour.

In the life of Marmaduke Rawdon of York,[5] the record of a day's hunting in the old park of Hemsley or Hamlake, in August 1664, is preserved. The park then belonged to the second Duke of Buckingham of the Villiers family.

In the north-eastern districts of the North Riding of Yorkshire, the following parks appear in the surveys of Saxton and Speed :—*Kirkby-Moreside, Synnynton, Blansby Park, Budik Park, Mulgrave Castle, Danby Park* (not impaled), and parks at the Castles of *Skelton* and *Kilton*.

Blansby is near Pickering, where Leland tells us there is 'a park by the castilleside, more than vii miles in compas, but it is not welle wooddid.'[6] This park was held under the Duchy of Lancaster, and in the first year of Edward VI. let to Armigill Wade, Gent., for forty-one years, at an annual rent of 11*l.* 5*s.* 4*d.*[7]

Near the town of Stokesley three ancient parks are also given in Saxton's Map,—*Aumond Park, Wharleton Castle*, and a park near the villages of Caythorne and Rudby.

An existing park is at *Stanwick*, the old seat of the Smithsons, now Dukes of Northumberland.

More to the west, and on the borders of the county of Durham, Leland more than once mentions a park by Greta Bridge 'waullid with stone, caullid *Bigenelle Park* (in another place, Brignel Parke, *latine brevis mons*), it longgith to

---

[1] Lambeth MSS. No. 709.
[2] Cal. Pat. Rolls, p. 191.
[3] Lambeth MSS. No. 709.
[4] Itin. vol. i. p. 67, fol. 73.

[5] Printed by the Camden Society in 1863, p. 123.
[6] Itin. vol. i. p. 66, fol. 72.
[7] Cotton MSS. Titus B. iv. f. 297.

the Lord Scrope.'[1] It does not appear in the ancient surveys.

Existing Deer Parks in the North Riding of Yorkshire.

1. HORNBY-CASTLE . The Duchess Dowager of Leeds.
2. SWINTON . . . Mrs. Danby Harcourt.
3. BOLTON CASTLE . Lord Bolton.
4. ALDBY . . . . Mr. Darley.
5. NEWBOROUGH . . Sir George Wombwell, Bart.
6. CASTLE HOWARD Earl of Carlisle.
7. DUNCOMBE . . . Lord Feversham.
8. STANWICK . . . Dowgr. Duchess of Northumberland.
9. BARNINGHAM . . Mr. Wyvill.

YORKSHIRE. EAST RIDING.

SEVEN parks only are given in Saxton's Survey as existing in the East Riding in the year 1577: one between *Kexby Bridge* and Church-Eaton on the banks of the Derwent ; one at *Everingham*, between Pocklington and Market-Wrighton, a still-existing park ; one at *Risby*, near Beverley ; one at *Burstwick*, near Headon ; the still-existing park at *Burton-Constable*, and the two Percy Parks of *Wresell* and *Leconfield*. The last-named parks are both noticed by Leland. Of Wresell (near Howden) he says, ' There is a parke hard by the castelle,' and of Leconfield (close to Beverley) he writes, ' The Park thereby is very fair and large and meetely welle woddid.'[2]

There were in 1512, as we know from the ' Northumberland Household Book,' two parks at *Wressel* ; the larger containing 42 red deer and 92 fallow-deer; and the smaller, probably a paddock near the castle, but 37 fallow-deer. Leconfield Park at the same period contained 249 fallow-deer. Leland mentions another park near Howden ' in the way to Wresell,' belonging to the Bishop of Durham, but it is not found marked in the Elizabethan surveys.

Close to Wressel also was the Earl of Northumberland's park of *Newsam*. Although not marked in the old maps as a park, it is repeatedly mentioned in the ' Household Book' already referred to, and, in 1512, 324 fallow-deer are said to have been here preserved.

Kexby Park is traced to a license granted to Thomas de Ughtred in the eighth of Edward III.[3]

The park of *Everingham* contains at present about 200 acres, and the same number of fallow-deer. The privileges of this park, which is undoubtedly very ancient, were confirmed by royal charter, by James II., in the year 1687.

North of Everingham is the park of *Londesborough*, and to the west, near

---

[1] Leland's Itin. vol. i. p. 89, fol. 95, and vol. v. p. 120, fol. 115.

[2] Itin. vol. i. p. 48, fol. 50 and p. 56, fol. 60.
[3] Cal. Pat. Rolls, p. 119

York, the modern park of Escrick, enclosed in the years 1823-4, and containing about 480 acres, and a herd of 400 fallow-deer.

I find *Burstwick Park* in 1604 is said to have contained 160 fallow-deer.[1] It appears then to have been held under the Crown.

The origin of the Park of *Burton-Constable* appears to be unknown: it is undoubtedly very ancient. At present it contains 290 acres, and herds of 160 red deer and 350 fallow-deer of all colours.

At *Rise* in this neighbourhood is a park belonging to Mr. Bethell, and more to the north, at *Sledmere*, another, the property of Sir Tatton Sykes, Bart.

Existing Deer Parks in the East Riding of Yorkshire.

1. EVERINGHAM . . . Lord Herries.
2. BURTON-CONSTABLE Sir Clifford Constable, Bart.
3. ESCRICK PARK . . Lord Wenlock.
4. RISE . . . . . . Mr. Bethell.
5. SLEDMERE . . . . Sir Tatton Sykes, Bart.

WESTMORELAND.

'THER be about Kendale divers fair wooddes, as Master Parris Parke, and many other,' is the remark of Leland in his 'Itinerary.'[2] A glance at Saxton's map, engraved in 1576, will prove the accuracy of the venerable topographer. Fifteen ancient parks will be found in that survey clustered about the town of Kendal. To the north, *Colnhead, Sterlmere,* and *Firbank.* To the west, *Camswick Park,* a park belonging to the castle of *Kendal.* South of the town, *Watlande, Seggeswick, Sisergh, Brigster Park, Levens, Witherslok, Betham,* and *Preston.*

Sisergh was imparked by license granted to Sir Walter de Strickland in the ninth of Edward III.[3]

Of these ancient parks *Levens* is the sole existing one. It was originally enclosed in the thirty-fourth year of Edward III., when Thomas de Strickland obtained a license to impark his woods here containing 300 acres of land.[4] Levens Park contains at present 178 acres, and a herd of 250 fallow-deer.

Betham Park, or *Bitham,* as he writes it, was noticed by Leland as 'a great parke and a goodly place yn hit of the Erle of Darby.'[5]

Preston appears to have been imparked by license granted to Richard de Preston in the forty-second of Edward III.[6]

To the east of Kendal, two other parks, at *Middleton* and *Barborn,* are given in Saxton's Survey.

An existing park, not given in the older

[1] Lambeth MSS. No. 709.
[2] Vol. v. p. 130, fol. 85.
[3] Burn's Westmoreland, vol. i. p. 87.

[4] Cal. Pat. Rolls, p. 173.
[5] Itin. vol. v. p. 100, fol. 85.
[6] Cal. Pat. Rolls, p. 184.

Q

map, is at *Dallam Tower*, in this neigh-bourhood. It was enclosed in 1720, and contains 300 acres and 150 head of deer. Another was once at *Troutbeck*, near Ambleside. This was a Royal park, of which the herbage and pannage was granted by Henry VI., in the twenty-fourth year of his reign, to Thomas Daniell, Esq., together with the windfalls and browsing, at the annual rent of 40*s*.[1]

In the north of this county, near Brougham Castle, on the borders of Cum-berland, is the Forest, or more properly the Chase, of *Whitfield*. Near it is the comparatively modern and magnificent Park of *Lowther*, belonging to the Earl of Lonsdale.

To the south, near Shap, was the an-cient Park of *Crosby-Ravensworth*, im-parked by license granted to William de Threkeld, in the tenth year of Edward III.[2]

Two other parks remain to be men-tioned; those at *Hartley Castle* and *Wharton Hall*, near the town of Kirkby-Stephen, on the borders of Yorkshire.

Existing Deer Parks in Westmoreland.

1. LEVENS . . . . The · Hon. Mrs.
        Howard.
2. DALLAM TOWER. Mr. G. Wilson.
3. LOWTHER . . . Earl of Lonsdale.

DURHAM.

THE Bishops of Durham from very early times appropriated to themselves several extensive parks within their palatine county. Besides that which was attached to their principal episcopal residence at *Bishops-Auckland*, and which existed till the death of Bishop Van Mildert in the year 1836, there were large parks at *Wol-singham* and *Stanhope*, in Wierdale Fo-rest, and at *Evenwood* and *Middleham*, nearer home. From a return of vert and venison, dated on the 15th of May 1457, and preserved in Surtees's 'History of Durham,'[3] it appears that there were at

that period in the Park of Auckland 100 fallow-deer; in that of Wolsingham, 140; in Stanhope, 200; and in Evenwood, 100. There is no return from Middleham, which probably at that time ceased to be an episcopal residence. Leland notices the fair park by the Castle of Akeland 'having falow dere, wild Bulles and kin.' He also observes that he left on his right hand one of the parks of Akeland (Auck-land), walled with stone (Wolsingham?). And of the park of *Stanhope* he writes : 'The Bishop of Duresme hath a praty square pile on the north side of the Were

---

[1] Cal. Pat. Rolls, p. 289.
[2] Ib. p. 126.

[3] I. clviii.

Ryver caullid the Westgate, and thereby is a parke rudely enclosid with stone of a 12 or 14 miles in compace, it is xii. miles up in Were-Dale from Akeland Castelle.'[1] At *Middleham* the old park wall is still perfect, and in summer, adds Surtees, is yellow with the blossom of stonecrop. ' Parcum muro inclusum,' is leased by the Bishop of Durham in 1521. It is still held under the see.[2]

The prior and convent of Durham had also their places of sylvan retirement. Near Durham was their large park of *Bear*, rectè *Beaurepaire.* The house and chapel of Beaurepaire were founded by Prior Bertram between 1244 and 1258, as a place of solace and retreat for himself and his successors. Hugh of Derlyngton, 1258–1274, enclosed the park, and that of *Muggleswick*, on the borders of Northumberland. Bishop Beke during his quarrel with the convent, broke down the fences and destroyed and drove out the game. In 1311 Bishop Kellawe granted license to Prior Tanfield to enlarge the park of Beaurepaire. In 1315 the Scotch, in their successful irruption into the bishoprick, destroyed almost the whole stock and store of game and cattle. The ruin is said to have been completed by the Scotch armies when they occupied Durham in 1641-1644.[3]

The prior and convent of Durham had also a deer park at *Hedworth* near Newcastle on Tyne, as early as the pontificate of Bishop Farnham (1241–1249). The new park seems alluded to in the last cited charter between the Prior and the Hedworths.[4]

In the northern parts of Durham ancient parks are marked in Saxton's Survey of 1576 at the castles of *Hilton* and *Lumley*, at *Beamish* and *Holmside*. 'The old park of *Beamish*,' writes Surtees, 'lies on upland ground to the south of the Team. In 1572 Queen Elizabeth granted to Sir Henry Gate, Knight, the Manor and Park of *Beamish*, and, in 1605, the park as now impaled was sold to Sir William Wray, Knight.[5]

The manor and park of *Lambton* lie on the Wear, to the north of Lumley. The park, including the plantations, contains nearly 1,200 acres.

South of Durham, at the castle of *Brancepeth*, were two parks, called the *East* and *West Parks.* Nearer Bishops-Auckland two others, at *Bedborn* and *Witton Castle.*

At *Raby Castle*, near Staindrop, were, in Leland's time, three parks, 'whereof,' adds the old topographer, 'too be plenished with dere, the middle park hath a lodge in it.'[6]

At *Barnard Castle* were two ancient parks, also noticed by Leland ; ' the one,' he adds, 'is called Marwood, and thereby is a chase that beareth also the name of Marwood, and that goeth on Tees ripe up into Teesdale.'[7] In 1602 a lease was made of these parks by the name of *Broad Park* and *Colt Park*, for twenty-one years, and in 1635, the custodie of Teesdale Forest and Marwood Chase was granted by the Crown to Sir Henry Vane, on his covenant to discharge all the Keepers' and Foresters' fees, and to restore the Game there for his Majesty's disport.[8]

[1] Leland's Itin. vol. i. p. 73, fol. 79.
[2] Surtees's Durham, vol. iii. p. 3.
[3] Ib. vol. ii. p. 373.
[4] Ib. p. 81.

[5] Surtees's Durham, vol. ii. p. 222.
[6] Itin. vol. i. p. 86, fol. 92.
[7] Ib. p. 87, fol. 93.
[8] Surtees's Durham, vol. iii. p. 120.

The park of *Ravensworth* near Newcastle, appears to have been enclosed by
license granted to Sir Henry Fitzhugh, in
the fourteenth of Richard II.[1]

Existing Deer Parks in Durham.

1. RABY CASTLE . Duke of Cleveland.
2. RAVENSWORTH. Lord Ravensworth.
3. WYNIARD PARK Earl Vane.

CUMBERLAND.

A FEW miles south of Carlisle was the
Royal Forest of Inglewood, and within its
limits *Wigton* and *Black Hall*, where
William de Wigton had license to impark in the fifty-third of Henry III., and
Dalston, where the Bishop of Carlisle had
a park which he was licensed to increase
in the twenty-third year of Edward I.[2]
The Patent Rolls contain several licenses
for hunting within this royal forest, granting ' to the Principal Forester, for the
Honor of the King, to give leave to
knights, " et probris hominibus," to Lords
and other nobles, also to sick and preg-
nant ladies, to have one course for a stag,
hind, buck, or doe, within the said forest.'
Two of these hunting licenses bear date in
the third and eighteenth of Edward III.[3]

To the east of Inglewood was the large
park of *Barrenwood*, and to the south,
the still larger park of *Greystock*. Both
are engraved in Saxton's survey of this
county in 1576; both are now without
deer. The ancient park of *Goborrow*,
however, still exists on the banks of
Ulleswater, belonging to Mr. Howard of
Greystock. That at *Stainton* near Dacre
in Saxton's map has disappeared. A
more modern park is at *Eden-Hall*, near

Penrith, the deer having been removed
from *Kirby*.

In the neighbourhood of Cockermouth
four ancient parks are given by Saxton,
one of them at *Cockermouth* itself. These
probably appertained to the great House
of Percy, of whose sylvan possessions we
have so interesting an account in the
'Northumberland Household Book.' From
' An Account of all the Deer in the
parks and forests in the north belonging
to the Earl of Northumberland, taken in
the fourth year of Henry VIII., Anno
1512,' it appears that there were in Cumberland 455 red and fallow-deer in the
Park of *Langstrothdale* ; 307 red and
fallow-deer in *Adylthorp Park* ; and 205
in the old park of that name ; and 230
red deer and 21 fallow-deer in *Wasdale*
(south of Egremont) ; and lastly 225 in
The West Ward. Both ancient and modern maps unite in noticing a park at
Uffay, now called *Ulpha Park*, on the
River Duddon, on the borders of the
county of Lancaster.

Existing Deer Parks in Cumberland.

1. GOBORROW . Mr. Howard of Greystock.
2. EDEN HALL Sir G. Musgrave, Bart.

---

[1] Cal. Pat. Rolls, p. 221.
[2] Ib. pp. 41, 57.

[3] Cal. Pat. Rolls, pp. 105, 149.

NORTHUMBERLAND.

EIGHT ancient parks are noticed in Sax-ton's Survey of this county, which was engraved probably about the year 1576, though the date is not given. None of them are mentioned in Leland's 'Itinerary,' though probably all were in existence in Henry VIII.'s time, the period of that venerable antiquary, who merely remarks, ' In Northumberland, as I heare say, be no Forests except Chivet Hills, and there is greate plenty of redd Dere and Roo Bukkes.'[1]

The most important parks were those which appertained to the Castle of Alnwick, belonging to the Earls of Northumberland. There were two principal parks, called *Hulme Park*, and *Cawledge* or *Callie Park*, on either side of the town of Aln-wick. From the account of the deer belonging to the Earl of Northumberland, taken in the fourth year of Henry VIII., in the year 1512, and preserved in the ' Northumberland Household Book,' it appears that there were at that period 879 fallow-deer in the former, and 586 in latter. These parks appear to have been disparked and destroyed after the Resto-ration of Charles II., by whose authority a warrant was issued to Robert Child and William Bowles, Master of the Toils, to order the taking of fallow-deer in the parks of the Earl of Northumberland, and to convey them to the Royal Parks.[2] Hulme

Park originally contained 3,500 acres; it was for many years let into farms, but part of it was restored and reimparked in the year 1824. The present park contains 134 acres of old grass, and 89 of moorland. There is a herd of 180 fallow-deer, and 22 white German deer or stags.

There was an ancient park also at *Warkworth Castle* in this neighbourhood, which contained in 1512, 150 fallow-deer; and also at *Acklington*, another old Percy park, not far distant, where there were at the same period 141 fallow-deer.[3] This park of Acklington appears to have been established by a license granted to Richard de Horsley in the thirty-fifth year of Edward I.[4] At *Widdrington Castle* in this part of the county, James I. is re-corded to have hunted, or rather to have killed two deer on his first progress into England, in April 1603. Sir Robert Cary was the owner of Widdrington at that time.[5]

Further south I find parks mentioned in Saxton's Map at *Cockley Tower*, *Bottle* or *Botthall Castle*, the *New Chapel*, and *Mitford*, all in the neighbourhood of Morpeth.

At *Dilston*, near Hexham, an ancient seat of the Radclyffe family, was a deer park which is given in Saxton's but not in Speed's Survey. It appears to have been destroyed and disparked long before

---

[1] Leland's Itin. vol. vii. p. 66, fol. 81.
[2] S. P. O. Domestic, July 7, 1662.
[3] Northumberland Household Book.

[4] Cal. Pat. Rolls, p. 67.
[5] Nichols's Progresses, vol. i. p. 68 ; see also ante, p. 44.

the fall of that right loyal and ancient house, though I find 'The Roe park wall' mentioned in the household expenses of Sir Francis Radclyffe, Bart., in 1686 and 1687.[1]

Among the parks in this county, which do not appear in the Elizabethan Maps, I may mention that at *Chillingham Castle*, in the northern part of it, famous for its breed of wild cattle, of which there is an account in Bewick's 'History of Quadru-

peds,'[2] and which have been already noticed under Lyme Hall, in Cheshire, and Chartley, in Staffordshire.

Existing Deer Parks in Northumberland.

1. ALNWICK CASTLE . The Duke of Northumberland.
2. CHILLINGHAM } Earl of Tanker-
   CASTLE } ville.

---

[1] In the Radclyffe Tracts, Newcastle-on-Tyne, 1859.

[2] P. 90.

CHAPTER XI.

ON THE MANAGEMENT OF DEER AND DEER PARKS

'A Park-keeper must be a careful vigilant man : He must daily take a turn round his Park, and keep a constant account of the number of his Deer.'—THE COMPLEAT SPORTSMAN, p. 67. *Anno* 1718.

Many times when I do find
Things go awry, and folk unkind,
To see the quiet Parks and Herds,
And hear the singing of the birds,
Do still my spirit more than words ;
    For I do see that 'tis our sin,
    Do make one's soul so dark within,
    When God would give us sunshine.

Altered from BARNES.

Fallow Deer led by the Power of Music. See page 253.

CHAPTER XI.

ERVASE MARKHAM, in his edition of Richard Surflet's translation of Liebault's 'Maison Rustique, or the Countrey Farme,' printed in 1616, has given in the nineteenth chapter of the second book some interesting matter 'of the situation of the parkes, and of the manner of ordering the wild beasts therein.' As this is not only, I believe, the earliest but also the most comprehensive essay which has been written on this subject, I shall make some considerable extracts from the work, which exhibits both the practice of our ancestors as regards their deer and deer parks, and also affords some valuable hints for the formation of parks and the management of red and fallow-deer. 'The parke,' he says, 'would be seated (if it be possible) within a wood of high and tall timber trees, in a place compassed about, and well fenced with walls made of rough stone and lime, or else of bricks and earth-lome, or else with poles made of oake plankes. You must foresee that there bee some little brooke of spring-water running along by the place; or, for want of spring-water and naturall streames, you must prepare ditches and pooles, walled and daubed in such sort as that they may receive and keepe the reine-water. Nor ought the parke to consist of one kind of ground only, as all of wood, all grasse, or all coppice, but of divers, as part high wood, part grasse or champion, and part coppice or under-wood, or thicke spring: nor must these severall grounds lie open, or as it were in a common one with another ; but they must be separated one from the other by a strong rale, through which deere or shepe (but no greater cattell) may passe, for they must have the full liberty of every place. Neither must the parke be situated upon any one entire hill, plaine, or else valley, but it must consist of divers hills, divers plains, and divers valleys ; the hills which are commonly called the viewes or discoveries of parkes, would bee all goodly high woods of tall timber, as well for the beauty and gracefulnesse of the parke, as also for the echoe and sound which will rebound from the same, when in the times of hunting, either the cries of the hounds, the winding of hornes, or the gibbetting of the huntsmen passeth through the same, doubling the musicke, and making it tenne times more delightfull : the plains which are called in parkes the lawnds, would be very champion and fruitfull, as well for the breeding of great store of grasse and hay for the feeding and nourishing of the deere or other wild beastes, as also for the pleasure of coursing with greyhounds, when at any time the owner shall be disposed to hunt in that manner ; for when the hounds shall have hunted the game from the thicks unto the lawnds, then the grey-hounds being placed thereupon, may in the view of the beholders course upon the same, and beget a delight past equall. The valleys which are

called the coverts or places of leare for wild beasts, would be all very thicke
sprung or under-wood, as well for the concealing of them from potchers and
purloyners, as for giving them rest and shadow in the day time, who cannot
indure to lie open to the view of passengers, or undefended by darknesse
and obscuritie : all these thicke coverts are defences for the wild beastes to
save them from the cunning sents or noses of hounds when they pursue
them, making their doubles and windings therein so intricate and cunningly,
that they scape many times their most mortallest mischiefe: also, in these
thicke coverts, the hunted deere finding an unhunted deere where he
lodgeth, will forthwith beate him up and lie downe himself in his place,
making the hounds undertake the fresh deere, and so escape his owne
danger, which in the open places he cannot doe: and the parke is a place
that must contrive all things for the good and safetie of the game it keepeth.
Thus you see the parke must consist of view, lawnd, and covert, and the
situation of hill, valley, and plaine. Now for the water, of which formerly
we spoake. You shall know it is very right necessarie in parkes, as well
for the reliefe and sustenance of wild beasts, as for the watering, washing,
and moistening of the grounds to make them fruitfull. Besides, whenso-
ever your game is extreamly hunted, and brought to the pinch of ex-
tremitie, then he will flie to the water, which is called the soile, and there
find reliefe and rescue: for, according to the saying of the profit David,
As the Hart desireth the water brooks, &c., so a deere in his greatest ex-
tremitie findeth reliefe and is refreshed by drinking and bathing in the
water. In the most convenientest lawnd of the parke, which is most
spatious and fruitfull, and which hath the greatest prospect into the parke,
and where the deere take greatest delight to feed, there you shall build the
lodge or house for the keeper to dwell in, and it shall by all means stand
cleare, and open every way, so as there may be no secret approach
made unto the same, but such as the keeper may easily behold from his.
windowes, and it shall stand so faire in the view of the lawnd, that from
thence a man may see every way round about the same, and some part up

into the high woods, and other most secret parts of the parke, so that when
the least disturbance or trouble is offerred unto the deere, a man may from
that lodge take notice of the same.' The author proceeds to give instructions for the defence of the lodge against malicious persons, and directs the
keeper how to defend himself by 'shooting with his bowes, casting stones,
or scalding water, to make them avoid from the same;' but passing by these
warlike devices as inapplicable and unnecessary at the present time, we
come to another part, where he gives instructions as to what trees should
be planted in the park, advising against fruit trees, 'for they are the occasion of much hurt and destruction to your pale, under the color of
gathering the fruit.' He then proceeds as follows: 'Yet I would not have
the parke unfurnished of all manner of fruit, for besides the pleasure
thereof, they are an excellent mast in which deere infinitely delight, and
are fed very much with the same. You shall not by any means in one
parke mixe the red deere and the fallow deere together, for the red deere
is a masterfull beast, and when the time of bellowing cometh, he growes
fierce and outragious, so that hee will be entire Lord of the field, and will
kill the fallow deere if they but crosse him in his walke : and therefore
each must be kept severally in severall parkes.'

    That such was the practice of the sixteenth and seventeenth centuries,
is proved by the ' Red Deer Parks,' distinct from parks for fallow-deer,
which are found in many of the great places of England, such as Badminton, in Gloucestershire, and Grimsthorpe, in Lincolnshire, where separate
parks for the different kinds of deer were formerly kept up : the present
practice appears to be generally to allow both red and fallow-deer to be
together, the danger alluded to in our author having been proved to be
exaggerated, if not without foundation. Regarding extraneous food to be
given in hard winter ' to the wild beasts,' the same writer observes : 'Notwithstanding, the good farmer must not content himselfe with the provision
which the ground bringeth forth of itselfe : but at such times as the earth
is barren, and when there is nothing to feed upon in the forests, they must

have given unto them of the harvest fruits, and be fed with barley, pure wheat, beanes, the *drosse of the wine presse*, and whatsoever else is good cheape.' The last paragraph betrays the foreign origin of Gervase Markham's 'Maison Rustique.' But parks on the Continent have been at all times so rare and uncommon that the author could have had but a limited experience in proving the correctness of his theories.

Following the example of the authors of ' The Countrey Farme,' it will be convenient, in the first place, to discuss the situation of a park, and afterwards to add a few words on the management of deer.

Variety of surface, and, if possible, a difference in the geological character of the soil, and consequently of the herbage, is, although not essential, a very desirable consideration in the choice of lands for the formation of a deer park; the ground should be broken up into wood and lawn, with a due proportion of under-wood, banks covered with whitethorn; rough grass, and more especially fern (*Pteris aquilina*), or common brakes, are very ornamental, and most useful as a covert to the does and fawns. Our ancestors were well aware of this: thus, in the licenses for Imparking, with which our ancient records abound, so many acres of woodland, so many acres of meadow, so much of under-wood and briars, are constantly noted, and the picturesque and beautiful situation of most of our ancient parks, the union of the fine and smooth turfed lawns, with the woody brakes and thickets which distinguish so many of these venerable enclosures, evince the judgment of the selection. One great object for the variety of surface, or ground broken up into woody glades and thickets, so much recommended for the situation of deer parks, is the more efficient shelter which is thereby afforded to the deer in winter. Shelter, indeed, in winter is of such importance that good judges prefer a park amply provided in this respect, but where no winter provision of food is made for the deer, to one where both hay and beans are given, but where they are left exposed, in consequence of the want of natural shelter, to the full severity of an English winter.[1]   Sheds are often erected in deer parks, for the purpose of feeding the deer in winter, and for the purpose of counteracting the natural deficiencies of the situation, as to covert and shelter; but these expedients partake too much of an artificial character to be in good keeping with the habits of what our ancestors called 'wild beasts,' and which are still considered to be feræ naturæ.

Before we consider the question of fences, it may be well to remember that parks, however wild and uncultivated, must not be wet and marshy. Deer, like sheep, will not thrive in a bog, and, like sheep, are apt to be affected by foot-rot, if left altogether in wet and undrained pastures : dry, and even poor land, is preferable to rich and valuable pastures, though the union of both, is much to be desired in a large and well-conditioned park. With regard to fencing, I confess to a prejudice in favour of the old English upright oak paling, with transverse bars at top, which is by far the most picturesque, and perfectly adapted to its purpose ; it has but one defect—its expense—though that is surpassed by its rival, the stone or brick wall.   A wall is, of course, the most durable; a good oak fence, however, will last for a century, and even after that period, some part of it will probably work up again, and be fit for further service.   A paling, moreover, has the advantage of allowing the traveller to peep at the park within ; for I think, with Washington Irving,[2] that parks should not be kept solely for the selfish gratification of the owner, and rejoice in seeing a public footpath across one of those ancient and aristocratic enclosures, where all may admire the scenery and the deer.   Where oak, as in many places, cannot be had for the whole fence, a substitute may be found as follows: the posts only oak, the rails and pales ash, or other timber, and the whole set in a whitethorn hedge ; if the hedge is entwined with the pales, and kept constantly clipped, it makes an excellent and permanent fence,

[1] Evelyn, in his Memoirs, tells us that in the year of the great frost, 1684, many parks of deer were entirely destroyed.
[2] Sketch Book, vol. ii. 2nd ed. p. 194.

though not so picturesque as the rough oak paling, grey with moss and lichen, which is so greatly to be admired at Charlecote, in Warwickshire, and at the far older park at Chartley, in Staffordshire. In wet countries, such as Ireland, a rough stone wall, no doubt, is the best and most proper fence for a park; and is there generally adopted; nor, indeed, when old, and partly covered with ivy, and topped with polipody, is it out of character with sylvan scenery; it has also great claims to antiquity, if, as is alleged, the enclosed grounds or parks of the priory of Croxton, in Leicestershire, were enclosed with a wall as early as the year 1162.[1]

As for the internal divisions of deer parks, I hold that continuous flat iron fencing, not wire, is by far the best; and of the different manufacturers, I would give the preference to Messrs. Hill and Smith, of Brierley Hill, near Dudley, Staffordshire, whose invention of a patent notched bar and joint is a great improvement, and tends to keep the uprights and bars in their proper position.

Having discussed the situation of the park, we come to our second subject—the management of the deer; and here I feel under great obligations to the Earl of Winchilsea, who, in some valuable notes on the subject of his noble park at Eastwell, in Kent, with which he has favoured me, observes: ' The true secret of a good park consists in a good original stock; soil not too rich, but various, with a short bite in most places; a well-kept-up succession of deer, so that none should be killed too early, or left until too late; quiet, shelter, and a good keeper, the last, not least; for who ever saw a good herd of deer under the management of any man that not only did not thoroughly understand but take pleasure in his business?' ' Never kill a deer,' Lord Winchilsea adds, ' before six years of age, as they make great improvement in the last year, particularly in weight, or keep them over till they are eight or nine years old, at which age they usually sink, and, moreover, get hard in their flesh.'

---

[1] Nichols's Leicestershire, vol. ii. part i. p. 151.

Fallow-deer differ considerably as to their size and weight; the lighter and spotted, or menil, deer are generally larger framed than the others, and a good fat buck will weigh from 100 to 120 pounds when prepared for venison ; the dark and dun kind do not weigh so much, though the former are generally admitted to be the hardier, and the latter, for their size, the fattest of the whole. Occasionally, however, these weights are greatly exceeded : a paddock-fed buck at Eastwell has been known to weigh 140 pounds, and even more; but when a buck has escaped from a park, and fattened upon forbidden pastures, a much greater weight has occasionally been attained; as much as 176 pounds was the weight of a seven year old buck, killed at Eastwell in the year 1863, which had escaped from the park, and lived at free commons on the crops during the whole summer. This buck may be compared with the account of that remarkable one, whose weight, however, is not recorded, mentioned in Dr. Comber's ‘Memoirs of Lord Deputy Wandesforde,’ and whose fat measured five inches in thickness.[1]

Here, perhaps, will be the place to say something as to the number of deer to be kept in a park, which, of course, must depend upon its size, and the nature of the soil; but the great point being not to overstock, it is a wise and safe rule never to allow more than one deer to the acre, and even a less proportion if sheep are suffered to be with them.[2] Cattle and horses, consuming, as they do, a coarser and different quality of grass than that eaten by the deer, have been considered of great use, and in some parks, after their introduction, the deer are said to have improved.[3]

In order to preserve a proper proportion of bucks and does—two-thirds to one-third is generally recommended—it is necessary, if possible,

[1] Wandesforde's Memoirs, Cambridge, 1778, p. 104.

[2] Mr. Downes stated in his evidence before the Select Committee of the House of Commons on Woods, &c., in 1848-9, that ‘he considered the keep of a buck is equal to the keep of eight or ten sheep ; he did not mean that eight or ten sheep could be kept with what would feed one buck, but that four changes are to be got from the sheep whilst one deer is coming to perfection ; and in addition to the buck must be added a doe to breed the buck.’

[3] This was the case in Hursley Park, in Hampshire.

to catch the fawns soon after they are dropped, and mark those which are intended to be preserved for stock by cropping one or both ears ; destroying the rest, except when it is desired that a few should be kept for table. It is better also to keep for stock those fawns which are first dropped ; the late fawns are generally the production of the older does. By this means a proper succession of deer, according to the size of the herd, will be preserved, and many of the does will consequently be in better condition when killed in winter ; the excellence of doe venison depending upon the does having either had no fawns or having lost them very early in the year. A certain proportion also of the buck fawns should be kept for 'haviars,'[1] that is, castrated deer, to come in late in the autumn, after the season of buck venison, and before the does are fit to be killed ; but the better plan is to make 'full-heads,' that is, deer not quite clean cut when fawns, as they not only throw up good horns, but are excellent venison, and generally thrive better than the 'haviars.' It is said that this plan was discovered accidentally by a keeper at Lord Middleton's park, at Wollaton, in Nottinghamshire, who, being often drunk when he went about in the fawning season to make haviars, did his work imperfectly. Several of the fawns thus treated threw up horns, and it was supposed that the keeper had failed entirely in his object ; but when they arrived at maturity, and came to be killed, it was found that all the purposes intended had been answered; so the system became established at Wollaton, and has since been practised in many other parks.[2]

The question of crossing the stock of deer from different parks remains to be noticed, and here there is much difference of opinion among the owners of parks, some of whom appear to be proud of having preserved their breed of deer without the admixture of foreign blood for a time beyond the memory of men, while others again consider that, unless the stock is occasionally crossed, the deer deteriorate both in size and

[1] Haviars, said to be derived from the French *hiver*, winter, because the venison is fit for use in winter.

[2] Information of the Earl of Winchilsea.

R

health by constantly breeding in and in, and this appears to be the more general opinion.   In support of the former practice, it is alleged that in very many parks no change has ever been made for very many years, and yet the deer remain perfectly healthy and free from disease; this has been accounted for by the fact that with deer those bucks only whose soundness in every respect has been most severely tried by a series of terrific duels, proving themselves the strongest, and masters of the whole herd, become the sires of the rising stock, and consequently a buck with the slightest constitutional defect is debarred from propagating a weak point among the species.[1]   To this it may be answered that in the end nevertheless the constant breeding in and in, is sure to tell to the disadvantage of the whole herd, though it may take a very long time to prove it; and, moreover, when we find, as is very constantly the case, that the introduction of fresh blood has been of the very greatest use to deer, both by improving their size and appearance, and particularly by being of service in removing the taint of 'rickback,' if not of other diseases to which deer are sometimes subject when the blood has not been changed, there can, I think, be no doubt but that a judicious cross with a good stock is of the greatest consequence, and is indeed essential, sooner or later, to the prosperity of every well-ordered park.

Among the several varieties of fallow-deer, the black and very dark, (supposed by some to be indigenous, by others to have come from Denmark)[2] are generally considered the hardiest and least subject to disease; they are, however, less in size than the lighter-coloured deer, which may be divided into the spotted, otherwise called menil or Manilla, deer,[3] the white and cream-coloured, the yellow or fallow, the skew or blue deer, and

---

[1] I am obliged to Viscount Falmouth for this argument.   It shows also that a good keeper should be careful to preserve one of the best framed and most healthy of his bucks for stock, and not kill all the best for venison.

[2] See p. 9.   They are sometimes, as at Annes-

ley, in Nottinghamshire, called the forest breed.

[3] From Manilla, the capital of the Philippine Islands, in the East Indies, from whence these deer are by some supposed to have been brought about the year 1730.   See Anderson's Recreations, vol. ii. p. 370.

the bald-faced, originally from Bosworth Park, in Leicestershire ; there are, besides, the dun, divided into the golden dun and the sooty dun, smaller and less common than some of the others, and generally the fattest. 'All these,' says Lord Winchilsea, 'we reckon good if the velvet of their horns be black, but dislike any whose horns throw up a white and coarse velvet.' The complaints to which deer are subject are various ; the most common appears to be foot-rot, caught sometimes from sheep, but not difficult of cure if the true remedy be taken, the perfect drainage of the land ;[1] the same remedy, without doubt, may be applied with the greatest advantage to parks where the deer suffer from liver complaints. At Earlstoke Park, in Wiltshire, the seat of Mr. Watson Taylor, the deer were affected by both these complaints, but since the drainage of the park, they have entirely disappeared. The rot, which is only an aggravated form of diseased liver, is also caused by want of drainage, and points to the same remedy ; about thirty years ago, the deer at Ashburnham, in Sussex, were attacked with this complaint, and cured by being supplied with branches of fir, which they eagerly devoured, preferring Scotch fir to spruce fir or any other ; the disease was removed immediately, and has never returned, the deer being now always supplied with an abundance of fir, especially in the spring and autumn. In this case, no doubt, the turpentine, which is known as a powerful ingredient in the medicine sold as a specific for the rot in sheep, was the cause of the cure.[2] At the Bishop of Winchester's park, at Farnham, in Surrey, the deer occasionally have the rot, rickback, and goitrous necks, after snow, and here it is to be observed there has been no change of blood for thirty years.

Rickbacked deer are too generally found in many parks ; this complaint is supposed to proceed from weakness, brought on both by breeding in and in, too much, and also by insufficient food ; those deer which are affected should be immediately destroyed, the breed crossed, and a more plentiful

[1] Foot-rot is also cured by placing quicklime in the most accustomed paths and passes of the deer.   [2] Information of the Earl of Ashburnham.

and invigorating diet (additional food), if in the winter, supplied. Deer are also subject to bowel complaints, known at Croxton Park, Leicestershire, as '*the mort*,' and at Garendon, in the same county, as '*the gurry*.' The only remedies are to feed on dry food, such as hay, beans, and acorns, with leaves of ivy and branches of ash. In a few parks also, (I allude to Hanbury, in Worcestershire, and to Calke, in Derbyshire,) the hoofs of the deer are frequently found to grow to an unnatural size, thereby causing lameness; the only remedy appears to be to catch the deer, and pare the hoof.

With regard to additional winter food, I have already observed that shelter is of much greater consequence; to this it may be added that much also depends upon the keep of the deer in summer, for if from want of grass they are allowed to get low in condition before a severe winter sets in, they often die, however well fed during the hard weather. Hay appears to be the most natural additional food that can be given to deer, and to this may be added horse and Spanish chestnuts, acorns, and beech masts,[1] which can be collected outside a deer park and kept for a winter supply at an expense very trifling compared with their value; at Escrick, in Yorkshire, what they call '*leafey hay*' is also made, that is, branches of deciduous trees cut down in the summer, and dried with the leaves on, like hay, and stacked in the same manner; deer are glad of it in the winter, and are known at all times to eat greedily the bark of all trees, particularly ash and willow, Scotch and spruce fir; perhaps ivy is their most favourite 'browse;'[2] but park-keepers should beware of yew. In the winter of 1865,

[1] It is very desirable to plant whitethorns in parks, the deer being very fond of the haws. Indeed, the excellence of doe venison in some parks has been ascribed to the hawthorns which grow in them.

[2] *Browse.*—Deer are most destructive to trees in the rutting season, and in the month of February, when they are very fond of barking ash trees, they have singular propensities for particular trees and spots in each wood or division of a park. Mr. Menzies, superintendent of Windsor Park, recommends a few of the bad trees to be cut down at these periods, and left in the most tempting places. 'The deer will,' he says, 'amuse themselves with them for hours together, butting at them, and tearing off the bark.' In the Royal Forests, '*browse wood*' for the winter feeding of the deer was formerly regularly cut. One of the keepers in the New Forest reported, in the year 1788, that, if the cutting of browse wood was stopped, it would require about three tons of hay yearly for each 100 deer, within his walk.—Appendix to 1st Report of the Surveyor-General of His Majesty's Land Revenues.

a large number of deer died at Badminton, in Gloucestershire, in consequence of having eaten the leaves and branches of a yew-tree, heavily weighed down by the snow outside the fence of this park.

A writer in ' Notes and Queries' has preserved a curious account of the effects of another evergreen upon deer. ' In the palmy days of Cranborne Chase,' he says, ' the season for killing " dry " does began at Martintide (Nov. 11), and ended at Candlemas (Feb. 2). Now it was customary with the keepers to produce the effect of natural sterility by inducing abortion in the female deer, and this they did by laying branches of mistletoe in their feeding grounds some two or three months before the season commenced. The plan succeeded, but it was said that the venison in such cases was deficient in flavour: this was probably a piece of woodcraft confined by traditional usage to this district.' [1]

After food of natural growth, we must not forget beans as the most valuable of that of artificial production, which are used most extensively in almost every park, and with the greatest advantage, particularly in spring, when it helps to correct the too great acidity of the young grass; when beans cannot be had, Indian corn is sometimes used, and also in one park (Chetwynd, in Shropshire), the refuse from the thrashing machine is found to be very excellent feeding for the deer in winter. Turnips and mangold-worzell are also extensively used for the winter feeding of deer, particularly in Ireland, and in those counties in England where beans are not very prevalent.

For stall and paddock feeding, swedes, hay, and beans are generally given, and with such advantage in Northwith Park, in Worcestershire, that thirty-five bucks are generally fat and fit to kill about the 21st of May. The same system is pursued in Duncombe Park, in Yorkshire (where corn also is given), and on a large scale at Eastwell and Godmersham Parks, in Kent. The manner in which the deer are caught in these parks for the purpose of being transferred to the paddocks is peculiar to them ; and

[1] Notes and Queries, 3rd series, vii. 227.

to the owners, the Earl of Winchilsea, and Mr. Knight, I am obliged for the following descriptive account :—

'To those who may not be acquainted with the mode of taking up deer for fattening, as practised at Eastwell and Godmersham, a few remarks may not be uninteresting. The best time is immediately after the close of the rutting season, say about the end of November. Three or four horsemen are sufficient for the purpose ; a larger number are likely to terrify the deer, and drive them about unnecessarily. To catch deer *secundum artem,* two dogs are required—one on each side. When the keeper has pointed out the deer he wishes to be taken up, a horseman rides into the herd in order to separate him from the others. This operation requires a horse well in hand, and well on his haunches, so as to turn quickly as the deer turns. The dogs also must be well trained, and under perfect command ;[1] they are loose, and follow the keeper's horse. As soon as the deer is singled out, he lays them on by giving the signal "Hold him up"; this may be done with steady dogs even if a few does should break away with the buck, as the dogs will take no notice of them, but stick to the male deer. If he happens to be strong, and in good condition, the course may last for about a mile, but in general the deer is brought to bay in a much shorter distance. The dogs are trained to seize him by the ear, and no well-bred dog will fasten on any other part; when two that understand their business have thus pinioned a deer, they hold him fast without a possibility of budging, until some one can jump off his horse, and, catching hold of the deer by his hind legs, just below his houghs, fling him on his side or back, in which position he is easily held, till more strength arrives.' In this manner about sixty deer are annually caught in the Park of Eastwell, and about twenty-five brace in that of Godmersham. Lord Winchilsea adds that he has known sixteen deer taken up, and turned out without an accident, in the course of one day's catching. His lordship also remarks upon the importance of *sewels,*

---

[1] The breed is peculiar to the parks of Eastwell and Godmersham, and described as smooth-haired powerful greyhounds.

that is, lengths of cord on spindles, with turkey feathers knotted on to them, at the interval of a couple of feet; it is found that deer are afraid of these strings of feathers, when stretched across a large park, and are by their means kept within a certain space for a day together, by this simple device, which, however, appears to be of little use in small parks, where it is found that deer take no heed of *sewels*, and where, therefore, it is useless to employ them.[1]

With regard to buck shooting, I am also obliged to Lord Winchilsea for the following observation :—

'To shoot a buck in the park with any reasonable chance of success, it is best for several people to get into a pony carriage, and liken themselves as much as possible to a party of strangers; by this means, and with due attention to the wind, the deer will usually let you approach within shot; but you must be quick about it, as nothing suspects danger sooner than a fat buck, and after a short period of uneasiness, he generally takes himself off, leaving you to follow at your leisure. This plan, however, will not do for more than once or twice, as they are soon up to it, and then the appearance of the carriage is enough to clear the horizon of all the deer within sight of it.'

The habits of deer are, of course, better observed in small rather than in large parks. The following interesting note was kindly sent me by the Earl Nelson, and relates to the deer in the little park or paddock of Brickworth, near Salisbury, in Wiltshire, belonging to the Dowager Countess Nelson. His lordship says that—'the deer go over the twenty-one acres of which the park consists twice in the twenty-four hours, with such regularity that you can tell the time of day by their position in the park. About 11 A.M. they leave off their feeding, and lie down in the middle of

---

[1] Deer may also be taken alive in traps, during hard weather : a circular hut is built divided into three or four equal sections, one section forming the trap, communicating right and left by means of sliding doors with the other compartments. The deer are enticed into it by hay or beans, and when once fairly inside, release by their weight the door of the trap, suspended by a rope and pulley, which should be made to slide in grooves like a portcullis.

the park; about 5, they resume it, and work up regularly, coming to the front of the house. Before rain, it has been also observed that you frequently see the does, followed by their fawns, dancing round the rookery, a group of trees in the centre of the park; in this sport they are not, however, joined by the bucks.' A remarkable incident, which took place some years ago in Donington Park, Leicestershire, has been recorded in the pages of 'The Reliquary,'[1] from whence the following is an extract :—

'Some timber was being felled in the park, and to one of the trees was attached a cord, by which the woodmen intended to pull it in a certain direction. At night, when the men went from their work, this cord was left dangling down to the ground, when a deer began to amuse himself by rubbing his horns against it. By and by, his horns got entangled, so that he could not loose them, but with the constant friction, through the night, of the rope against the tree, as he tossed his head to and fro, the rope broke, leaving a considerable portion wrapped about his horns. As he was roaming about the park, another deer attacked him, and by butting their heads together, the second deer managed to unwrap several yards of the rope, and also to noose himself; so that the two deer were tied together by a cord of perhaps three yards in length. Feeling themselves fettered, both animals became furious, and must have attacked each other with tremendous force for a long time, when the strength of one failed him, who sunk down, no more to renew the combat. The live deer was found tethered to the dead one, being unable either to extricate himself from his dead companion or drag him about.'[2]

The doe brings forth her young in the month of June, and occasionally much later,[3] at which time she seeks a retired spot among fern, or other

[1] The Reliquary, vol. i. p. 239.
[2] An incident of the same description between two bucks in the Home Park at Hampton Court was described by a writer in the newspapers in October 1865.
[3] In the year 1861, on November 3, a living

fawn was dropped in the Park of Eatington, in Warwickshire. The period of gestation in the doe is eight months; she brings forth generally one, not unfrequently two; and sometimes three, fawns at a birth.

cover, where she drops her fawn, which for a day or two, until it is able to follow her, she leaves, and feeds on some adjacent spot within the hearing of its voice, should it be attacked, and returns to suckle it occasionally, or to protect it if alarmed. The first year, whether male or female, it is called a *fawn* — from the French *fan, faon,* which it has been said is derived from the Latin *Infans*—and has no horns; the second year, the male is called a *pricket,* with horns about four or five inches long, terminating in a single point. The third year, his horns are renewed, and increase in length; they now divide at the top, with a small spur at bottom, called an *antler;* and he takes the name of *sorel;* which in the fourth year is changed to that of *sore,* when his horns receive an addition both in length and branches. In the fifth year, he arrives at the honour of being called *a buck of the first head,* and his horns now take the palmated form. Buck is probably from *bocker,* to strike, and is therefore an animal that strikes with the horns; and thence it has become the general name of the male of the beasts of the chase, even of those which have no horns, as the hare and the rabbit.[1] In the sixth year, he is accounted fit to be killed, and is called an *old* or *great buck.* Thus, in the quaint language of 'The Book of St. Alban's,' printed in 1496, we read :—

The dyscrpnynge of a bucke.

And ye speke of y bucke the fyrste yere he is :
A fawne soukynge on his dame say as I you wys :
The seconde yere a Prycket the thyrde yere a Sowrel :
A soure at the fourth yere the trouth I you tell.
The fyfth yere calle hym a Bucke of the fyrst heve.
The syrte yere calle him a Bucke and doo as I you reve :

Of the hornys of a bucke.

The hornes of a grete bucke or he soo be
Must be summonyd as I saye herkenyth to me.

---

[1] Bell's Quadrupeds, p. 406.

𝕮𝖜𝖔 𝖇𝖗𝖆𝖓𝖈𝖍𝖊𝖘 𝖋𝖞𝖗𝖘𝖙𝖊 𝖕𝖆𝖜𝖒𝖕𝖉 𝖍𝖊 𝖒𝖚𝖘𝖙 𝖍𝖆𝖚𝖊 :
𝕬𝖓𝖉 𝖋𝖔𝖚𝖗𝖊 𝖆𝖇𝖆𝖚𝖓𝖈𝖊𝖗𝖘 𝖙𝖍𝖊 𝖘𝖔𝖙𝖍 𝖞𝖋 𝖞𝖊 𝖜𝖔𝖑𝖑 𝖘𝖆𝖚𝖊.
𝕬𝖓𝖉 𝖝𝖝𝖎𝖎𝖎𝖎 𝖊𝖘𝖕𝖊𝖑𝖊𝖗𝖘 𝖆𝖓𝖉 𝖙𝖍𝖊𝖓𝖓𝖊 𝖞𝖊 𝖒𝖆𝖞𝖊 𝖍𝖞𝖒 𝖈𝖆𝖑𝖑 :
𝖂𝖍𝖊𝖗𝖊 𝖘𝖔 𝖞𝖊 𝖇𝖊 𝖆 𝖌𝖗𝖊𝖙𝖊 𝖇𝖚𝖈𝖐𝖊 𝕴 𝖙𝖊𝖑𝖑 𝖞𝖔𝖚 𝖆𝖑𝖑.

In the second year, the female of the fallow-deer is called a *teg*, and in the third, and afterwards, a *doe*. This is the Anglo-Saxon *da*. The word *fallow*, it may be observed, describes the prevailing colour of the animal. Anglo-Saxon ꝼalepe, which Somner translates *helvus*, *gilvus*, fallow colour.

'How does your *fallow* greyhound, Sir?'—SHAKESPERE.

But it has been long used in contradistinction to the red deer or stag. Thus Lord Clarendon wrote :—'The king, who was excessively affected to hunting, had a great desire to make a great park for red as well as *fallow* deer, between Richmond and Hampton Court.'

The buck sheds his horns annually, towards the end of April and beginning of May ; soon after which there spring up, from the same place to which these had formerly adhered, two soft bumps covered with a velvet-like down, which gradually push out in height till they attain their full size, and suffer a succession of changes of the following nature.[1]

During the early period of their growth nothing can be more soft and tender than these are; nor can anything exceed their sensibility at this period of their growth, as evident by the great solicitude the animal displays to guard them then from every species of injury. The blood-vessels at this time much abound in this tender organ; and it is well known by epicures that at this period, when properly dressed, it furnishes a most delicate morsel of food.[2] As it advances in growth, it acquires a firmer consistence, the blood-vessels diminish in size, and become more rigid, till

[1] The following description is from the 1st vol. of Anderson's Recreations (London, 1799), p. 262.
[2] See for many curious old receipts for dressing venison, 'Wyl Bucke His Testament. The Legacies palatably prepared for the Legatees.' Pr. pr. at the Chiswick Press, 1827.

they by degrees are so much contracted as totally to disappear, and become at length a solid horny substance of great firmness. As this rigidity increases the acuteness of their sensibility decreases ; probably the animal then experiences a sensation like itchiness in that organ, which induces him to rub it against trees and other solid substances he meets with ; that rubs off the down, and sharpens the points of this weapon with which nature has provided him, seemingly to give him power during the rutting season, at which time it has acquired its highest degree of perfection. From that period it becomes gradually ossified and insensible, till at length, the blood-vessels being entirely obliterated, it loses all connection with the animal, and finally drops off from it, to make way for a fresh crop during the succeeding year, when the procreating power is by nature intended to return.

The fallow-deer is easily tamed, and feeds upon a variety of things which the stag refuses, as I have already shown. They are gregarious to a great extent, associating in large herds, the bucks apart from the does, excepting during the pairing season, and in the winter, during which season they associate promiscuously.

Towards the beginning of October, their throats begin to swell, when they make a noise called groaning, with a kind of rattling in the throat, which they do at no other season. They then associate with the does, when the oldest and strongest, as has been already observed, becoming masters of the herd, keep the younger male deer at a distance. At this period, called 'the rutting season,' they neglect their food, and become exceedingly lean ; and it has been observed that the more they are wasted at this season the finer and fatter will be the venison, for the most part, in the summer following.[1] About November, they separate from the does till the following autumn.

The season for killing deer in the Royal parks before the alteration of the style in the year 1752, was, for the buck, from June 24 to September

[1] Anderson's Recreations, vol. ii. p. 369.

14, and the doe from November 1 to Candlemas day (February 2) ; which,' as it is impossible to alter seasons with dates, may now be deferred to the old style—eleven days later.

This accords exactly with Dame Juliana Berner's verses in ' The Book of St. Alban's ' :—

> Marke well thyse seasons folowynge
> Tyme of grece begynnyth at Mydsomer daye :
> And tyll holy Rode daye lastyth as I you saye.
> The season of the doo begynnyth at Mygbelmas :
> And it shall endure and laste untyll Candylmas.

The same venerable authority, with the pedantic accuracy which was the delight of our ancestors, informs us—

> Of the cryenge of thyse bestys
> An harte belowyth and a bucke groynyth I fynde :
> And eche roobucke certayn bellyth by kynde.
> The noyse of thyse bestys thus ye shall call :
> For pryde of theyr make they use it all.
> Saye chylde where ye goo : your dame taught you so.

And again—

> My chylde callyth herdys of harte and of hynde
> And of bucke and of doo where ye theym fynde.
> Twenty is a lytyll herde though it be of hyndys
> And three score is a myddyll herde to call hem by kyndys.
> And foure score is a grete herde call ye them soo :
> Be it harte, be it hynde, bucke or else doo.

It remains to mention the age of deer, and here there is a considerable difference between the red deer and the fallow-deer; the former are known to have attained to the age of thirty-five or forty years, the latter never exceed twenty.

With a curious anecdote, quoted by Bell from Playford's ' Introduction to Music,' I will conclude these few remarks on the management of deer, which I recommend to the favourable and indulgent notice of the owners of parks.

' Travelling some years since, I met on the road near Royston a herd of about twenty bucks following a bagpipe and violin, which, while the music played, went forward, when it ceased, they all stood still ; and in this manner they were brought out of Yorkshire to Hampton Court.' [1]

[1] See the woodcut at the beginning of this chapter.

INDEX.

INDEX.

T

LONDON

PRINTED BY SPOTTISWOODE AND CO.

NEW-STREET SQUARE

www.ingramcontent.com/pod-product-compliance
Lightning Source LLC
Chambersburg PA
CBHW030345270326
41926CB00009B/973